INTERNET OF THINGS

Dr.M.Karthi

Dr.V.Vanneswari

Mrs.M.Shiyamala

Mrs.P.Manju

Internet of Things

Copyright © 2025 Dr.M.Karthi, Dr.V.Vanneswari, Mrs.M.Shiyamala, Mrs.P.Manju

All rights reserved. No part of this book may be reproduced, stored in a retrieval system, or transmitted in any form or by any means, electronic, mechanical, photocopying, recording, or otherwise, without the prior written permission of the author.

This book is sold as is, without any warranties, express or implied. The author and publisher are not responsible for any problems that may arise from using this book. If you have a problem with the book, your only option is to return it for a refund. The author agrees to protect the publisher from any legal issues that may arise from the book's content. Any legal disputes about this book will be handled according to the laws of the constitution of India

Publisher: Inkscirbe Publishing Pvt Ltd

ISBN Number: 978-1-966421-17-7

PREFACE

The Internet of Things (IoT) has become a cornerstone of technological innovation in recent years, fundamentally altering the way we interact with the physical and digital worlds. From smart homes and wearable health monitors to intelligent transportation systems and industrial automation, IoT is revolutionizing every sector. This book, Internet of Things, is written to provide a comprehensive and accessible foundation for students, researchers, and professionals seeking to understand and apply the concepts of IoT.

The idea for this book emerged from a collective realization of the growing need for a structured, up-to-date, and practical resource in this domain. As the lead author, I have taken the primary initiative in developing the conceptual framework, organizing the chapters, and writing the major portions of this book. My experience in teaching, research, and hands-on implementation of IoT systems has greatly shaped the structure and content presented here.

Each chapter in this book is designed to build progressively—from the basic principles of IoT to more advanced topics such as protocols, architecture, cloud integration, security, and real-world applications. Case studies and illustrative examples are included to help readers bridge theory with practice.

This book is a collaborative effort, and I am fortunate to be joined by three dedicated co-authors (my friends) who contributed

their support, technical input, and peer reviews have been invaluable in enriching the quality and depth of this book. I extend my sincere thanks to each of them for their commitment to this project.

We collectively hope this book will serve as a valuable academic and professional resource for readers who are keen to explore the possibilities of IoT. Whether used as a textbook, a reference guide, or a self-learning tool, it is our aspiration that this work inspires further learning, innovation, and application in the field of IoT.

Dr.M.Karthi,
Dr.V.Vanneswari,
Mrs.M.Shiyamala,
Mrs.P.Manju

CONTENTS

1. INTRODUCTION TO IOT 11
2. IOT DEVELOPMENT 121
3. IOT SECURITY AND PRIVACY 185
4. IOT APPLICATIONS AND USE CASES 221
5. IOT DATA ANALYTICS AND AI 293

INTERNET OF THINGS

CHAPTER 1

INDEX

INTRODUCTION TO IOT

1.1 Introduction to the Internet of Things (IoT) 11
    1.1.1 What is IoT? 11
    1.1.2 The Evolution of IoT 14
    1.1.3 Key Features and Characteristics of IoT 18
    1.1.4 IoT in Everyday Life 24
    1.1.5 Importance of IoT 25

1.2 IoT Architecture 27
    1.2.1 Components of IoT Systems 27
    1.2.2 IoT Architecture Layers 31
    1.2.3 Sensor Networks and Actuators 32
    1.2.4 Cloud, Edge, and Fog Computing in IoT 35
    1.2.5 Elements of an IoT Ecosystem 40
    1.2.6 Convergence of IT and IoT 42
    1.2.7 Technology Drivers 46
    1.2.8 Business Drivers 49

1.3 IoT Communication Protocols 50
    1.3.1 Overview of Communication Technologies 50
    1.3.2 Wireless Communication Protocols 52
    1.3.3 Cellular Networks for IoT 59
    1.3.4 Short-Range vs Long-Range Communication 61

1.3.5 Network Topologies 63

IoT Devices and Sensors 72

    1.4.1 Types of IoT Devices.. 72

    1.4.3 Types of Sensors and their Applications.. 90

    1.4.4 ChoosingThe Right Sensor For Your IoT Project:........................ 93

    1.4.5 Powering IoT Devices 93

1.5 History and Evolution of IoT Standards 96

    1.5.1 Early Beginnings of IoT 96

    1.5.2 Role of Standardization 97

1.6. Internet Connectivity 99

    1.6.1 IP Addressing.. 99

    1.6.2 Data Acquiring.. 104

    1.6.3 Organizing the data... 111

CHAPTER 1

INTRODUCTION TO IOT

1.1 Introduction to the Internet of Things (IoT)

1.1.1 What is IoT?

The **Internet of Things (IoT)** refers to a **network of interconnected physical devices** that are embedded with **sensors, software, and communication technologies**, enabling them to collect, exchange, and process data over the internet. These devices range from household appliances and wearable gadgets to industrial machinery and smart infrastructure. The goal of IoT is to **bridge the gap between the physical and digital worlds**, allowing devices to work seamlessly together with minimal human intervention. By automating tasks and optimizing processes, IoT enhances efficiency, reduces costs, and improves the overall quality of life.

IoT systems function by collecting data through **sensors** that measure various environmental factors such as temperature, humidity, motion, and pressure. This data is transmitted via **wireless or wired networks**, where it is processed using **cloud computing, artificial intelligence (AI), and data analytics**. Once analyzed, the system can make intelligent decisions and trigger specific actions, such as adjusting a smart thermostat, sending maintenance alerts for industrial machines, or optimizing traffic flow in smart cities. The ability of IoT to operate autonomously and provide **real-time insights** makes it a transformative force across multiple industries.

One of the key advantages of IoT is its ability to **enhance automation and control**. For example, in smart homes, IoT-enabled appliances like refrigerators, security systems, and lighting controls can be remotely monitored and operated through mobile applications. In the healthcare sector, wearable devices continuously track vital signs and alert doctors in case of abnormalities, improving patient care. Similarly, **industrial IoT (IIoT)** enables manufacturers to implement **predictive maintenance**, where machines detect potential failures before they occur, reducing downtime and increasing efficiency.

IoT is also playing a crucial role in **urban development**, contributing to the rise of **smart cities**. By integrating IoT technology into traffic management, waste disposal, and energy grids, cities can optimize resources and enhance public services. For instance, **smart traffic lights** can adjust signal timings based on real-time congestion levels, while **smart waste bins** can notify collection teams when they are full, ensuring efficient garbage disposal. The agricultural sector is also leveraging IoT through **smart farming techniques**, where sensors monitor soil moisture levels and automate irrigation systems, improving crop yields and reducing water wastage.

Despite its numerous benefits, IoT comes with certain challenges, particularly in terms of **data security and privacy**. As more devices become connected, the risk of cyber threats and unauthorized access increases. Ensuring robust encryption, authentication, and network security measures is essential to protect sensitive information. Moreover, the rapid growth of IoT devices necessitates **scalability and interoperability**, requiring standardization across different platforms and networks.

As technology advances, the future of IoT will be shaped by **artificial intelligence (AI), 5G connectivity, blockchain, and edge computing**. These innovations will further enhance the capabilities of IoT, making devices smarter, more responsive, and highly autonomous. The **continuous expansion of IoT applications** across industries will revolutionize how we interact with technology, paving the way for a **more connected, efficient, and intelligent world**.

Examples of IoT networks in action

IoT networks and the data they produce are at work in virtually all aspects of modern life – in our homes, our cars, our stores, and even on our bodies.

Smart homes: Many people are already intimately familiar with IoT networks in their own homes. Through smart switches, sensors, and devices that communicate through protocols like Z-Wave or Zigbee, home automation systems can be used to monitor and control things like lighting, climate, security systems, appliances, and more – even from afar. If you forget to turn off the lights or your oven before leaving the house, you can do it from your phone through IoT-enabled devices.

Smart grids: Combined with AI and advanced analytics technology, smart grids use IoT solutions to help integrate technology to help consumers better ration and understand the energy they're using – and even producing – through solar panels and other means. IoT sensors across the grid can detect potential risks earlier so that power can be redistributed as needed to prevent or minimise outages and other issues. Sensors can also detect mechanical problems and alert technicians as needed for repairs, all of which helps energy consumers have better control and insight.

Smart cities: According to the Smart City Index (SCI), a smart city is "an urban setting that applies technology to enhance the benefits and diminish the shortcomings of urbanization." Increasing populations, traffic congestion, and aging infrastructures are all among some of the challenges that the IoT is helping to address. Using sensors, meters, and other IoT devices, city planners can monitor and collect data to proactively address issues. For example, sensors placed in storm drains can detect water levels and automate actions to help prevent flooding when levels get too high.

Connected cars: Today, virtually all new cars roll off the line with IoT and smart functionality, with 5G cars expected to grow in ubiquity over the next five years and beyond. Advanced driver assistance systems (ADAS) that use IoT technology help drivers avoid collisions, plan routes, squeeze into tight spots, and much more. And as automotive IoT develops, we are increasingly seeing connectivity with external devices such as traffic lights, pedestrians, news and weather sources, and streaming entertainment providers.

IoT in retail: Customer-facing IoT solutions are increasingly being used to enhance in-store experiences. Motion-activated smart cameras, smart shelves, beacon, and RFID technologies can help shoppers locate items through a mobile app. They make it easy to share stock information, and even send in-context promotions to customers while they are browsing in store. And as the lines blur between in-store and online shopping experiences, IoT solutions can help improve customer experiences by tracking delivery and shipping vehicles, allowing customers to better customise their shopping plans.

Telehealth: It is increasingly common to see IoT-driven consumer medical devices like smart watches and medication dispensers that help doctors to monitor patients remotely. But some of the most fascinating advances in telehealth are coming via smart surgical tools. This is particularly relevant for patients in remote or under-developed areas. These tools allow remote doctors to connect with some of the best surgeons in the world, to perform guided surgeries, remote diagnoses, and even monitor anesthetized patients during that critical time.

Traffic management: Through a network of sensors, cameras, and other devices, IoT technology can be used to reduce traffic congestion and help to provide workable rerouting options. For example, real-time data feeds can be used to adjust the timing of signals to ensure a smooth flow of traffic in dynamic conditions. Light sensors can detect and adjust lighting brightness for optimal visibility while road sensors can detect accidents and automatically report issues.

How does IoT work?

IoT devices are our eyes and ears when we can't physically be there – capturing whatever data they are programmed to gather. That data can then be collected and analysed to help us inform and automate subsequent actions or decisions. There are four key stages in this process:

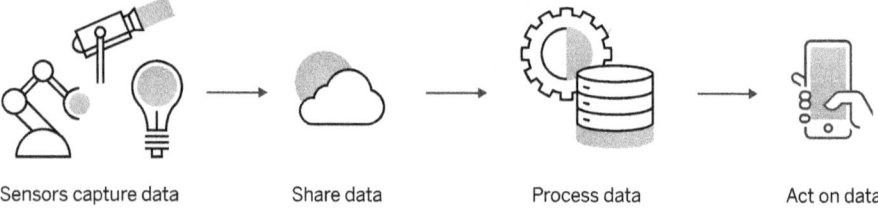

Sensors capture data Share data Process data Act on data

1. **Capture the data.** Through sensors, IoT devices capture data from their environments. This could be as simple as the temperature or as complex a real-time video feed.

2. **Share the data.** Using available network connections, IoT devices send this data to a public or private cloud system (device-system-device) or to another device (device-device), or store it locally as directed for processing at the edge.

3. **Process the data.** At this point, software is programmed to do something based on that data – such as turn on a fan or send a warning.

4. **Act on the data.** Accumulated data from all devices within an IoT network is analysed. This delivers powerful insights to inform confident actions and business decisions.

1.1.2 The Evolution of IoT

The Internet of Things (IoT) has evolved from a futuristic concept to an integral part of modern life, connecting billions of devices and revolutionizing how people interact with technology. The development of IoT spans several decades, and its journey is marked by breakthroughs in computing, networking, and sensing technologies. Here's an overview of the evolution of IoT:

1.Early Concepts and Origins (1980s-1990s)

The Vision: The idea of interconnected devices has its roots in the 1980s when researchers envisioned a world where everyday objects could communicate with each other. Early pioneers saw potential in embedding sensors and communication systems into devicesallowing them to interact autonomously.

First "Smart" Devices: In the 1990s, the first internet-connected appliances began to appear. One early example was a connected Coca-Cola vending machine at Carnegie Mellon University, which allowed users to check the status of the machine remotely via the internet.

RFID and Ubiquitous Computing: In the late 1990s, Radio Frequency Identification (RFID) technology gained attention as a way to track objects and information. Mark Weiser's concept of "ubiquitous computing" laid the foundation for IoT, envisioning a world where computing would be embedded into the environment.

2.The Birth of IoT (1999-2010)

The Term "Internet of Things": The term "Internet of Things" was coined in 1999 by Kevin Ashton, a British technologist who worked on RFID technology. He envisioned a future where the internet would extend beyond computers to include physical objects and everyday devices.

Advances in Wireless Technology: The early 2000s saw significant advancements in wireless technologies like Wi-Fi, Bluetooth, and cellular networks, which provided the backbone for IoT connectivity. These wireless protocols enabled devices to communicate more easily and cost-effectively.

M2M Communication: Machine-to-Machine (M2M) communication emerged as a precursor to IoT, particularly in industries like manufacturing, where connected sensors were used to monitor and control machinery remotely. This form of communication paved the way for more complex IoT ecosystems.

3. The Rise of Smart Devices (2010-2015)

Consumer IoT: The 2010s marked a significant rise in consumer IoT devices, driven by the increasing availability of affordable sensors, microcontrollers, and connectivity options. Devices like smart thermostats (Nest), smart speakers (Amazon Echo), and fitness trackers (Fitbit) became mainstream.

Mobile Revolution: The rapid growth of smartphones and mobile apps played a pivotal role in IoT adoption. Mobile devices provided a gateway for controlling and interacting with IoT systems, giving users real-time access to connected devices.

Cloud Computing: The development of cloud computing services enabled IoT devices to offload processing tasks and store large amounts of data. This allowed for real-time analytics, remote monitoring, and data storage, further enhancing the capabilities of IoT ecosystems.

4. IoT Expansion and Integration (2015-2020)

Edge Computing: With the explosion of IoT data, edge computing became crucial. Edge computing refers to processing data closer to the source, at the "edge" of the network. This reduces latency, enhances real-time processing, and lowers the burden on central cloud servers, which is essential for applications like autonomous vehicles and industrial automation.

Industrial IoT (IIoT): IoT found extensive applications in industrial sectors, including manufacturing, logistics, and energy. IIoT uses connected sensors and analytics to optimize production, prevent equipment failure, and increase efficiency. The concept of smart factories and Industry 4.0 emerged, integrating IoT with robotics, AI, and big data analytics.

Smart Cities: Governments and municipalities began adopting IoT technologies to develop smart cities. These cities use IoT to improve infrastructure, traffic management, energy efficiency, and public safety. Smart sensors monitor air quality, manage waste, and optimize water usage, while connected streetlights and traffic systems improve urban living conditions.

5G Networks: The emergence of 5G technology provided the necessary bandwidth, speed, and low-latency connectivity required for more advanced IoT applications. 5G enables the deployment of massive IoT networks, supporting millions of devices in densely populated areas like smart cities.

5. IoT in Healthcare and Wearables

Remote Monitoring: IoT has transformed healthcare by enabling remote patient monitoring and telemedicine. Wearable devices such as smartwatches and health sensors collect real-time data on vital signs, activity levels, and sleep patterns. This data can be analysed to monitor chronic conditions or detect early signs of health issues.

Connected Medical Devices: Hospitals use IoT-enabled devices to track medical equipment, monitor patients in real-time, and automate inventory management. Smart devices such as insulin pumps and pacemakers are becoming more connected, allowing for more personalized and data-driven care.

Pandemic Response: The COVID-19 pandemic accelerated IoT adoption in healthcare. From contact tracing apps to smart temperature monitors, IoT technologies were widely used to manage the crisis, monitor patient conditions, and track the spread of the virus.

6. The Current IoT Landscape (2020-Present)

AI Integration: Artificial Intelligence (AI) and machine learning are increasingly integrated into IoT ecosystems, allowing for predictive analytics, intelligent automation, and advanced decision-making. AI-driven IoT systems are used in areas like autonomous vehicles, smart grids, and personalized marketing.

Cybersecurity Challenges: With the growth of IoT devices, concerns about security and privacy have increased. IoT devices are vulnerable to hacking, data breaches, and malware attacks, making cybersecurity a major challenge. The industry is working to improve IoT security through standards, encryption, and device authentication measures.

Environmental IoT: IoT technologies are being leveraged to address environmental challenges, such as monitoring ecosystems, optimizing resource usage, and reducing carbon footprints. Smart farming, water management, and energy conservation are examples of how IoT is contributing to sustainability.

7. Future of IoT: What Lies Ahead?

Massive IoT Networks: As 5G networks become widespread, IoT networks will scale to support billions of devices globally, from smart homes to autonomous factories. This massive IoT infrastructure will be the foundation for a more interconnected and data-driven world.

Autonomous Systems: IoT will be integral to the future of autonomous systems, from self-driving cars to drones and robots. These systems will rely on real-time data from connected sensors, allowing them to navigate and operate independently.

Interoperability and Standardization: One of the key challenges for the future of IoT is creating standard protocols for devices from different manufacturers to communicate with each other seamlessly. As IoT ecosystems become more complex, standardization will be crucial for ensuring compatibility and security across devices.

IoT and AI Synergy: The combination of IoT and AI will enable smarter, more adaptive systems. IoT will continue to generate massive amounts of data, which AI algorithms can analyze and act upon in real time, enabling everything from predictive maintenance to personalized customer experiences.

Privacy and Ethics: As IoT continues to grow, concerns over data privacy, surveillance, and the ethical use of connected devices will need to be addressed. Regulatory frameworks and transparent practices will be essential to balancing innovation with consumer protection.

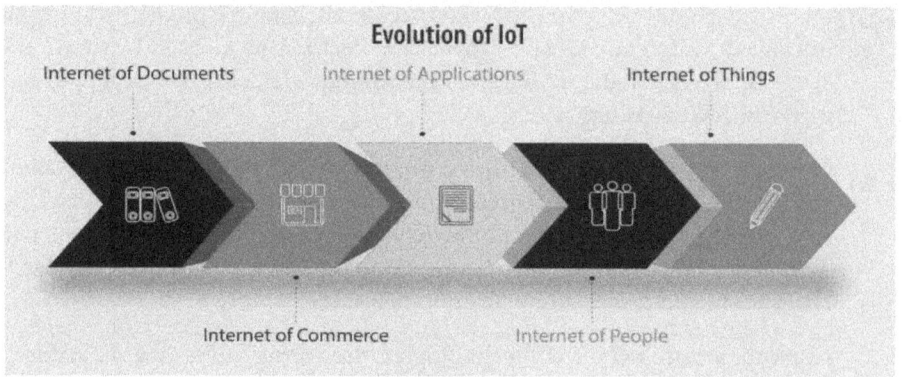

1.1.3 Key Features and Characteristics of IoT

The Internet of Things (IoT) is characterized by the following key features that are mentioned below.

1. Connectivity

Connectivity is an important requirement of the IoT infrastructure. Things of IoT should be connected to the IoT infrastructure. Anyone, anywhere, anytime can connect, this should be guaranteed at all times. For example, the connection between people through Internet devices like mobile phones, and other gadgets, also a connection between Internet devices such as routers, gateways, sensors, etc.

2. Intelligence and Identity

The extraction of knowledge from the generated data is very important. For example, a sensor generates data, but that data will only be useful if it is interpreted properly. Each IoT device has a unique identity. This identification is helpful in tracking the equipment and at times for querying its status.

3. Scalability

The number of elements connected to the IoT zone is increasing day by day. Hence, an IoT setup should be capable of handling the massive expansion. The data generated as an outcome is enormous, and it should be handled appropriately.

4. Dynamic and Self-Adapting (Complexity)

IoT devices should dynamically adapt themselves to changing contexts and scenarios. Assume a camera meant for surveillance. It should be adaptable to work in different conditions and different light situations (morning, afternoon, and night).

5. Architecture

IoT Architecture cannot be homogeneous in nature. It should be hybrid, supporting different manufacturers 'products to function in the IoT network. IoT is not owned by anyone engineering branch. IoT is a reality when multiple domains come together.

6. Safety

There is a danger of the sensitive personal details of the users getting compromised when all his/her devices are connected to the internet. This can cause a loss to the user. Hence, data security is the major challenge. Besides, the equipment involved is huge. IoT networks may also be at risk. Therefore, equipment safety is also critical.

7. Self Configuring

This is one of the most important characteristics of IoT. IoT devices are able to upgrade their software in accordance with requirements with a minimum of user participation. Additionally, they can set up the network, allowing for the addition of new devices to an already-existing network.

8. Interoperability

IoT devices use standardized protocols and technologies to ensure they can communicate with each other and other systems. Interoperability is one of the key characteristics of the Internet of Things (IoT). It refers to the ability of different IoT devices and systems to communicate and exchange data with each other, regardless of the underlying technology or manufacturer.

Interoperability is critical for the success of IoT, as it enables different devices and systems to work together seamlessly and provides a seamless user experience. Without interoperability, IoT systems would be limited to individual silos of data and devices, making it difficult to share information and create new services and applications.

To achieve interoperability, IoT devices, and systems use standardized communication protocols and data formats. These standards allow different devices to understand and process data in a consistent and reliable manner, enabling data to be exchanged between devices and systems regardless of the technology used.

9. Embedded Sensors and Actuators

Embedded sensors and actuators are critical components of the Internet of Things (IoT). They allow IoT devices to interact with their environment and collect and transmit data.

Sensors are devices that can detect changes in the environment, such as temperature, light, sound, or movement. In IoT systems, sensors are embedded into devices, allowing them to collect data about the environment.

Actuators are devices that can interact with the environment, such as turning on lights, opening or closing doors, or controlling the speed of a motor. In IoT systems, actuators are embedded into devices, allowing them to perform actions based on data collected by sensors.

Together, sensors and actuators allow IoT devices to collect data about the environment, process that data, and take action based on the results. This makes it possible to automate a wide range of processes and tasks, such as home automation, energy management, and predictive maintenance.

In order to ensure that sensors and actuators can communicate with each other and with other devices and systems, they use standardized communication protocols, such as Bluetooth Low Energy (BLE), Zigbee, or Wi-Fi.

Overall, embedded sensors and actuators are essential components of IoT systems, enabling them to collect and process data and interact with their environment in new and innovative ways.

IoT devices are equipped with sensors and actuators that allow them to collect and transmit data, as well as to interact with the environment.

10. Autonomous operation

Autonomous operation refers to the ability of IoT devices and systems to operate independently and make decisions without human intervention. This is a crucial characteristic of the Internet of Things (IoT) and enables a wide range of new applications and services.

In IoT systems, devices and systems are equipped with sensors, actuators, and processing power, allowing them to collect and process data about the environment, make decisions based on that data, and take action accordingly.

For example, an IoT system might use sensors to detect changes in temperature or light levels in a room, and then use actuators to adjust the temperature or turn on the lights based on that data. This allows for the automation of many tasks, such as energy management, home automation, and predictive maintenance.

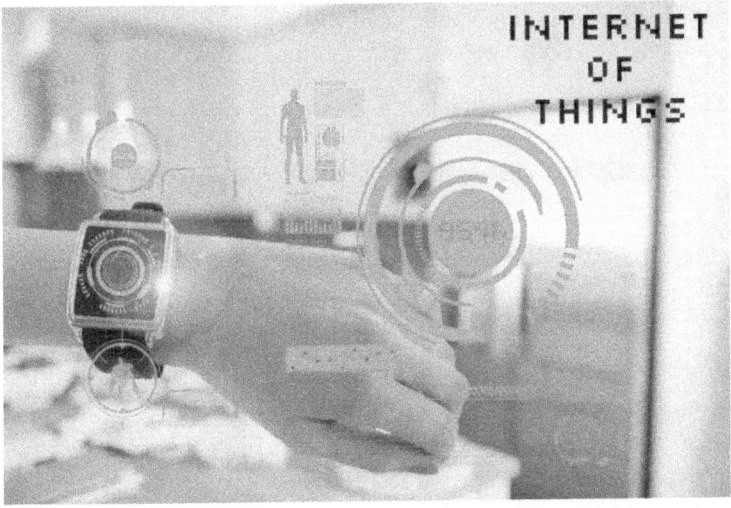

Another example of autonomous operation in IoT is self-healing networks, where IoT devices can automatically detect and repair problems, such as network outages, without human intervention.

Autonomous operation is made possible by advances in artificial intelligence, machine learning, and cloud computing, which enable IoT devices and systems to process and analyse large amounts of data in real time and make decisions based on that data.

Overall, the autonomous operation is an important characteristic of IoT systems, allowing them to deliver new and innovative services and applications that can improve efficiency, reduce costs, and enhance the user experience. IoT devices are designed to operate autonomously, without direct human intervention, making it possible to automate a wide range of processes and tasks.

11. Data-driven

Data-driven is a key characteristic of the Internet of Things (IoT). IoT devices and systems collect vast amounts of data from sensors and other sources, which can be analyzed and used to make data-driven decisions.

In IoT systems, data is collected from embedded sensors, actuators, and other sources, such as cloud services, databases, and mobile devices. This data is used to gain insights into the environment, improve operational efficiency, and make informed decisions.

For example, an IoT system might use data from sensors to monitor the temperature and humidity levels in a building, and then use that data to optimize heating, cooling, and ventilation systems. This can result in significant energy savings and improved indoor air quality.

Another example of data-driven IoT is predictive maintenance, where data from sensors and other sources is used to predict when equipment is likely to fail, allowing for proactive maintenance and reducing the risk of unplanned downtime.

Data-driven IoT is made possible by advances in big data technologies, such as distributed data processing and cloud computing, which allow for the efficient analysis and management of large amounts of data in real time.

Overall, data-driven is an important characteristic of IoT systems, allowing organizations to make informed decisions and achieve new levels of efficiency, cost savings, and innovation. IoT devices generate vast amounts of data, which is analyzed to drive improvements in efficiency, performance, and user experience.

12. Security

Security is a critical concern for the Internet of Things (IoT), as IoT devices and systems handle sensitive data and are connected to critical infrastructure. The increasing number of connected devices and the amount of data being transmitted over the Internet make IoT systems a prime target for cyberattacks.

To secure IoT systems, multiple layers of security are necessary, including physical security, network security, and data security.

Physical security involves protecting the physical devices from unauthorized access or tampering. This can be achieved through measures such as secure enclosures, access controls, and tamper-proofing.

Network security involves protecting the communication networks that connect IoT devices, including Wi-Fi networks, cellular networks, and wired networks. This can be achieved through encryption, secure authentication, and firewalls.

Data security involves protecting the data collected and transmitted by IoT devices and systems. This can be achieved through encryption, secure storage, and access controls.

In addition to these technical measures, it is also important to have robust policies and procedures in place to ensure the security of IoT systems, such as incident response plans and regular security audits.

Overall, security is a critical concern for IoT systems, and it is essential to implement multiple layers of security to protect against cyberattacks and ensure the confidentiality, integrity, and availability of sensitive data. IoT systems are designed to be secure, protecting against unauthorized access, hacking, and other security threats.

13. Ubiquity

Ubiquity refers to the widespread and pervasive presence of the Internet of Things (IoT) devices and systems in our daily lives. The goal of IoT is to create a seamless and interconnected world where devices and systems can communicate and share data seamlessly and transparently.

Ubiquity is achieved through the widespread deployment of IoT devices, such as sensors, actuators, and other connected devices, as well as the development of IoT networks and infrastructure to support communication and data exchange.

In a ubiquitous IoT environment, devices and systems can be accessed and controlled from anywhere, at any time, using a variety of devices, such as smartphones, laptops, and other connected devices.

For example, in a smart home, a person could use their smartphone to control the temperature, lighting, and other systems in their home, even when they are away.

In addition, ubiquity is also achieved through the integration of IoT with other technologies, such as artificial intelligence, big data, and cloud computing, which allow for the creation of more advanced and sophisticated IoT systems and applications.

Overall, ubiquity is a key characteristic of the IoT, and it is essential for realizing the full potential of IoT and creating a truly interconnected and smart world. IoT devices are widely distributed and can be found in a variety of environments, from homes and workplaces to public spaces and industrial settings.

14. Context Awareness

Context awareness refers to the ability of Internet of Things (IoT) devices and systems to understand and respond to the environment and context in which they are operating. This is achieved through the use of sensors and other technologies that can detect and collect data about the environment.

Context awareness is a critical aspect of IoT, as it enables IoT devices and systems to make decisions and take actions based on the context in which they are operating.

For example, in a smart home, a context-aware IoT system could adjust the temperature, lighting, and other systems based on the time of day, the presence of people in the home, and other factors.

In addition, context awareness is also used to improve the efficiency and effectiveness of IoT systems by reducing the amount of data that needs to be transmitted and processed. For example, a context-aware IoT system might only collect and transmit data when it is relevant to the current context, such as when a person is in the room or when the temperature changes significantly.

Overall, context awareness is a key aspect of IoT and is essential for realizing the full potential of IoT and creating truly intelligent and responsive systems. IoT devices are designed to be context-aware, taking into account the environment and context in which they are operating in order to provide more relevant and useful information and services.

1.1.4 IoT in Everyday Life

The Internet of Things, or IoT, is a network of objects like cars, buildings, utilities, and other devices connected to the internet. They have sensors, electronics, software, and other components that enable this connection. These objects can collect and exchange data, allowing them to interact with each other and the external environment. This technology can potentially revolutionise everyday life, from energy management to healthcare to transportation.

Sensors, detectors, and embedded devices comprise most IoT systems. These systems also have communication hardware and software, which enables them to connect with the cloud through the internet. IoT devices collect and analyse data locally or on the cloud system. Using this data, IoT systems can either make decisions on their own or react to environmental changes. Users can also control their IoT devices remotely through the cloud

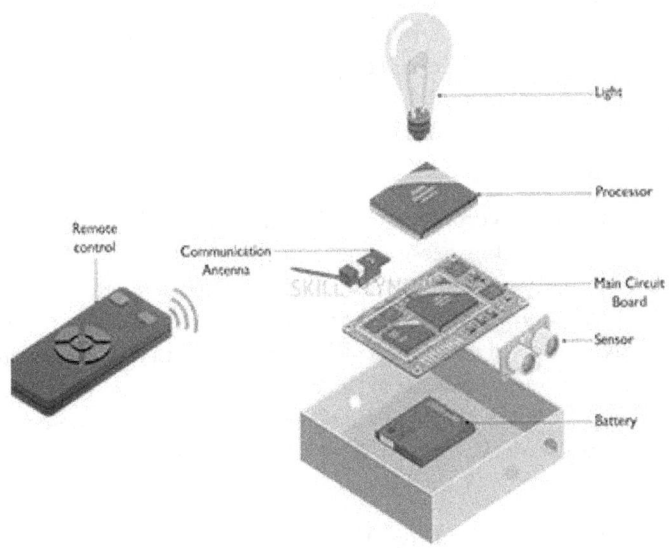

Applications of the Internet of Things

The applications of IoT in everyday life are vast. Here is an overview of some of the most common IoT uses in daily living.

- ➢ IoT in Healthcare
- ➢ IoT in the House
- ➢ IoT in Transportation
- ➢ IoT in Wearables

1.1.5 Importance of IoT

The **Internet of Things (IoT)** is a groundbreaking technology that connects everyday objects, industrial machines, and digital systems to the internet, enabling them to communicate, exchange data, and perform intelligent actions without human intervention. From smart homes and wearable devices to industrial automation and healthcare innovations, IoT is transforming multiple sectors, making life more efficient, productive, and sustainable.

1. Driving Automation and Efficiency: One of the biggest advantages of IoT is its ability to automate tasks and optimize resource usage. Smart home devices, such as voice-controlled assistants, smart thermostats, and security systems, improve convenience by learning user behaviors and adjusting settings automatically. In industries, IoT-driven automation reduces manual labor, minimizes errors, and enhances production efficiency. Manufacturing plants use IoT sensors to monitor machinery performance, detect faults in real time, and schedule predictive maintenance, preventing costly breakdowns.

2. Enhancing Data-Driven Decision Making: IoT generates vast amounts of real-time data that businesses and individuals can leverage to make informed decisions. For example, in agriculture, IoT-enabled sensors track soil moisture levels, temperature, and weather patterns, allowing farmers to optimize irrigation and increase crop yields. In retail, smart shelves equipped with RFID tags monitor inventory levels, reducing stock shortages and improving supply chain management. Real-time data analysis helps businesses identify trends, optimize operations, and improve customer experiences.

3. Cost Reduction and Resource Optimization: IoT plays a crucial role in minimizing costs and reducing waste. Smart energy management systems monitor electricity consumption in homes and offices, adjusting usage based on occupancy and weather conditions. IoT-enabled smart grids optimize energy distribution, preventing overloads and reducing energy wastage. Similarly, in transportation, IoT-driven fleet management systems track vehicle performance, optimize fuel consumption, and reduce operational costs for logistics companies.

4. Strengthening Security and Safety: Security is a growing concern in the digital age, and IoT contributes to enhanced protection in both personal and professional environments. Smart surveillance cameras, motion detectors, and biometric authentication systems improve home and office security. In the healthcare sector, IoT-powered medical devices monitor patient vitals, send alerts in emergencies, and enable remote diagnostics, improving patient care and reducing hospital visits. IoT is also used in smart cities to detect air pollution, monitor structural health in buildings, and enhance disaster preparedness.

5. Improving Quality of Life: IoT significantly enhances the daily lives of individuals through smart wearables, connected vehicles, and digital assistants. Fitness trackers and smartwatches monitor heart rate, activity levels, and sleep patterns, helping users maintain a healthy lifestyle. Connected cars use IoT to provide real-time navigation, predictive maintenance alerts, and accident detection, making driving safer and more efficient. Virtual assistants like Amazon Alexa and Google Assistant integrate IoT functionalities, offering voice-controlled automation for tasks like controlling home appliances, setting reminders, and accessing online services.

6. Enabling Smart Cities and Sustainable Living: IoT plays a key role in developing **smart cities**, where interconnected devices improve urban planning, infrastructure, and sustainability. Intelligent traffic management systems use real-time data from IoT sensors to reduce congestion and improve road safety. Smart waste management systems notify collection teams when bins are full, optimizing collection routes and reducing environmental impact. By improving resource allocation, IoT contributes to a more sustainable, eco-friendly future.

7. Empowering Businesses and Innovation: Businesses across industries are leveraging IoT to enhance operational efficiency, improve customer engagement, and unlock new revenue streams. Retailers use IoT-powered analytics to personalize shopping experiences, while e-commerce companies utilize IoT in warehouses for smart inventory tracking. The logistics sector benefits from real-time shipment tracking, predictive maintenance, and autonomous vehicle technology. As IoT continues to evolve, new business models and innovative solutions will reshape industries, fostering economic growth and technological advancement.

1.2 IoT Architecture

1.2.1 Components of IoT Systems

An **IoT system** consists of several interconnected components that enable devices to collect, process, and transmit data. These components work together to create a seamless network that allows smart devices to communicate and operate autonomously. The key components of an IoT system include:

1. Sensors and Actuators: Sensors and actuators are fundamental components of any IoT system, enabling devices to interact with the physical world. **Sensors** collect real-time data from the environment by detecting changes in parameters such as temperature, humidity, light, motion, pressure, and gas levels. This data is then processed and transmitted to IoT systems for analysis. **Actuators**, on the other hand, convert digital signals into physical actions, responding to the data collected by sensors. They can control devices such as motors, valves, switches, or relays to perform specific tasks. For example, in a smart home, a temperature sensor can detect a rise in room temperature, prompting an actuator to turn on the air conditioning system. The seamless interaction between sensors and actuators enables automation, efficiency, and real-time control in various IoT applications, including smart cities, healthcare, industrial automation, and agriculture.

Example: In a smart home, a temperature sensor detects room temperature, and an actuator (thermostat) adjusts the air conditioning accordingly.

2. Edge Devices and Gateways: Edge devices and gateways play a crucial role in IoT ecosystems by bridging the gap between sensors and cloud-based systems. **Edge devices** are computing units located close to the data source, capable of processing, filtering, and analyzing data before transmitting it to the cloud. This reduces latency, conserves bandwidth, and enhances real-time decision-making. **Gateways**, on the other hand, act as intermediaries that facilitate communication between IoT devices and external networks. They handle protocol translation, security enforcement, and data aggregation, ensuring seamless connectivity between different IoT components. For instance, in an industrial IoT system, an edge device can monitor machine performance and detect anomalies locally, while a gateway securely transmits only relevant insights to cloud analytics platforms. By decentralizing processing and improving connectivity, edge devices and gateways enable efficient, scalable, and secure IoT implementations across industries.

Example: In an industrial IoT system, an edge device processes vibration data from machines and alerts maintenance teams if abnormal patterns are detected.

3. Connectivity and Communication Protocols: Connectivity and communication protocols are the backbone of IoT systems, enabling seamless data exchange between devices, gateways, and cloud platforms. IoT devices use various **wired and wireless communication protocols** based on factors such as range, power consumption, and data transmission speed. **Short-range protocols** like Wi-Fi, Bluetooth, Zigbee, and Z-Wave are commonly used in smart homes, wearables, and industrial automation. **Long-range protocols** such as LoRaWAN, NB-IoT, and Sigfox are ideal for applications like smart agriculture and asset tracking, where devices need to communicate over extended distances with low power consumption. Cellular networks (4G/5G) provide high-speed connectivity for mission-critical IoT applications like autonomous vehicles and healthcare monitoring. These communication protocols ensure reliable and efficient data transfer, enabling IoT devices to function effectively in real-time, automated environments.

Example: A wearable fitness tracker uses Bluetooth to sync health data with a smartphone, while a smart agriculture system uses LoRaWAN to send soil moisture data to a remote server.

4. Cloud Computing and Data Storage: Cloud computing and data storage are essential components of IoT systems, providing the infrastructure needed to process, store, and analyze vast amounts of data generated by connected devices. Cloud platforms offer **scalability, flexibility, and remote accessibility**, allowing IoT devices to send data to centralized servers where advanced analytics, machine learning, and decision-making processes occur. Various cloud service models, such as **Infrastructure as a Service (IaaS), Platform as a Service (PaaS), and Software as a Service (SaaS)**, support IoT applications based on their processing and storage needs. Additionally, cloud storage solutions ensure **data security, redundancy, and real-time accessibility**, enabling seamless operation of smart applications like smart cities, healthcare monitoring, and industrial automation. By leveraging cloud computing, IoT systems can efficiently handle large-scale data, enhance system reliability, and enable intelligent decision-making across various industries.

Example: A smart city's traffic management system collects data from IoT-enabled traffic lights and analyzes patterns in the cloud to optimize traffic flow.

5. IoT Platforms and Data Analytics: IoT platforms and data analytics play a crucial role in managing connected devices, processing data, and extracting valuable insights from IoT ecosystems. **IoT platforms** provide a centralized framework for device management, data integration, real-time monitoring, and application development. Popular platforms like **AWS IoT, Google Cloud IoT, and Microsoft Azure IoT** enable seamless connectivity, security enforcement, and remote control of IoT devices. **Data analytics**, powered by machine learning and artificial intelligence, helps organizations analyze vast amounts of sensor data to detect patterns, predict outcomes, and optimize processes. For example, predictive maintenance in industrial IoT uses analytics to identify early signs of equipment failure, reducing downtime and operational costs. By combining IoT platforms with advanced data analytics, businesses can improve efficiency, enhance decision-making, and unlock new opportunities for automation and innovation.

Example: In predictive maintenance, an IoT platform processes real-time data from factory machines, identifies unusual patterns, and schedules maintenance before breakdowns occur.

6. User Interface (UI) and Applications: The **User Interface (UI)** in IoT systems serves as the bridge between users and connected devices, enabling seamless interaction, monitoring, and control. UI can take various forms, including **mobile applications, web dashboards, voice assistants, and touchscreen interfaces**, depending on the IoT application. A well-designed UI ensures **usability, accessibility, and real-time responsiveness**, allowing users to visualize data, configure device settings, and receive alerts effortlessly. For instance, a smart home app lets users control lighting, temperature, and security cameras remotely, while an industrial IoT dashboard provides real-time analytics on machine performance. The effectiveness of an IoT system largely depends on its UI, as it enhances user experience and enables intuitive control over complex IoT networks, driving convenience, automation, and efficiency in everyday applications.

Example: A smart irrigation system sends notifications to a farmer's smartphone app, showing real-time soil moisture levels and allowing remote control of water valves.

7. Security and Privacy: As the Internet of Things (IoT) continues to grow, security and privacy have become significant concerns. With billions of interconnected devices transmitting sensitive data, ensuring the safety of these systems is critical. IoT devices are often vulnerable to cyberattacks due to weak authentication, outdated software, and insecure communication protocols. Hackers can exploit these vulnerabilities to gain unauthorized access, disrupt services, or steal personal information. Privacy issues also arise as IoT devices collect vast amounts of personal data, from health metrics to location information, creating the risk of data breaches or misuse. Protecting IoT systems requires a combination of strong encryption, regular software updates, secure authentication mechanisms, and robust data management practices. Additionally, clear privacy policies and user consent are essential to ensure that personal information is handled responsibly. As IoT technologies evolve, addressing security and privacy concerns is paramount to maintaining trust and ensuring the safe deployment of IoT applications across industries.

Example: A smart door lock uses encrypted communication and biometric authentication to prevent unauthorized access.

1.2.2 IoT Architecture Layers

Internet of Things (IoT) technology has a wide range of applications and the use of the Internet of Things is growing so faster. It is the networking of physical objects that contain electronics embedded within their architecture to communicate and sense interactions amongst each other or to the external environment. The architecture of IoT is divided into 4 different layers i.e. Sensing Layer, Network Layer, Data processing Layer, and Application Layer.

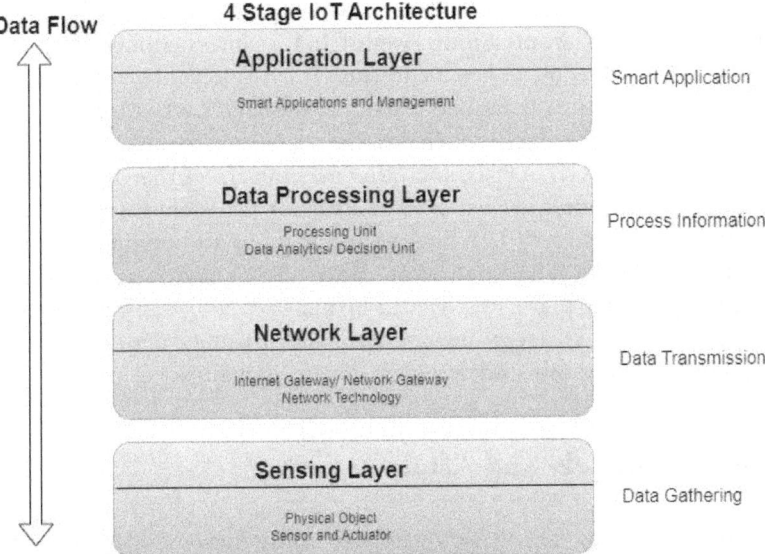

Sensing Layer: The sensing layer is the first layer of the InternetofThings architecture and is responsible for collecting data from different sources. This layer includes sensors and actuators that are placed in the environment to gather information about temperature, humidity, light, sound, and other physical parameters. Wired or wireless communication protocols connect these devices to the network layer.

Network Layer: The network layer of an IoT architecture is responsible for providing communication and connectivity between devices in the IoT system. It includes protocols and technologies that enable devices to connect and communicate with each other and with the wider internet. Examples of network technologies that are commonly used in IoT include Wifi, Bluetooth, Zigbee, and cellular networks such as 4G and 5G technology. Additionally, the network layer may include gateways and routers that act as intermediaries between devices and the wider internet, and may also include security features such as encryption and authentication to protect against unauthorized access.

Data processing Layer: The data processing layer of IoT architecture refers to the software and hardware components that are responsible for collecting, analyzing, and interpreting data from IoT devices. This layer is responsible for receiving raw data from the devices, processing it, and making it available for further analysis or action. The data processing layer includes a variety of technologies and tools, such as data management systems, analytics platforms, and machine learning algorithms. These tools are used to extract meaningful insights from the data and make decisions based on that data. Example of a technology used in the data processing layer is a data lake, which is a centralized repository for storing raw data from IoT devices.

Application Layer: The application layer of IoT architecture is the topmost layer that interacts directly with the end-user. It is responsible for providing user-friendly interfaces and functionalities that enable users to access and control IoT devices. This layer includes various software and applications such as mobile apps, web portals, and other user interfaces that are designed to interact with the underlying IoT infrastructure. It also includes middleware services that allow different IoT devices and systems to communicate and share data seamlessly. The application layer also includes analytics and processing capabilities that allow data to be analyzed and transformed into meaningful insights. This can include machine learning algorithms, data visualization tools, and other advanced analytics capabilities.

1.2.3 Sensor Networks and Actuators

Sensor and actuators are basic elements in numerous electrical and mechanical structures. On the same note, sensors are tasked with the responsibility of identifying changes within an environment while actuators are tasked with the responsibility of performing certain actions in response to these detections. It is important for anyone who is employed in certain professions, to have clear distinctions between these two, should work within robotics, automation, as well as control systems.

Sensor: Sensor is a device used for the conversion of physical events or characteristics into the electrical signals. This is a hardware device that takes the input from environment and gives to the system by converting it. For example, a thermometer takes the temperature as physical characteristic and then converts it into electrical signals for the system.

Types of Sensors

> **Temperature Sensors:** Take temperatures.

> **Light Sensors:** Light intensity sensors: It has the function of detecting the intensity of the light.

> **Pressure Sensors:** To use it to measure pressure in gases or liquids.

> **Motion Sensors:** Recognize motion in an established region.

Advantages of Sensors

> Offer timely and accurate information as this is a critical requirement by the high release frequency.

> Support automation and management of systems.

> Improve safety by maintaining check on important parameters.

Disadvantages of Sensors

> Sometimes can be costly particularly the high precision sensors.

> It can sometimes need some adjustments and can also probably require maintenance in the long run.

> Interference from the environment is easy in this process.

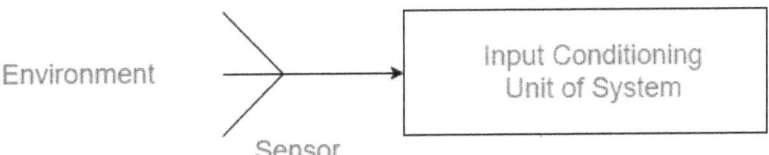

Actuator: Actuator is a device that converts the electrical signals into the physical events or characteristics. It takes the input from the system and gives output to the environment. For example, motors and heaters are some of the commonly used actuators.

Types of Actuators

> **Linear Actuators:** Utilize a linear motion to convert energy, Kinetic/pendulum.

> **Rotary Actuators:** This will affect the creation of rotational motion.

> **Hydraulic Actuators:** How does fluid power gives motion.

> **Pneumatic Actuators:** Function with use of compressed air.

Advantages of Actuators

> Assist in providing a fine level of control of mechanical installations.

> They should enable automation and therefore minimize the need for intervention of human participants.

> Available in a range of variations and suitability in multiple operations ranging from everyday uses to industrial use.

Disadvantages of Actuators

> May consume much power in its operation particularly when used in places that involve much power such as in large industries.

> May be large and costly to both install and maintain.

> As a disadvantage there is a circumstance that, with time the component is liable to mechanical wear and tear.

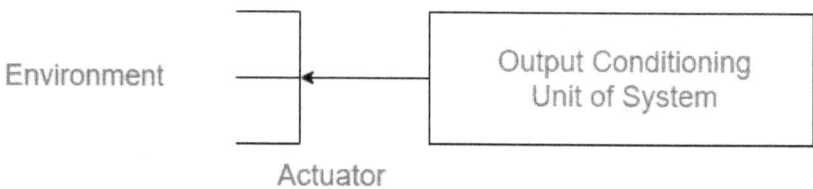

Actuator

Difference between Sensor and Actuator

Sensor	Actuator
It converts physical characteristics into electrical signals.	It converts electrical signals into physical characteristics.
It takes input from environment.	It takes input from output conditioning unit of system.
It gives output to input conditioning unit of system.	It gives output to environment.
Sensor generated electrical signals.	Actuator generates heat or motion.
It is placed at input port of the system.	It is placed at output port of the system.
It is used to measure the physical quantity.	It is used to measure the continuous and discrete process parameters.
It gives information to the system about environment.	It accepts command to perform a function.

| Example: Photo-voltaic cell which converts light energy into electrical energy. | Example: Stepper motor where electrical energy drives the motor. |

1.2.4 Cloud, Edge, and Fog Computing in IoT

Cloud Computing

Cloud Computing is a model for delivering information technology services over the internet. Users can now access and use shared pools of reconfigurable computing resources, including as servers, storage, databases, OS, and applications, without worrying about maintaining the underlying infrastructure.

The way that organizations and people access and use computing resources has been changed by cloud computing. They can rent computer resources from a cloud provider like Amazon Web Services rather than purchasing and maintaining their own hardware and software. Scalability, cost savings, increased agility, improved reliability, and global access are a few advantages of cloud computing.

Advantages of Cloud Computing

- ➢ **Scalability:** Without having to invest in pricey hardware, cloud computing enables businesses to effortlessly scale up or down their computer capabilities as needed. This enhances an organization's agility and enables swift responses to shift business requirements.

- ➢ **Cost-Effectiveness:** For small and medium-sized organizations in particular, cloud computing can be more affordable than traditional computer methods. This is because economies of scale allow cloud companies to offer computing power at a reduced price.

- ➢ **High Availability:** Cloud computing is capable of providing high availability, and most cloud providers offer uptime guarantees of a specific standard. This makes it perfect for applications that need constant availability, such as online stores or banking services.

Disadvantages of Cloud Computing

- ➢ **Security Risks:** Cloud computing can create additional security concerns, especially if the security precautions taken by the cloud provider are moderate. Data leaks, unauthorized access, and other cyber-attacks fall under this category.

- **Dependent Internet Connectivity:** Internet connectivity is necessary for cloud computing to access computing resources and data. If the internet connection is inconsistent or slow, this could be a drawback as it could result in lost productivity or stopped service.
- **Restricted Control:** The rate of control that companies have over their computing resources and data may be limited as a result of cloud computing. Because they depend on cloud service providers to manage and maintain their computer infrastructure, businesses may not be able to fully personalize and improve their systems.

Edge Computing

Edge Computing is a distributed computing architecture that brings computing and data storage closer to the source of data. Data processing takes place at the network's edge, adjacent to the device that generated the data, as opposed to a central location, such as a data center. Reduced latency and bandwidth needs are desired outcomes of edge computing when transferring large amounts of data to a processing center. Edge computing facilitates real-time decision-making by processing data close to the edge and accelerating data transfer to and from the cloud.

IoT devices, automated vehicles, and augmented reality/virtual reality (AR/VR) systems require low latency benefits, particularly from edge computing. Applications that produce a lot of data, such as those used in industry, video and image analysis, and intelligent

Advantages of Edge Computing

- **Reduced Latency:** Edge Computing makes it possible to process and analyze data more quickly at the point of origin, which cuts down on the time it takes for data to be transported to the cloud and back. Due to the huge reduction in latency, this is perfect for real-time decision-making applications like robotics, industrial automation, and automated cars.
- **Increased Security:** By enabling data processing and analysis close to the data's origin and reducing the quantity of data that must be transferred to the cloud, edge computing can increase security. As a result, it is more difficult for hackers to hack the system because the attack surface and potential vulnerabilities are reduced.
- **Greater Bandwidth Efficiency:** By enabling local data processing and analysis, edge computing can lessen the quantity of data that needs to be transported to the cloud. Better bandwidth efficiency as

a result can lower data transmission costs and enable quicker processing.

Disadvantages of Edge Computing

> **Low Processing Power:** With compare to cloud computing infrastructure, edge computing devices often have less processing power and storage space. The types of apps that can be used on edge devices may be constrained as a result.

> **Increased Complexity:** Edge computing implementation can be trickier than standard cloud computing strategies. This is due to the requirement of edge computing, which can be difficult to manage and maintain, to install processing and storage resources closer to the source.

> **Increased Costs:** In terms of hardware and maintenance costs, edge computing can be more expensive than cloud computing. This is because Edge Computing necessitates the deployment of processing and storage resources across several numbers which can be more expensive to set up and maintain.

Difference between Edge Computing and Cloud Computing

Parameter	Edge Computing	Cloud Computing
Definition	Edge Computing is a distributed computing architecture that brings computing and data storage closer to the source of data.	Cloud Computing is a model for delivering information technology services over the internet.
Location of Processing	Processing is done at the edge of the network, near the device that generates the data.	Data Analysis and Processing are done at a central location, such as a data centre.
Bandwidth Requirements	Low bandwidth is required, as data is processed near the source.	Higher bandwidth is required as compared to edge computing, as data must be transmitted over the network to a central location for processing.
Costs	Edge Computing is more expensive, as specialized hardware and software	Cloud Computing is less expensive, as users only pay for the resources they actually use.

		may be required at the edge.	
Scalability		Scalability for Edge Computing can be more challenging, as additional computing resources may need to be added at the edge.	Easier, as users can quickly and easily scale up or down their computing resources based on their needs.
Use Cases		Applications that require low latency and real-time decision-making, such as IoT devices, autonomous vehicles, and AR/VR systems.	Applications that do not have strict latency requirements, such as web applications, email, and file storage.
Data Security		Data security can be improved, as data is processed near the source and is not transmitted over the network.	Data Security is more challenging, as data is transmitted over the network to a central location for processing.

Fog Computing

Fog computing is a decentralized computing infrastructure or process in which computing resources are located between the data source and the cloud or any other data center. Fog computing is a paradigm that provides services to user requests at the edge networks. The devices at the fog layer usually perform operations related to networking such as routers, gateways, bridges, and hubs. Researchers envision these devices to be capable of performing both computational and networking operations, simultaneously. Although these devices are resource-constrained compared to the cloud servers, the geological spread and the decentralized nature help in offering reliable services with coverage over a wide area. Fog computing is the physical location of the devices, which are much closer to the users than the cloud servers.

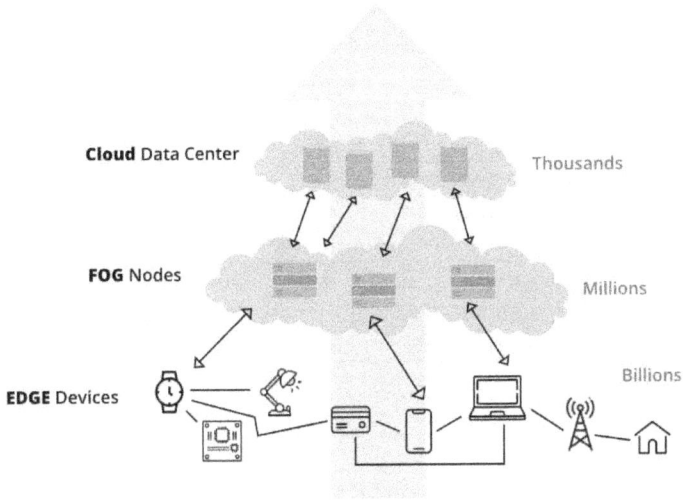

Differences between Cloud Computing and Fog Computing:

Feature	Cloud Computing	Fog Computing
Latency	Cloud computing has high latency compared to fog computing	Fog computing has low latency
Capacity	Cloud Computing does not provide any reduction in data while sending or transforming data	Fog Computing reduces the amount of data sent to cloud computing.
Responsiveness	Response time of the system is low.	Response time of the system is high.
Security	Cloud computing has less security compared to Fog Computing	Fog computing has high Security.
Speed	Access speed is high depending on the VM connectivity.	High even more compared to Cloud Computing.
Data Integration	Multiple data sources can be integrated.	Multiple Data sources and devices can be integrated.
Mobility	In cloud computing mobility is Limited.	Mobility is supported in fog computing.
Location Awareness	Partially Supported in Cloud computing.	Supported in fog computing.

Number of Server Nodes	Cloud computing has Few numbers of server nodes.	Fog computing has large number of server nodes.
Geographical Distribution	It is centralized.	It is decentralized and distributed.
Location of service	Services provided within the internet.	Services provided at the edge of the local network.
Working environment	Specific data center building with air conditioning systems	Outdoor (streets, base stations, etc.) or indoor (houses, cafes, etc.)
Communication mode	IP network	Wireless communication: WLAN, WIFI, 3G, 4G, ZigBee, etc. or wired communication (part of the IP networks)
Dependence on the quality of core network	Requires strong network core.	Can also work in Weak network core.

1.2.5 Elements of an IoT Ecosystem

The Internet of Things (IoT) ecosystem refers to the interconnected network of physical devices, vehicles, buildings, and other objects that are embedded with sensors, software, and connectivity. These devices can communicate with each other and with the internet, exchanging data and performing tasks autonomously or with minimal human intervention.

The Internet of Things (IoT) ecosystem refers to the interconnected network of physical devices, vehicles, buildings, and other objects that are embedded with sensors, software, and connectivity. These devices can communicate with each other and with the internet, exchanging data and performing tasks autonomously or with minimal human intervention.

Here are some key components of IoT Ecosystem –

- ➢ **Devices and Sensors** – IoT devices are embedded with sensors, actuators, and other components that enable them to collect and transmit data. Examples of IoT devices include smart home appliances, wearables, industrial machines, and vehicles.

- **Communication Networks** – IoT devices require connectivity to communicate with each other and with the internet. This can be achieved through various means such as Wi-Fi, Bluetooth, cellular networks, and satellite communications.

- **Cloud Computing** – IoT platforms often include cloud-based services that enable data storage, analytics, and visualization. The cloud provides a scalable and flexible infrastructure for managing the large amounts of data generated by IoT devices.

- **Data Analytics and Machine Learning** – IoT generates vast amounts of data that can be analyzed to derive insights and make informed decisions. Data analytics and machine learning techniques are used to process and analyze the data to extract meaningful insights.

- **Applications and Services** – IoT applications are the software programs that enable users to interact with the IoT ecosystem. These applications can be designed for specific use cases such as smart home automation, healthcare monitoring, or industrial automation. Services such as device management, security, and data processing are also important components of the IoT ecosystem.

Here are some key benefits of IoT Ecosystem –

- **Increased Efficiency** – IoT devices and sensors can automate and streamline many processes, reducing the need for human intervention and improving efficiency. For example, in industrial settings, IoT can help optimize production lines, reduce downtime, and improve supply chain management.

- **Improved Safety and Security** – IoT can enhance safety and security in a variety of settings. For instance, in the healthcare industry, IoT can be used for remote patient monitoring, ensuring that patients receive timely care. In the home, IoT devices can provide enhanced security through surveillance cameras, door locks, and alarms.

- **Enhanced Customer Experience** – IoT can provide a more personalized and convenient experience for customers. For instance, in retail settings, IoT can be used to provide personalized recommendations and improve the shopping experience. In the hospitality industry, IoT can be used to provide guests with personalized services and amenities.

> **Cost Savings** – IoT can help organizations save money by reducing waste, improving efficiency, and optimizing processes. For example, in the energy industry, IoT can help optimize energy usage and reduce costs. In transportation, IoT can help optimize logistics and reduce fuel consumption.

Here are few examples of IoT Ecosystem –

> **Smart Homes** – Smart homes are an example of how IoT technology can be used to improve daily life. IoT devices such as smart thermostats, lighting, security cameras, and voice assistants are used to automate and control various aspects of the home. These devices can be controlled through mobile apps, voice commands, or automated schedules, providing greater convenience and energy efficiency.

> **Industrial IoT** – Industrial IoT is another example of how IoT technology can be used to improve efficiency and productivity in industrial settings. IoT sensors and devices are used to monitor and optimize manufacturing processes, track inventory and assets, and manage supply chains. This technology can help reduce downtime, optimize energy usage, and improve safety.

> **Healthcare IoT** – Healthcare IoT is a rapidly growing area that involves the use of IoT technology in healthcare settings. IoT devices such as wearables and remote monitoring devices can be used to monitor patients' vital signs, track medication adherence, and provide real-time feedback to healthcare providers. This technology can help improve patient outcomes and reduce healthcare costs.

1.2.6 Convergence of IT and IoT

What is operational technology (OT)?

OT, short for operational technology, is defined by the ISA95 standard as the devices, assets, and systems used in the physical process (level 0), sensing and manipulation (level 1), supervisory control (level 2), and manufacturing operations management (level 3). OT includes equipment and devices used in the physical process—pipes, belts, machines, robots, sensors, controllers, etc., and the systems used to control equipment—HMI, SCADA, MES, etc.

What's the difference between IT and OT?

OT is focused on manufacturing and industrial operations, whereas IT is focused on the physical and digital assets and processes used to create, process, store, and secure electronic data.

OT departments are primarily concerned with availability, uptime, and data quality and reliability of systems.

IT is typically more concerned with the security, standardization, and scalability of systems.

What is IT/OT convergence?

IT/OT convergence breaks down the barriers between OT and IT systems. Now the operational technology running in your machines, on your equipment, and across your production lines can securely inform your IT systems. These OT systems—and the rich data they generate—can access and fuel advanced IT systems. The powerful processing potential of these business applications can now reach the core of your operations—your OT systems and data.

By connecting systems that control manufacturing processes with those that control data storage, communications, and computing, you can finally apply your most advanced IT resources to improve your most mission critical operations.

Connecting IT and OT systems ensures assets are running to intended spec, output, uptime, and SLAs. It improves visibility and responsiveness to avoid unplanned downtime. It allows full control over parameters, specs, rules, constraints, and policies—revealing not only how equipment is running at all times, but also when an incident may occur based on historical data and conditions.

IT/OT convergence strategy also improves scalability of your digital transformation initiatives. By extending and standardizing data access, you can more readily deploy and scale powerful new solutions, without fear of being trapped in a pilot purgatory.

The types of IT/OT convergence

Process convergence

Process convergence is the unification of workflows across IT and OT. Both departments need to revise their procedures and policies to drive visibility, alignment, and ultimately understanding. The convergence of processes represents an organizational convergence, addressing the internal business structures. For example, a company may have established SOPs for cybersecurity, these processes and procedures should consider and protect OT networks.

Software and data convergence

Software and data convergence brings together IT and OT systems into an architecture that is seamless, secure, and scalable to meet the needs of the enterprise. This convergence allows OT data from the manufacturing shop floor to be leveraged in IT systems, such as the cloud or IoT platforms, for visibility and insights into performance.

Physical convergence

Physical convergence refers to physical devices being retrofitted with newer hardware to accommodate the addition of IT to OT. Examples of this include investments in networking equipment for OT.

What are the benefits of IT/OT convergence?

Operational efficiency

IT/OT convergence empowers manufacturers with enhanced visibility into operations, utilizing OT data for insights. This enables improved efficiency, cost reduction, enhanced OEE, decreased defects, and optimized throughput.

Enhanced cybersecurity

IT/OT convergence reduces cybersecurity risks by implementing unified security policies, enhancing monitoring, and enabling collaborative threat management between IT and OT teams.

Faster time to market

IT/OT convergence accelerates time to market by streamlining data integration and automation, enhancing real-time analytics for faster decision-making, and facilitating agile development and deployment of new technologies and products.

Improved automation

IT/OT convergence enhances automation by enabling seamless data exchange and control across production. This integration boosts efficiency, reduces manual tasks, and supports advanced automation like predictive maintenance and adaptive control systems.

Reduced costs

IT/OT convergence cuts costs by eliminating duplicate systems, optimizing resources, automating operations, enabling predictive maintenance to prevent downtime, and reducing overhead through unified monitoring and management.

Increased compliance

IT/OT convergence enhances compliance by centralizing data management, ensuring consistent regulatory adherence across systems, and improving visibility for audits. Real-time monitoring and reporting enable proactive compliance measures.

Increased IT and OT department collaboration

IT/OT convergence enhances collaboration by integrating systems and data, facilitating communication and knowledge sharing, aligning goals, and enabling cross-functional teams to work more effectively toward common objectives.

The role of IoT in IT/OT convergence

IoT platforms bring together IT and OT data into a single interface. Sourcing OT data from industrial connectivity and IT data from integrations, IoT platforms enable a variety of use cases, including asset and performance monitoring, connected work cell, and predictive maintenance.

IT/OT convergence best practices

Communicate goals: Understand the business objective, set measurable and realistic goals, and then communicate clearly across teams.
Provide training: Cross-training OT and IT teams on the responsibilities and priorities of each team can help improve understanding and collaboration.
Show overlap: Identify and communicate the areas of shared responsibility, especially in terms of systems and security.
Use the right tools: Determine and deploy the right toolset to enable discovery, configuration, management, and security.
Define roles and responsibilities: Clearly communicate the roles and responsibilities for each team, and the opportunities and areas for collaboration.

1.2.7 Technology Drivers

5 key drivers of IoT for Smart Buildings

Facility management is undergoing a complete transformation, as smart facilities and IoT technologies continue to evolve. Buildings are becoming streamlined operational ecosystems capable of collecting more actionable data, being more environmentally friendly, and significantly increasing resource efficiencies.

There is no doubt that IoT is increasingly bridging the gaps between the physical and digital world, so here's our take on the 5 key drivers in the smart facilities mix.

This may mean tracking the amount of traffic in the building, the number of people in the meeting rooms, free workspaces, facility air quality, and temperature. This can be achieved by the installation of wireless IoT sensors. One thing is certain, <u>smart facilities are the future.</u>

Based on our years of experience with our facility customers, here are five key drivers setting the momentum of IoT and smart facilities:

- ➢ Scalability
- ➢ Easy installation and maintenance
- ➢ Reliability
- ➢ IoT security
- ➢ Integration

1. Scalability, the practical driver

The first key driver is perhaps not the most exciting, but probably the most practical: scalability. Creating a small proof of concept using widely available DIY (Do It Yourself) IoT kits is relatively easy, but **when you need to scale the implementation to thousands or hundreds of thousands of sensors, things get a little more complicated.**

A well designed IoT solution ensures that your solution is easy and fast to scale, secure, easy to use, and of course, cost-efficient.

The challenges with scalability are not only about adding more devices but also about maintaining them. Consider what it takes to keep the IoT devices on several locations operating effectively: monitoring their battery levels and replacing batteries, ensuring consistent and strong connectivity, dealing with each sensor's reporting intervals, as well as remote firmware updates over the entire lifecycle.

Although these issues seem to add some complications to the mix when you consider implementing IoT to your operations, the efforts will be more than rewarded in the savings received.

2. Easiness of installation and maintenance

Easy installation and scale are paramount for smart facilities. A wonderful instant benefit of IoT is that its hardware, including sensors and gateways, are easy to install and user-friendly for the technicians. For example, wireless sensor installation should be as easy as mounting the sensor to walls, ceilings, under tables, etc. in a matter of seconds and validating the connectivity with a smartphone. Also, there should be no need to involve building IT infrastructure when connecting devices with mobile gateways.

When considering different IoT solutions, one must remember that **the amount of installation time per sensor will mirror directly to the overall cost.** The instructions must be straightforward for technicians and easy to understand. Also, the instructions should be easily available in, for example, a mobile app that can guide the technicians through both installation and maintenance procedures.

3. Reliability

Buildings are built to last, and that's how the design for sensors and gateways should be approached as well. Batteries in sensors last for several years, therefore requiring very little maintenance. Once installed, the sensor maintenance should be minimal.

As the installed sensor base scales, the less you need to worry about their connectivity, battery levels and signal strengths, the more time you have analyzing the data they give.

Reliable maintenance makes sure that the dataflow is constant, all the devices are in operation and where they should be, and that nothing comes in the way of getting the most out of IoT in your smart facilities solution.

4. IoT Security

The quality of security is one of the major key drivers of any type of development, and IoT data collection platforms are designed with privacy and security in mind. End-to-end security is employed from the sensors to the cloud application in terms of software, and from the factory to the location with no unknown software layers. Comprehensive security allows for protected integration to your cloud platform and ensures the continuity of its transmission.

We at Haltian are overseeing security all the way from the manufacturing, where customer-specific encryption keys are installed in the software ensuring data integrity. We don't use any unknown software layers and interfaces.

Our cloud partner for sensor operations is Amazon Web Services which means that our solution has gone through a thorough validation process and is tested regularly.

5. Easily integrated IoT ecosystem

IoT ecosystem and value chains are rather long and complex, hence implementing that IoT solutions require various layers to talk to each other. A system that can deliver a cost-effective data collection solution for smart facilities with full integration to any cloud-based application is a massive forward driver.

Haltian's Thingsee solution includes various sensors, gateways, cellular connectivity and software for device cloud. Our customers can have an IoT platform or cloud-based solution from another vendor, to which we integrate easily. The beauty of running a cloud-based solution is the ease of integration!

1.2.8 Business Drivers

Business drivers for the Internet of Things (IoT) include technological advancements, cost reduction, data insights, and the need for improved efficiency, customer experience, and operational performance. Specifically, the falling cost of sensors, processing power, and cloud storage, coupled with increased sensor availability, are key enablers. These advancements are driving the adoption of IoT solutions across various industries, including manufacturing, retail, healthcare, and transportation.

Here's a more detailed look at the business drivers for IoT:

1. Technological Advancements:

Reduced Costs: The cost of sensors, processing power, and storage has decreased significantly, making IoT solutions more affordable and accessible.

Increased Sensor Density: The availability of a wider variety of sensors with improved capabilities has enabled the collection of more data and the monitoring of a wider range of parameters.

Cloud and Big Data: Cloud computing and big data analytics have provided the infrastructure for storing, processing, and analyzing the large amounts of data generated by IoT devices.

5G and Improved Connectivity: The emergence of 5G technology has provided faster and more reliable connectivity for IoT devices, enabling real-time data transmission and control.

2. Business Benefits:

Data-Driven Decision Making: IoT enables businesses to collect and analyze real-time data, leading to more informed decisions and optimized operations.

Improved Efficiency and Productivity: IoT solutions can automate tasks, streamline processes, and improve resource utilization, leading to increased efficiency and productivity.

Enhanced Customer Experience: IoT data can be used to personalize customer experiences, improve service quality, and build stronger customer relationships.

Cost Reduction: IoT can help businesses identify areas for cost optimization, reduce operational expenses, and improve resource management.

New Revenue Streams: IoT can enable businesses to create new product and service offerings, generate new revenue streams, and expand their market reach.

3. Industry-Specific Applications:

Manufacturing: IoT can be used to monitor equipment performance, predict maintenance needs, optimize production processes, and improve quality control.

Retail: IoT can be used to optimize inventory management, improve store layouts, personalize customer experiences, and track customer behavior.

Healthcare: IoT can be used to monitor patient health, improve diagnostics, personalize treatment plans, and automate tasks.

Transportation: IoT can be used to improve fleet management, optimize routes, monitor vehicle performance, and enhance safety.

1.3 IoT Communication Protocols

1.3.1 Overview of Communication Technologies

The Internet of Things (IoT) is a technology that has transformed the way we live and work. It is a network of interconnected devices that exchange data and perform various tasks with one another.

In IoT communication refers to the exchange of information and data between various devices, systems, and networks. Internet of Things devices, such as actuators, sensors, and other smart devices, rely on communication to interact with one another and external systems, such as cloud-based platforms and mobile apps. Communication is an important aspect of IoT because it allows devices to collaborate to achieve common goals.

For example, Sensors in an IoT system, might collect data on environmental conditions like temperature, humidity, and light levels and send it to a cloud platform for storage and analysis. The platform may then share that data with other IoT devices, such as a smart thermostat or lighting system, allowing them to make adjustments to the environment based on the data. At its core, IoT is a system of interconnected devices that communicate with each other to exchange data and perform various tasks. However, not all IoT communications are the same.

In IoT, several types of communications occur, including –

Device-to-Device Communication

The most common type of communication in IoT is device-to-device. This type of communication takes place between two or more Internet of Things (IoT) devices, such as a smart thermostat that's communicating with a smart lighting system to adjust the lighting and temperature in a room. The devices communicate with one another to coordinate their actions in response to environmental factors like temperature and light levels.

This type of communication is important in the IoTs because it enables devices to collaborate to achieve common goals. A smart home system, for example, may include several devices such as a thermostat, a lighting system, and a safety system. These devices have to interact with each other in order to keep the home safe, comfortable, and secure.

Device-to-Cloud Communication

Device-to-cloud communication is another crucial type of communication in IoT. This type of communication occurs between an IoT device and a cloud-based platform, in which the device sends data to the cloud for storage and analysis. A smart home security camera, for example, sends video to a cloud-based platform for remote viewing and storage. This type of communication is critical in IoT because it allows devices to store and analyze data in the cloud, which can be accessed from anywhere in the world. This allows users to remotely monitor and control their IoT devices even when they are away from home.

Cloud-to-Device Communication

Cloud-to-device communication is the inverse of device-to-cloud communication. This kind of communication takes place when a cloud-based platform sends data or commands to an IoT device. A weather tracking platform, for example, may send commands to a smart irrigation system to adjust watering schedules based on upcoming weather conditions. This type of communication is important in IoT because it allows users to control their IoT devices from anywhere in the world. This can be useful in scenarios where users need to make changes to their IoT devices in response to changing conditions or events.

Peer-to-Peer Communication

Another form of communication in IoT is peer-to-peer communication. This type of communication takes place between IoT devices without the use of a cloud platform. This is useful in situations where cloud-based communication is not possible or desirable, such as in remote or secure locations. A group of IoT devices, for example, may communicate with one another in a peer-to-peer network to share data and coordinate their actions. This is useful in manufacturing, where machines must communicate with one another to optimize production processes.

Machine-to-Machine Communication

Machine-to-machine communication is one type of IoT communication. This type of communication takes place between machines without the need for human intervention. Communication between IoT devices and non-IoT machines, such as a manufacturing robot communicating with a conveyor belt system to optimize production processes, is one example. This type of communication is critical in IoT because it enables machines to collaborate to achieve common goals without the need for human intervention. This is useful in situations where human intervention is neither practical nor desirable, such as manufacturing or logistics.

1.3.2 Wireless Communication Protocols

IoT (Internet of Things) has power to make the complete system automatic. There are various **IOT communication protocols** which are used in communication between devices in the IoT network. **The wireless communication protocol** is a standard set of rules with reference to which various electronic devices communicate with each other wirelessly. Since there are many wireless communication protocol available to use for your product, it becomes difficult for the product designers to choose the correct one but once the scope of IoT application is decided it would become easier to select the right protocol. Here we are briefly explaining some **protocols used in IOT** with their features and applications.

Wi-Fi: Wi-Fi (Wireless Fidelity) is the most popular **IOT communication protocols** for wireless local area network (WLAN) that utilizes the IEEE 802.11 standard through 2.4 GHz UHF and 5 GHz ISM frequencies. Wi-Fi provides Internet access to devices that are within the range of about 20

40 meters from the source. It has a data rate upto 600 Mbps maximum, depending on channel frequency used and the number of antennas. In terms

of using the Wi-Fi protocol for IOT, there are some pros & cons to be considered. The infrastructure or device cost for Wi-Fi is low & deployment is easy but the power consumption is high and the Wi-Fi range is quite moderate. So, the Wi-Fi may not be the best choice for all types of IOT applications but it can be used for applications like Home Automation.

There are many development boards available that allow people to build IOT applications using Wi-Fi. The most popular ones are the Raspberry Pi and Node MCU. These boards allow people to build IOT prototypes and also can be used for small real-time applications. Likewise, is the Marvell Avastar 88W8997 SoC, which follows the Wi-Fi's IEEE 802.11n standard. The chip has applications like wearables, wireless audio & smart home.**ESP32** and **ESP8266** are the most commonly use wifi modules for embedded applications.

Bluetooth: Bluetooth is a technology used for exchanging data wirelessly over short distances and preferred over various **IOT network protocols**. It uses short-wavelength UHF radio waves of frequency ranging from 2.4 to 2.485 GHz in the ISM band. The Bluetooth technology has 3 different versions based on its applications:

> **Bluetooth:** The Bluetooth that is used in devices for communication has many applications in IOT/M2M devices nowadays. It is a

technology using which two devices can communicate and share data wirelessly. It operates at 2.4GHz ISM band and the data is split in packets before sending and then is shared using any one of the designated 79 channels operating at 1 MHz of bandwidth.

- **BLE (Bluetooth 4.0, Bluetooth Low Energy):** The BLE has a single main difference from Bluetooth that it consumes low power. With that, it makes the product of low cost & more long-lasting than Bluetooth.

- **iBeacon:** It is a simplified communication technique used by Apple and is completely based on Bluetooth technology. The Bluetooth 4.0 transmits an ID called UUID for each user and makes it each to communicate between iPhone users

Bluetooth has many applications, such as in telephones, tablets, media players, robotics systems, etc. The range of Bluetooth technology is between 50 – 150 meters and the data is being shared at a maximum data rate of 1 Mbps.

After launching the BLE protocol, there have been many new applications developed using Bluetooth in the field of IOT. They fall under the category of low-cost consumer products and Smart-Building applications. Like Wi-Fi, **Bluetooth also has a module Bluetooth HC-05 that can be interfaced with development boards like Arduino or Raspberry Pi to build DIY projects**. When it comes to Real-time applications, Marvell's Avastar 88W8977 comes with Bluetooth v4.2 and has features like high speed, mesh networking for IOT. Another product, M5600 is a wireless pressure transducer with a Bluetooth v4.0 embedded in it.

Zigbee: ZigBee is another **IoT wireless protocols** has features similar to the the Bluetooth technology. But it follows the IEEE 802.15.4 standard and is a high-level communication protocol. It has some advantages similar to Bluetooth i.e. low-power consumption, robustness, high security, and high scalability.

Zigbee offers a range of about 10 – 100 meters maximum and data rate to transfer data between communicated devices is around 250 Kbps. It has a large number of applications in technologies like M2M & IOT.

Having limitations in regards to data rate, range, and power consumption, Zigbee is only appropriate for Small-Scale Wireless applications. Though having some limitations, **it provides a 128-bit AES encryption and is giving a big hand in making secure communication for home automation & small Industrial applications**. Zigbee too has its DIY module named **XBee** & **XBee Pro** which can be interfaced with Arduino or Raspberry Pi boards to make simple projects or application prototypes.

The company Develco has made products using Zigbee technologies like Sensors, gateways, meter interfaces, smart plugs, smart relays, etc which all work on the Zigbee wireless Mesh network, consuming low power and free from external interferences. Another company, Datanet has Zigbee based products which are used in real-time applications already, like the DNL910 & DNL920.

Z-Wave: Z-Wave is a communication protocol specially designed for Home Automation products and it is also known as a low-power RF communications technology. The data packets are exchanged at data rates of 100kbps maximum and the protocol operates at a frequency of 900 MHz in the ISM band. It has a distance range of up to 30 meters maximum. It supports control of up to 232 devices. The only maker of chips for this technology is Sigma Designs.

The Z-Wave has module ZIY (Z-Wave It Yourself) which is an Arduino & Raspberry Pi compatible board and can be used for Home Automation applications. Silicon Labs has a product Z-Wave 700, **specially developed for Smart Home applications having features like long battery life** (10 years) and improved range to about 100 meters. Also, the company has launched a Z-Wave 700 Development Kit which includes Z-Wave software, sample code and the module with an adapter, enabling others to develop Z-Wave based application products

6LoWPAN: 6LowPAN (IPv6 Low-power Wireless Personal Area Network) is a network protocol that supports data encapsulation and header compression mechanisms with other applications like that of Bluetooth & ZigBee. The standard can be used across multiple communications platforms, including Ethernet, Wi-Fi, IEEE 802.15.4 and sub-1GHz ISM.

It can be adapted as Bluetooth 4.0 or ZigBee and operate at 2.4 GHz or 900 MHz, respectively. It consumes low power and can be used in a wide number of IOT and M2M applications.

6LoWPAN protocol has a 6LoWPAN L-Tek Arduino Shield that can be connected with Arduino board to get 6LoWPAN connectivity at a frequency band of 900 MHz. The users can **develop application prototypes using the module**. Talking about modules, Melange Systems has Tarang UT20 &TarangMini SM modules that have the connectivity to 6LoWPAN protocol. Microchip has developed SmartConnect 6LoWPAN for IP mesh connectivity over 802.15.4 links in 2.4GHz frequency band. IDT has ZWIR45xx series modules that are used for 6LoWPAN protocol applications.

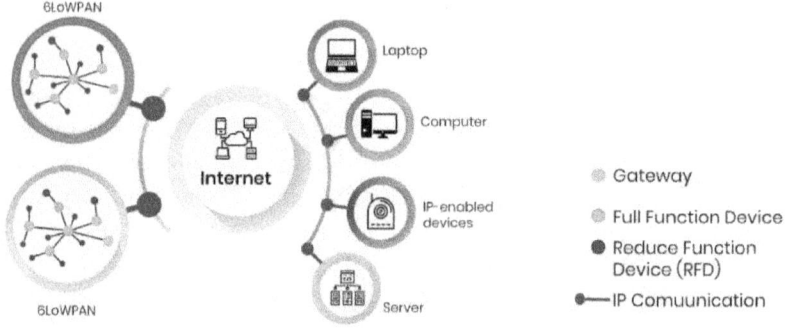

6LoWPAN Architecture

RFID: Radio-frequency identification (RFID) is a technology that uses electromagnetic fields to identify objects or tags which contains some stored information. The range of RFID varies from about 10cm to 200m maximum and such a long difference makes the two range have names like short-range distance and long-range distance. Since the range has a huge difference, the frequency at which the RFID operates has a huge difference too i.e. it starts from KHz and ranges till GHz or can be said as frequency ranges from Low frequency (LF) to Microwave depending upon the application and distance of communication.

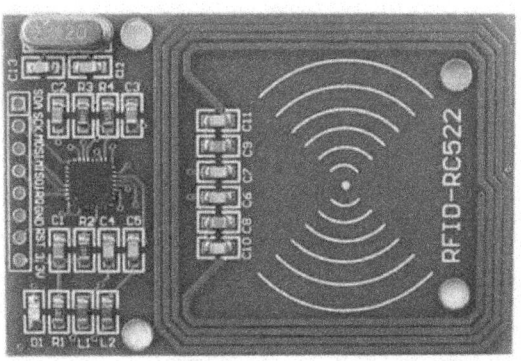

Cellular: The cellular network has been in use since the last 2 decades and comprises of GSM/GPRS/EDGE(2G)/UMTS or HSPA(3G)/LTE(4G) communication protocols. This protocol is generally **used for long-distance communications**. The data can be sent of large size and with high speeds compared to other technologies.

The operating frequencies range from 900 – 2100 MHz with a distance coverage of 35km to 200km and the data rates i.e. the speed of transferring data is from 35 Kbps to 10 Mbps. A company Quectel has cellular IOT products like EC21, EC23, EG91 and many more LTE standard products working on 4G. UMTS/HSPDA UC15, UC20, UC15 Mini & UC20 Mini are the 3G based IOT module launched by the same company.

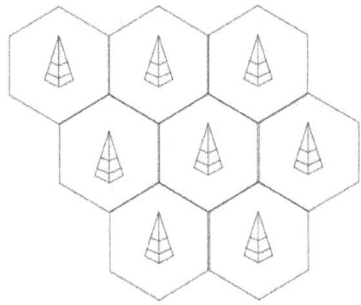

NB-IOT

NB-IOT stands for **Narrow Band Internet of Things**, is an LPWAN i.e. Low Power Wide Area Network technology. The technology can be used for applications requiring low power consumption, long-distance communication and for a long time (large battery life). The advantage of NB-IOT is that it has good coverage capacity i.e. the signal can transmit through walls or in underground areas where normal cellular signals won't reach. It has a distance coverage of around 10 Kms maximum. Quectel has launched NB-IOT modules like LTE BC95, LTE BC68 and many more modules that can be used to build real-time products in the field of IOT.

NFC: NFC (Near Field Communication) is a protocol used for enabling simple and safe two-way interactions between electronic devices. It has mostly smartphones based applications like allowing contactless payment transactions, accessing digital content and connecting various electronic devices.

It operates at a frequency of 13.56MHz in the ISM band and the maximum distance range is about 10cm with a data rate of 100–420kbps. It replaces the card swiping payment transaction and can be used for wireless payment like some magic.

Being a good protocol for IOT technology, there are various modules and real-time products that follow the NFC protocol. Like the Seeed Studio NFC shield, DFRobot NFC module, Grove NFC, and all 3 of them are Arduino and Raspberry Pi compatible. For real-time products, NFC has CLRC663 plus, MFRC630, NTAG I²C plus products.

LoRaWAN: LoRa is getting popular now days and used in **IOT network protocol**. LoRaWAN (Long Range Wide Area Network) has applications for long distances and is designed to **provide low-power for communication in IoT, M2M applications**. It has a capacity of connecting millions of devices with data rates ranging from 0.3 kbps to 50 kbps. The distance for LoRaWAN application ranges from 2   5km for the urban environment & maximum 15km for the suburban environment.

1.3.3 Cellular Networks for IoT

"Cellular networks for IoT" refers to using existing cellular networks (like 2G, 3G, 4G, and 5G) to connect Internet of Things (IoT) devices, leveraging their wide coverage and reliability to enable connectivity for a variety of applications across diverse locations, with the most common cellular IoT technologies being LTE-M (Long Term Evolution for Machines) and NB-IoT (Narrowband IoT) which are specifically designed for low power consumption and extensive coverage needs of IoT devices.

Key points about cellular networks for IoT:

Wide Coverage: Cellular networks provide extensive geographic coverage, making them suitable for IoT devices deployed in remote areas where other connectivity options might be limited.

Reliability: Cellular networks are known for their stability and reliability, crucial for critical IoT applications that require consistent connectivity.

Low Power Consumption: Technologies like NB-IoT are specifically designed to operate on low power, extending battery life for IoT devices.

M2M SIMs: IoT devices typically use dedicated "M2M" SIM cards to manage connectivity and data usage within a cellular network.

Application Examples: Cellular IoT is used in applications like smart meters, asset tracking, industrial monitoring, agricultural sensors, wearable devices, and connected vehicles.

Main Cellular IoT Technologies:

LTE-M (LTE-Cat M1): Offers faster data rates compared to NB-IoT, suitable for applications requiring moderate data transfer.

NB-IoT (Narrowband IoT): Focuses on extended coverage and low power consumption, ideal for devices that only need to send small amounts of data at infrequent intervals.

Types of Cellular IoT Networks

The Global System for Mobile Communications (GSMA) is the globally adopted standard for cellular communication. The cellular networks have exponentially developed from 2G, 3G, and 4G, to 5th Generation- 5G NR and 5G RedCap -the technology that most industrial people look forward to. LPWAN technology is also a major technology in connecting IoT devices that requires minimal power. This low-power wide area network is great for sending bits of data, like sensors readings, making it ideal for massive IoT with low power consumption.

2G: The second generation (2G) served us for three decades. 2G connectivity deployments are simple, affordable, and easy to implement. 2G cellular networks were implemented for logistics, telematics applications where devices transmit basic alerts, status updates, and location data with less power consumption.

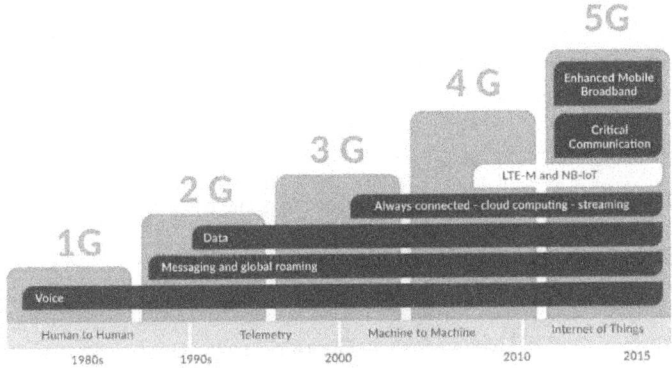

3G: 3G cellular IoT networks provide faster data transmission. 3G facilitates more advanced processes like file sharing, streaming, analytics, and remote device management with Universal Mobile Telecommunications System. It is commonly used in consumer IoT devices and smart grids.

4G: 4G LTE (long-term evolution) is capable of accommodating more sophisticated IoT solutions. 4G network data speeds are 10x faster than 3G. Using 4G LTE technology, cellular IoT devices can make low bandwidth voice calls (VoLTE), and enable video conferencing facilities. It is widely used in security cameras, healthcare.

5G: 5G (5th generation mobile network) is the new global wireless standard after 4G networks. 5G technology, with a peak speed of 20 Gbps, is all set to outperform 4G networks (1 Gbps). 5G wireless technology delivers peak data speeds, lower latency, more reliability, and massive network capacity, streamlining IoT businesses and other digital experiences such as online gaming, videoconferencing, and autonomous cars. The two derivatives of 5G networks 5G NR and 5G RedCap are all prepared to bridge the gaps in the existing cellular networks and build an efficient connected ecosystem. To know more, read more on our blog on 5G NR and 5G RedCap.

1.3.4 Short-Range vs Long-Range Communication

IoT devices communicate using a variety of wireless technologies, which can be broadly classified into **short-range** and **long-range** communication. The choice between them depends on factors such as range, power consumption, data rate, and application requirements.

Short-Range Communication

Short-range communication technologies are ideal for localized IoT applications where devices are close to each other or connected to a central hub. These technologies offer high data rates but have limited coverage.

Examples:

- **Wi-Fi** – High-speed data transfer for smart homes and offices.
- **Bluetooth & BLE (Bluetooth Low Energy)** – Low-power communication for wearables and IoT sensors.
- **Zigbee & Z-Wave** – Mesh networking for smart home automation.
- **Near Field Communication (NFC)** – Ultra-short-range for contactless payments and authentication.

Pros:

- High data rates (suitable for video streaming, real-time control).
- Lower latency and faster response times.
- Energy-efficient options (e.g., BLE, Zigbee).

Cons:

- Limited range (typically a few meters to a few hundred meters).
- Requires dense infrastructure (Wi-Fi routers, Bluetooth hubs).

Long-Range Communication

Long-range technologies are designed for IoT applications that require wide-area coverage, such as smart cities, agriculture, and industrial monitoring. These technologies prioritize range and power efficiency over data rates.

Examples:

- **Cellular (LTE-M, NB-IoT, 5G)** – Reliable connectivity for large-scale IoT deployments.
- **LoRaWAN (Long Range Wide Area Network)** – Low-power, long-range communication for remote monitoring.
- **Sigfox** – Ultra-low-power connectivity for small data transmissions.
- **Satellite IoT** – Connectivity for remote locations without cellular coverage.

Pros:

- Wide-area coverage (up to several kilometers or even global with satellites).
- Suitable for remote and outdoor applications.
- Low-power options available (LoRa, NB-IoT).

Cons:

- Lower data rates compared to short-range technologies.
- Higher latency in some cases (e.g., satellite IoT).
- More expensive deployment and infrastructure costs.

Feature	Short-Range (Wi-Fi, Bluetooth)	Long-Range (Cellular, LoRa)
Range	Up to 100m (Wi-Fi), ~10m (BLE)	Several km to global (satellite)
Power Consumption	Low to moderate	Low (LoRa, NB-IoT) to high (5G)
Data Rate	High (Wi-Fi: up to 10 Gbps)	Low to moderate (NB-IoT: ~100 kbps, 5G: Gbps)
Latency	Low (milliseconds)	Varies (low for cellular, high for satellite)
Use Cases	Smart homes, wearables, automation	Smart cities, industrial IoT, remote monitoring

1.3.5 Network Topologies

Network topology is the way devices are connected in a network. It defines how these components are connected and how data transfer between the network. Understanding the different types of network topologies can help in choosing the right design for a specific network.

There are two major categories of Network Topology i.e. Physical Network topology and Logical Network Topology. Physical Network Topology refers to the actual structure of the physical medium for the transmission of data. Logical network Topology refers to the transmission of data between devices present in the network irrespective of the way devices are connected. The structure of the network is important for the proper functioning of the network. one must choose the most suitable topology as per their requirement.

Types of Network Topology

Point to Point Topology

Point-to-point topology is a type of topology that works on the functionality of the sender and receiver. It is the simplest communication between two nodes, in which one is the sender and the other one is the receiver. Point-to-Point provides high bandwidth.

Point to Point

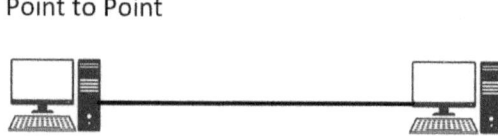

Mesh Topology

In a mesh topology, every device is connected to another device via a particular channel. Every device is connected to another via dedicated channels. These channels are known as links. In Mesh Topology, the protocols used are AHCP (Ad Hoc Configuration Protocols), DHCP (Dynamic Host Configuration Protocol), etc.

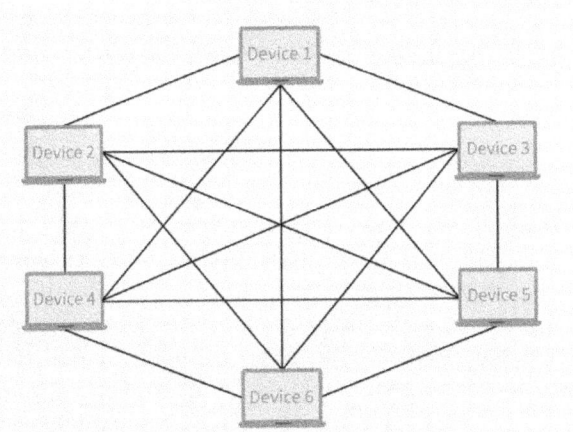

- Suppose, the N number of devices are connected with each other in a mesh topology, the total number of ports that are required by each device is N-1. In Figure 1, there are 5 devices connected to each other, hence the total number of ports required by each device is 4. The total number of ports required = N * (N-1).

- Suppose, N number of devices are connected with each other in a mesh topology, then the total number of dedicated links required to connect them is N C 2 i.e. N(N-1)/2. In Figure 1, there are 5 devices connected to each other, hence the total number of links required is 5*4/2 = 10.

Advantages of Mesh Topology

- Communication is very fast between the nodes.
- Mesh Topology is robust.
- The fault is diagnosed easily. Data is reliable because data is transferred among the devices through dedicated channels or links.
- Provides security and privacy.

Disadvantages of Mesh Topology

- Installation and configuration are difficult.
- The cost of cables is high as bulk wiring is required, hence suitable for less number of devices.
- The cost of maintenance is high.

A common example of mesh topology is the internet backbone, where various internet service providers are connected to each other via dedicated channels. This topology is also used in military communication systems and aircraft navigation systems.

Star Topology

In Star Topology, all the devices are connected to a single hub through a cable. This hub is the central node and all other nodes are connected to the central node. The hub can be passive in nature i.e., not an intelligent hub such as broadcasting devices, at the same time the hub can be intelligent known as an active hub. Active hubs have repeaters in them. Coaxial cables or RJ-45 cables are used to connect the computers. In Star Topology, many popular Ethernet LAN protocols are used as CD(Collision Detection), CSMA (Carrier Sense Multiple Access), etc.

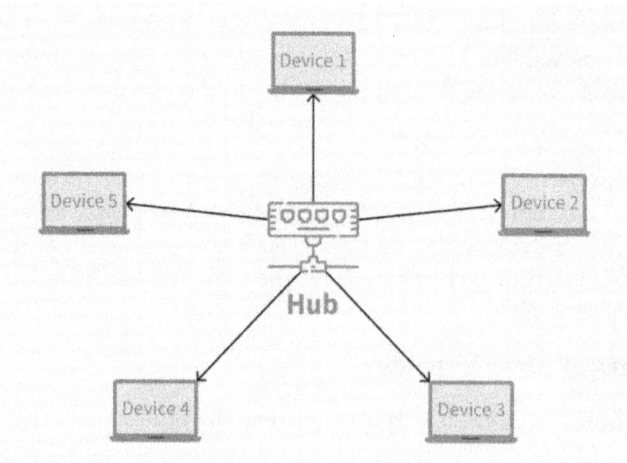

Advantages of Star Topology

➤ If N devices are connected to each other in a star topology, then the number of cables required to connect them is N. So, it is easy to set up.

➤ Each device requires only 1 port i.e. to connect to the hub, therefore the total number of ports required is N.

➤ It is Robust. If one link fails only that link will affect and not other than that.

➤ Easy to fault identification and fault isolation.

➤ Star topology is cost-effective as it uses inexpensive coaxial cable.

> **Disadvantages of Star Topology**

> If the concentrator (hub) on which the whole topology relies fails, the whole system will crash down.

> The cost of installation is high.

> Performance is based on the single concentrator i.e. hub.

A common example of star topology is a local area network (LAN) in an office where all computers are connected to a central hub. This topology is also used in wireless networks where all devices are connected to a wireless access point.

Bus Topology

Bus Topology is a network type in which every computer and network device is connected to a single cable. It is bi-directional. It is a multi-point connection and a non-robust topology because if the backbone fails the topology crashes. In Bus Topology, various MAC (Media Access Control) protocols are followed by LAN ethernet connections like TDMA, Pure Aloha, CDMA, Slotted Aloha, etc.

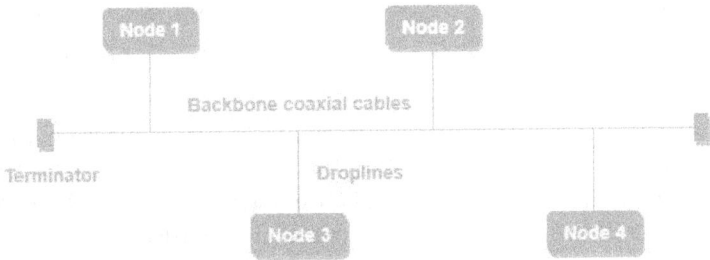

Advantages of Bus Topology

> If N devices are connected to each other in a bus topology, then the number of cables required to connect them is 1, known as backbone cable, and N drop lines are required.

> Coaxial or twisted pair cables are mainly used in bus-based networks that support up to 10 Mbps.

> The cost of the cable is less compared to other topologies, but it is used to build small networks.

> Bus topology is familiar technology as installation and troubleshooting techniques are well known.

> CSMA is the most common method for this type of topology.

Disadvantages of Bus Topology

- ➤ A bus topology is quite simpler, but still, it requires a lot of cabling.
- ➤ If the common cable fails, then the whole system will crash down.
- ➤ If the network traffic is heavy, it increases collisions in the network. To avoid this, various protocols are used in the MAC layer known as Pure Aloha, Slotted Aloha, CSMA/CD, etc.
- ➤ Adding new devices to the network would slow down networks.
- ➤ Security is very low.

A common example of bus topology is the Ethernet LAN, where all devices are connected to a single coaxial cable or twisted pair cable. This topology is also used in cable television networks.

Ring Topology

In a Ring Topology, it forms a ring connecting devices with exactly two neighbouring devices. A number of repeaters are used for Ring topology with a large number of nodes, because if someone wants to send some data to the last node in the ring topology with 100 nodes, then the data will have to pass through 99 nodes to reach the 100th node. Hence to prevent data loss repeaters are used in the network.

The data flows in one direction, i.e. it is unidirectional, but it can be made bidirectional by having 2 connections between each Network Node, it is called Dual Ring Topology. In-Ring Topology, the Token Ring Passing protocol is used by the workstations to transmit the data.

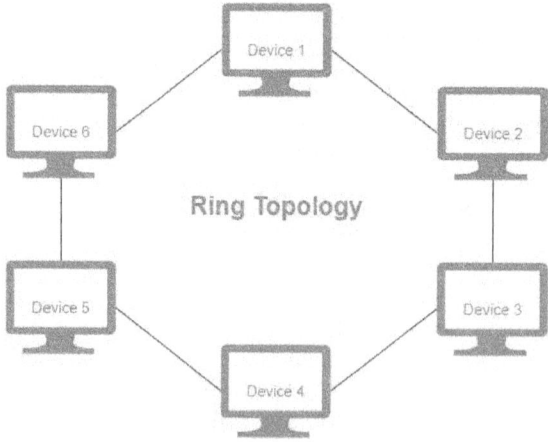

The most common access method of ring topology is token passing.

- **Token passing:** It is a network access method in which a token is passed from one node to another node.
- **Token:** It is a frame that circulates around the network.

Operations of Ring Topology

- One station is known as a **monitor** station which takes all the responsibility for performing the operations.
- To transmit the data, the station has to hold the token. After the transmission is done, the token is to be released for other stations to use.
- When no station is transmitting the data, then the token will circulate in the ring.
- There are two types of token release techniques: **Early token release** releases the token just after transmitting the data and **Delayed token release** releases the token after the acknowledgment is received from the receiver.

Advantages of Ring Topology

- The data transmission is high-speed.
- The possibility of collision is minimum in this type of topology.
- Cheap to install and expand.
- It is less costly than a star topology.

Disadvantages of Ring Topology

- The failure of a single node in the network can cause the entire network to fail.
- Troubleshooting is difficult in this topology.
- The addition of stations in between or the removal of stations can disturb the whole topology.
- Less secure.

Tree Topology

Tree topology is the variation of the Star topology. This topology has a hierarchical flow of data. In Tree Topology, protocols like DHCP and **SAC (Standard Automatic Configuration)** are used.

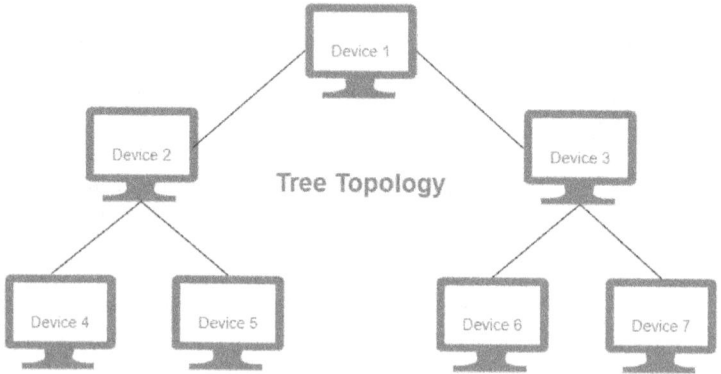

In tree topology, the various secondary hubs are connected to the central hub which contains the repeater. This data flow from top to bottom i.e. from the central hub to the secondary and then to the devices or from bottom to top i.e. devices to the secondary hub and then to the central hub. It is a multi-point connection and a non-robust topology because if the backbone fails the topology crashes.

Advantages of Tree Topology

- It allows more devices to be attached to a single central hub thus it decreases the distance that is traveled by the signal to come to the devices.
- It allows the network to get isolated and also prioritize from different computers.
- We can add **new devices to the existing network.**
- **Error detection** and **error correction** are very easy in a tree topology.

Disadvantages of Tree Topology

- If the central hub gets fails the entire system fails.
- The cost is high because of the cabling.
- If new devices are added, it becomes difficult to reconfigure.

A common example of a tree topology is the hierarchy in a large organization. At the top of the tree is the CEO, who is connected to the different departments or divisions (child nodes) of the company. Each department has its own hierarchy, with managers overseeing different teams (grandchild nodes). The team members (leaf nodes) are at the bottom of the hierarchy, connected to their respective managers and departments.

Hybrid Topology

Hybrid Topology is the combination of all the various types of topologies we have studied above. Hybrid Topology is used when the nodes are free to take any form. It means these can be individuals such as Ring or Star topology or can be a combination of various types of topologies seen above. Each individual topology uses the protocol that has been discussed earlier.

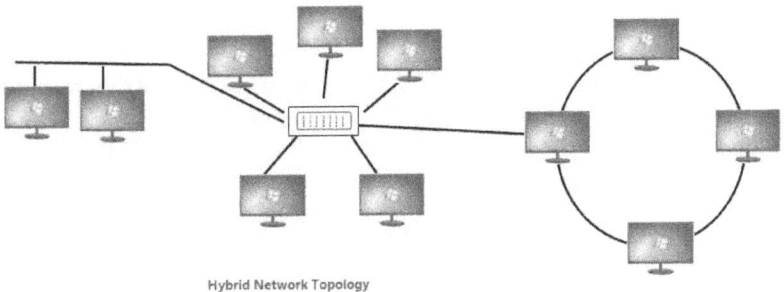

Hybrid Network Topology

Advantages of Hybrid Topology

➤ This topology is **very flexible**.

➤ The size of the network can be easily expanded by **adding new devices.**

Disadvantages of Hybrid Topology

➤ It is challenging **to design the architecture** of the Hybrid Network.

➤ **Hubs** used in this topology are **very expensive.**

➤ The infrastructure cost is very high as a hybrid network **requires a lot of cabling and network devices**.

A common example of a hybrid topology is a university campus network. The network may have a backbone of a star topology, with each building connected to the backbone through a switch or router. Within each building, there may be a bus or ring topology connecting the different rooms and offices. The wireless access points also create a mesh topology for wireless devices. This hybrid topology allows for efficient communication between different buildings while providing flexibility and redundancy within each building.

IoT Devices and Sensors

1.4.1 Types of IoT Devices

IoT devices come in various forms, designed for different applications across industries. These devices collect, process, and transmit data to improve efficiency, automation, and decision-making. Below are the main types of IoT devices categorized based on their functions and use cases.

Consumer IoT Devices

Consumer IoT devices are used in homes and personal applications, enhancing convenience, security, and entertainment.

Examples:

- **Smart Home Devices** – Smart thermostats (Nest), smart lights (Philips Hue), and smart locks.
- **Wearables** – Smartwatches (Apple Watch, Fitbit), fitness trackers, and smart glasses.
- **Smart Appliances** – IoT-enabled refrigerators, washing machines, and coffee makers.
- **Voice Assistants** – Amazon Alexa, Google Assistant, and Apple Siri.

Use Cases:

- Home automation and security.
- Health tracking and fitness monitoring.
- Smart entertainment systems.

2. Industrial IoT (IIoT) Devices

IIoT devices are used in industries like manufacturing, energy, and logistics to optimize operations and improve safety.

Examples:

- **Smart Sensors** – Temperature, humidity, vibration, and pressure sensors for monitoring machinery.
- **Predictive Maintenance Devices** – Sensors that detect wear and tear in machines to prevent failures.
- **Asset Tracking Devices** – GPS-enabled trackers for logistics and supply chain management.
- **SCADA Systems** – Supervisory Control and Data Acquisition (SCADA) devices for industrial automation.

Use Cases:

- Predictive maintenance to prevent equipment failure.
- Automated monitoring in factories and warehouses.
- Real-time tracking of goods and machinery.

3. Healthcare IoT (IoMT) Devices

The Internet of Medical Things (IoMT) includes devices that assist in remote health monitoring, diagnostics, and patient care.

Examples:

- **Wearable Health Monitors** – Smart ECG monitors, glucose monitors, and pulse oximeters.
- **Smart Insulin Pens** – Connected insulin pens that track dosage and timing.
- **Remote Patient Monitoring (RPM) Devices** – IoT-enabled devices for tracking vital signs remotely.
- **Connected Medical Equipment** – Smart infusion pumps, pacemakers, and hospital beds.

Use Cases:

- Continuous monitoring of patients with chronic conditions.
- Real-time alerts for abnormal health parameters.
- Remote diagnosis and telemedicine applications.

4. Smart City IoT Devices

IoT devices in smart cities help improve urban infrastructure, transportation, and public services.

Examples:

- **Smart Streetlights** – Adaptive lighting that saves energy and reduces costs.
- **Traffic Management Sensors** – IoT-enabled traffic lights and vehicle tracking systems.
- **Air Quality Monitors** – Devices that measure pollution levels and send real-time alerts.
- **Smart Parking Systems** – Sensors that guide drivers to available parking spots.

Use Cases:

- Reducing energy consumption with adaptive lighting.
- Traffic optimization and congestion reduction.
- Real-time environmental monitoring.

5. Agricultural IoT Devices (AgriTech)

IoT in agriculture helps farmers optimize resources, monitor crops, and increase yields.

- ### Examples:
- **Soil Moisture Sensors** – Measure soil conditions and optimize irrigation.
- **Automated Irrigation Systems** – Smart irrigation systems that adjust water usage based on weather data.
- **Livestock Monitoring Devices** – GPS collars and biometric sensors for tracking animal health.
- **Drones** – Used for aerial surveillance, crop monitoring, and pesticide spraying.

Use Cases:

- Precision farming to maximize crop yield.

- Remote monitoring of livestock health.
- Automated irrigation and resource management.

6. Automotive and Transportation IoT Devices

IoT in transportation enhances vehicle safety, efficiency, and fleet management.

Examples:

- **Connected Vehicles** – Cars with real-time diagnostics and navigation (Tesla, BMW).
- **Fleet Management Systems** – GPS trackers and telematics for logistics companies.
- **V2X Communication Devices** – Vehicle-to-everything (V2X) systems that enable communication between cars and infrastructure.
- **Smart Dashcams** – AI-powered dashcams for driver monitoring and accident detection.

Use Cases:

- Real-time vehicle tracking and diagnostics.
- Autonomous and semi-autonomous driving.
- Improved road safety with smart traffic systems.

7. Enterprise IoT Devices

Businesses use IoT to improve efficiency, security, and workplace automation.

Examples:

- **Smart Office Devices** – IoT-enabled HVAC systems, smart lighting, and occupancy sensors.
- **Connected Security Systems** – IoT-based surveillance cameras and biometric access control.
- **Inventory Management Systems** – RFID and barcode scanners for warehouse tracking.
- **AI-Powered Chatbots and Assistants** – Automated customer support and office management tools.

Use Cases:

- Energy savings through automated lighting and HVAC systems.
- Enhanced security with IoT-based surveillance.
- Smart inventory tracking and automation.

1.4.2 Basic Electronics:

For designing this hardware many types of devices are used to make it perfectly working. All the devices are purchased from different manufacturers. These components are soldered on a soldering board. The following list of hardware are required for this system.

- Power supply
- Microcontroller ATMEGA328
- GPS module
- GSM module
- Max232
- RS232

Power supply: It consists of step down transformer, bridge rectifier, capacitors and voltage regulator ICs. 230V AC is converted to 12V DC using transformer and bridge rectifier. This 12VDC is further reduced to 5V DC using voltage regulator IC.

Resistors: A resistor is a passive two-terminal electrical component that implements electrical resistance as a circuit element. Resistors act to reduce current flow, and, at the same time, act to lower voltage levels within circuits.

In electronic circuits resistors are used to limit current flow, to adjust signal levels, bias active elements, terminate transmission lines among other uses. High-power resistors that can dissipate many watts of electrical power as heat may be used as part of motor controls, in power distribution systems, or as test loads for generators.

Fixed resistors have resistances that only change slightly with temperature, time or operating voltage.

Variable resistors can be used to adjust circuit elements (such as a volume control or a lamp dimmer), or as sensing devices for heat, light, humidity, force, or chemical activity.

Resistors are common elements of electrical networks and electronic circuits and are ubiquitous in electronic equipment. Practical resistors as discrete components can be composed of various compounds and forms. Resistors are also implemented within integrated circuits.

The electrical function of a resistor is specified by its resistance: common commercial resistors are manufactured over a range of more than nine orders of magnitude. The nominal value of the resistance will fall within a manufacturing tolerance.

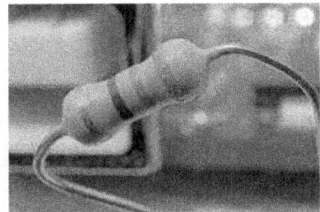

FIG: AXIAL LEAD RESISTOR

Resistor is a circuit element having the function of introducing electrical resistance in to the circuit. There are three basic types of resistor.

(a) Fixed resistor

(b) Rheostat

(c) Potentiometer

A fix resistor is a two terminal device which electrical resistance is constant.

A rheostat is a resistor that can be changed in resistance value without opening the circuit to make adjustment.

A potentiometer is an adjustable resistor with three terminals, on at each end of the resistor element and thin movable along its length.

There are three basic types of resistors:

1. Carbon composite resistors

2. Wire wound resistors

3. Carbon-Film resistors.

In the circuit we use carbon composition resistors

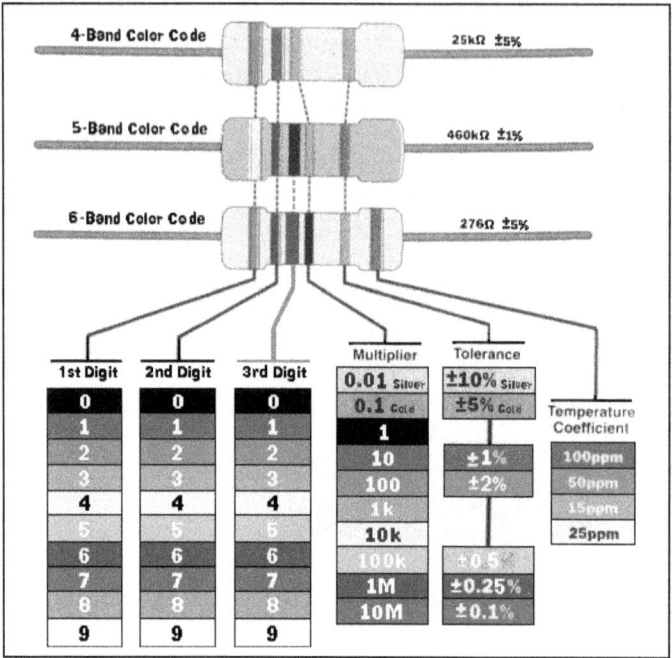

FIG: COLOUR CODING IN A RESISTOR

Capacitor:

A **capacitor** (originally known as a **condenser**) is a passive two-terminal electrical component used to store energy electrostaticallyin an electric field. The forms of practical capacitors vary widely, but all contain at least two electrical conductors (plates) separated by a dielectric (i.e. insulator). The conductors can be thin films, foils or sintered beads of metal or conductive electrolyte, etc. The nonconducting dielectric acts to increase the capacitor's charge capacity. A dielectric can be glass, ceramic, plastic film, air, vacuum, paper, mica, oxide layer etc. Capacitors are widely used as parts of electrical circuits in many common electrical devices. Unlike aresistor, an ideal capacitor does not dissipate energy. Instead, a capacitor stores energy in the form of an electrostatic field between its plates.

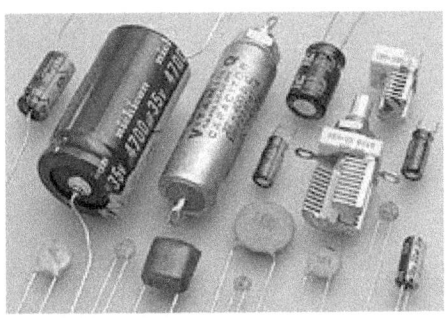

FIG: CAPACITORS

IC LM7805:

7805 is a **voltage regulator** integrated circuit. It is a member of 78xx series of fixed linear voltage regulator ICs. The voltage source in a circuit may have fluctuations and would not give the fixed voltage output. The **voltage regulator IC** maintains the output voltage at a constant value. The xx in 78xx indicates the fixed output voltage it is designed to provide. 7805 provides +5V regulated power supply. Capacitors of suitable values can be connected at input and output pins depending upon the respective voltage levels.

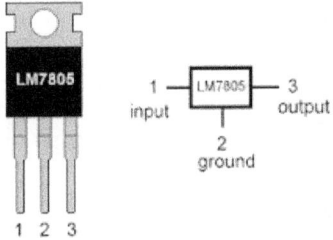

FIG: 7805 PIN DIAGRAM

W10M Bridge Rectifier

A **bridge rectifier** is an arrangement of four or more diodes in a **bridge** circuit configuration which provides the same output polarity for either input polarity. It is used for converting an alternating current (AC) input into a direct current (DC) output.

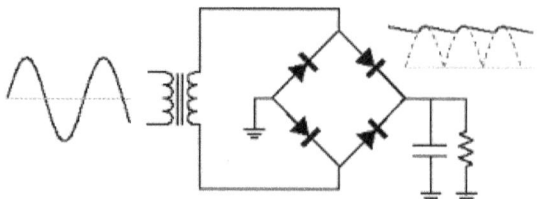

FIG: CIRCUIT DIAGRAM OF BRIDGE RECTIFIER

MICROCONTROLLER ATMEGA328:

The Atmel AVR core combines a rich instruction set with 32 general purpose working registers. All the 32 registers are directly connected to the Arithmetic Logic Unit (ALU), allowing two independent registers to be accessed in one single instruction executed in one clock cycle. The resulting architecture is more code efficient while achieving throughputs up to ten times faster than conventional CISC microcontrollers

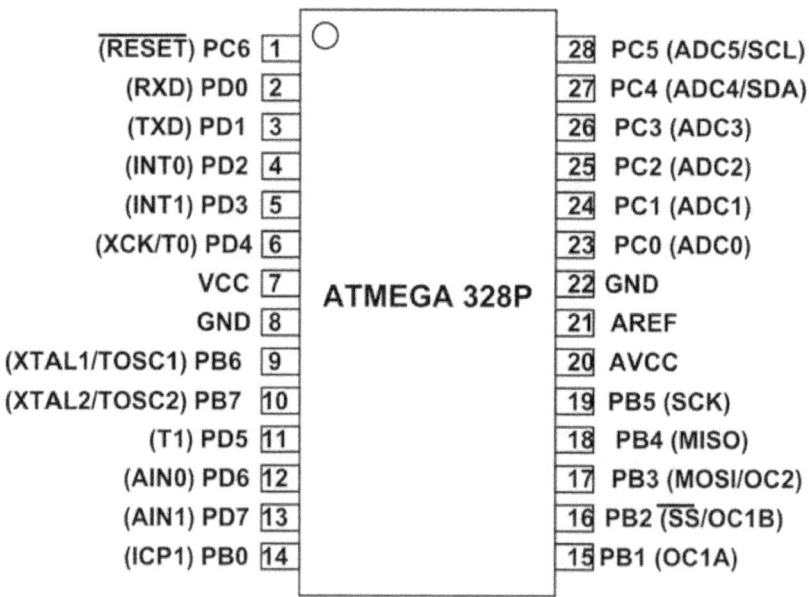

The Atmega168 provides the following features: 16 Kbytes of In-System Programmable Flash with Read-While-Write capabilities, 512 bytes of EEPROM, 1 Kbyte of SRAM, 23 general purpose I/O lines, 32 general

purpose working registers, three flexible Timer/Counters with compare modes, internal and external interrupts, a serial programmable USART, a byte oriented Two wire Serial Interface, a 6-channel ADC (eight channels in TQFP and QFN/MLF packages) with 10-bit accuracy, a programmable Watchdog Timer with Internal Oscillator, an SPI serial port, and five software selectable power saving modes. The Idle mode stops the CPU while allowing the SRAM; Timer/Counters, SPI port, and interrupt system to continue function

FIG: ATMEGA328

The Power down mode saves the register contents but freezes the Oscillator, disabling all other chip functions until the next Interrupt or Hardware Reset. In Power-save mode, the asynchronous timer continues to run, allowing the user to maintain a timer base while the rest of the device is sleeping. The ADC Noise Reduction mode stops the CPU and all I/O modules except asynchronous timer and ADC, to minimize switching noise during ADC conversions. In Standby mode, the crystal/resonator Oscillator is running while the rest of the device is sleeping. This allows very fast start-up combined with low-power consumption.

GPS MODULE:
A **GPS navigation device** is a device that accurately calculates geographical location by receiving information from GPS satellites. Initially it was used by the United States military, but now most receivers are in automobiles and smartphones.
The Global Positioning System (GPS) is a satellite-based navigation system made up of a network of a minimum of 24, but currently 30, satellites placed into orbit by the U.S. Department of Defense. Military action was the original intent for GPS, but in the 1980s, the U.S. government decided to allow the GPS program to be used by civilians. The satellite data is free and works anywhere in the world.
GPS devices may have capabilities such as:

- maps, including streets maps, displayed in human readable format via text or in a graphical format,
- turn-by-turn navigation directions to a human in charge of a vehicle or vessel via text or speech,
- directions fed directly to an autonomous vehicle such as a robotic probe,
- traffic congestion maps (depicting either historical or real time data) and suggested alternative directions,
- information on nearby amenities such as restaurants, fueling stations, and tourist attractions.

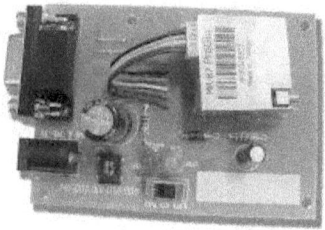

FIG: GPS MODULE

GSM/GPRS Module

GSM GPRS Modules are one of the commonly used communication modules in embedded systems. A GSM GPRS Module is used to enable communication between a microcontroller (or a microprocessor) and the GSM / GPSR Network. Here, GSM stands for Global System for Mobile Communication and GPRS stands for General Packet Radio Service.

A GSM GPRS MODEM comprises of a GSM GPRS Module along with some other components like communication interface (like Serial Communication – RS-232), power supply and some indicators. With the help of this communication interface, we can connect the GSM GPRS Module on the GSM GPRS MODEM with an external computer (or a microcontroller).

What is GSM?

GSM or Global System for Mobile Communication is a Wireless Communication standard for mobile telephone systems. It was developed by the European Telecommunications Standards Institute (ETSI) as a replacement to the 1st Generation Analog Cellular Network.

Hence, GSM is often called as the 2nd Generation Digital Cellular Network or simply 2G. From its deployment in Finland in the year 1991, GSM has grown rapidly with an estimated market share of over 90% in more than 200 countries.

What is GPRS?

GPRS or General Packet Radio Service is an extension of the GSM Network. GPRS is an integrated part of the GSM Network which provides an efficient way to transfer data with the same resources as GSM Network.

Originally, the data services (like internet, multimedia messaging etc.) in the GSM Network used a circuit – switched connection. In this type, the access time for the network are long and the charges for the data were based on the connection time. Also, this type of connection is not suitable for transmitting bursts of data.

With the integration of GPRS, a packet – switching based data service, in to the GSM Network, the scene of data services has changes. In GPRS based packet – switching networks, the user device doesn't hold the resources for a continuous time but efficiently uses a common pool.

The access time in GPRS is very small and the main advantage is that it allows bursts of data to be transmitted. Also, the charges for data are based on the usage and not on the connection time.

MAX232:

The MAX232 is an IC, first created in 1987 by Maxim Integrated Products, that converts signals from an RS-232 serial port to signals suitable for use in TTL compatible digital logic circuits. The MAX232 is a dual driver/receiver and typically converts the RX, TX, CTS and RTS signals.

The drivers provide RS-232 voltage level outputs (approx. ± 7.5 V) from a single + 5 V supply via on-chip charge pumps and external capacitors. This makes it useful for implementing RS-232 in devices that otherwise do not need any voltages outside the 0 V to + 5 V range, as power supply design does not need to be made more complicated just for driving the RS-232 in this case.

The receivers reduce RS-232 inputs (which may be as high as ± 25 V), to standard 5 V TTL levels. These receivers have a typical threshold of 1.3 V, and a typical hysteresis of 0.5 V.

FIG: MAX232 IC   FIG: PIN DIAGRAM OF MAX232 IC

RS232:

In telecommunications systems used today RS-232 is a standard for serial communication transmission of data. It formally defines the signals connecting between a DTE (data terminal equipment) such as a computer terminal, and a DCE (data circuit-terminating equipment, originally defined as data communication equipment), such as a modem.

The RS-232 standard is commonly used in computer serial ports. The standard defines the electrical characteristics and timing of signals, the meaning of signals, and the physical size and pinout of connectors. The current version of the standard is TIA-232-F Interface Between Data Terminal Equipment and Data Circuit-Terminating Equipment Employing Serial Binary Data Interchange, issued in 1997.

An RS-232 serial port was once a standard feature of a personal computer, used for connections to modems, printers, mice, data storage, uninterruptible power supplies, and other peripheral devices. However, RS-232 is hampered by low transmission speed, large voltage swing, and large standard connectors.

In modern personal computers, USB has displaced RS-232 from most of its peripheral interface roles. Many computers do not come equipped with RS-232 ports and must use either an external USB-to-RS-232 converter or an internal expansion card with one or more serial ports to connect to RS-232 peripherals. Nevertheless, RS-232 devices are still used, especially in industrial machines, networking equipment and scientific instruments.

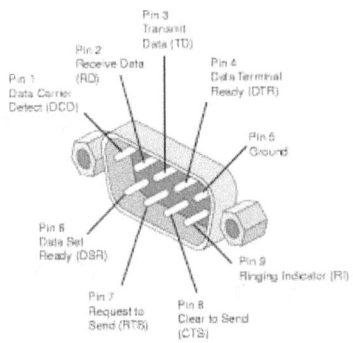

FIG: PIN DIAGRAM OF RS232 CONNECTOR

PCB CONSTRUCTION:

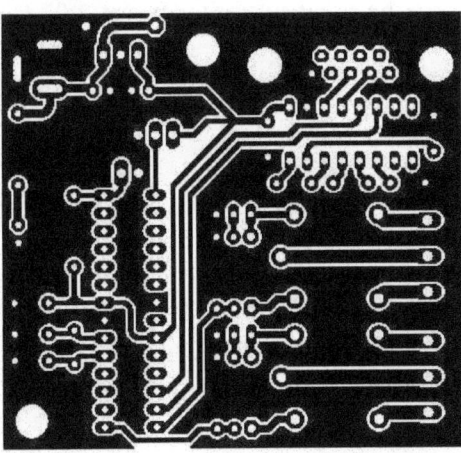

PCB Layout
No device can work if its connections are not according to specification, and if the proper resistance, capacitance, inductance etc. are not connected to the

place where required. Thus a PCB designer has to first think of the very possible combination of voltages that are required by the circuit and make them available at points where they are needed with the minimum use of jumpers and keeping the circuit size compact and yet effective.

The layout of PCB has to incorporate all the information on the board before one can go on the artwork preparation. This means that a concept, which clearly defines all the details of the circuitry and partly of final equipment, is a prerequisite before the actual layout can start.

For PCB layout, the following points ought to be considered carefully

1. Record size of components used.

2. Overall area covered is normally kept rectangular or square.

3. Vcc and ground lines should be provided at the sides to facilitate external connection.

4. Input and output terminals may be placed giving through to external connection.

5. Make a rough sketch placing components and interconnect components with jumpers.

6. Do not place components pointing in differed direction unless needed. Make them parallel to the either side of the board.

7. Make the neat final scaled sketch on the inch graph sheet.

8. Lines mounted are of uniform width.

9. Invest the layout to confirm that all the components are connected properly and given sufficient place in the layout.

Note: While following the above rule, a design must be chosen to minimize the total circuit area used.

Tracing

After the circuit layout has been prepared on the tracing paper, inverting the tracing paper onto the PCB so that the side that had been traced faces the

PCB copper coating. Then trace the layout onto the PCB placing a carbon paper in between the two.

Painting

Paint must be uniformly applied. Use 0 number painting brushes for painting PCB layout.

Etching

In all PCBs, etching is the most important step. The final copper pattern is formed by selective removal of all unwanted copper which is not protected by an etch resist. Amongst the Enchants, $FeCl_3$ (Ferric Chloride) is commonly used for small PCBs where etching is only out carried out occasionally for a small number of boards.

For etching, the solution is made, wherein sample and standard solution are in 2*1 dilutions. In order to increases the copper dissolution capacity and to bring the etching time slightly down, HCL is added. Etching temperature should be in the ranges of 20°C to 45°C. $FeCl_3$ is an enchant used in small-scale PCB production. In high volume production $FeCl_3$ is of not much importance because it cannot be regenerated and it attacks the common metal etch resist.

PROCEDURE

To etch 1 kg of copper, 5.1 kg of Ferric Chloride is consumed. In order to increase the copper dissolving capacity and to bring the etching time slightly down, often HCL is added. HCL acts simultaneously against excessive sludge formation.

After etching is over the Ferric Chloride contained surface should be first cleaned by spraying water, which is not enough. Then we dip it in a 5% (by volume) in the solution of oxalic acid to remove iron and copper salts and final water rinsed vigorously. Then we rinse it by using petrol so that the paint comes out and copper remains intact where the paint was applied. The copper acts as conduction path for flow of signals.

The high corrosive nature of Ferric chloride leads to short etching time and avoid under etching.

Chemistry

Due to hydrolysis reaction, free acid is formed which reacts with copper.

$$FeCl_3 + 3H_2O = Fe(OH)_3 + 3HCl$$

The copper is oxidized by Ferric ion forming cuprous chloride.

Drilling

Drilling of holes for mounting components is important mechanical operation in PCB production process. The importance of hole drilling into PCB's has further gone up with electronic components miniaturization. After rinsing drilling is done using bit as per the circuit provided. The diameters of holes generally accepted are as follows.

1. $D = 0.8$ mm

2. $D = 1.1$ mm

3. $D = 1.5$ mm

4. $D = 3.2$ mm

Where,

D = Hole diameter.

Component Mounting

1. Before mounting any components, examine the PCB carefully for any cracks, beaks or other defects in conduction paths.

2. The leads of components like resistors and capacitors should be fully inserted into the mounting holes taking care to mount the components so that any information written on the components is clearly visible.

3. Carefully cut the leads of components so that about 3 mm of the end extended beyond the wiring side of the PCB. The ends of the leas are bent at right angles to make a firm contact with the surface where it is to be soldered.

4. In case of semiconductor devices like transistors and diodes, the length of the leads extending above the component side of the PCB should be about 1 cm. if transistor leads are too short we use a base. Metal cap should touch

if they are not at ground potential. The right terminals should be at right places.

5. Certain components like transformers, potentiometers and variable capacitors, which are meant for use with PCB, are provided with pin type terminals that can be simply inserted into the hole in the PCB and soldered.

6. Use IC base for IC.

Soldering

PCB soldering required proper soldering technique, as explained below:

1. A light duty soldering iron of 25W or 30 W rating should be used to prevent damage to the printed circuit wiring due to excessive heating. The tip of soldering iron should not have an oxide coating. Clean it using sand paper.

2. Do not use excess solder to avoid solder flouring to adjacent conducing paths forming bridges, which cause short circuits.

3. Clean the surface of traces before you start soldering. It is advisable to use flux.

Layout of desired circuit diagram and preparation is first and most important operation in any printed circuit board manufacturing process. First of all layout of component side is to be made in accordance with available components dimensions. The following points are to be observed while forming the layout of P.C.B:

1. Between two components, sufficient space should be maintained.

2. High wattage/max, dissipated components should be mounted at a sufficient distance from semiconductors and electrolytic capacitors.

3. the most important point is that the components layout is making proper compression with copper side circuit layout.

Printed circuit board (P.C.B's) is used to avoid most or all the disadvantages of conventional bread board. These also avoid the use to thin wired for connecting (the components they are small in size and efficient in performance) the two most popular boards are widely used for general purpose application where the cost is to be low and the layout is simple

1.4.3 Types of Sensors and their Applications

Sensors are the devices that can detect and response to changes in the environment. These changes can be in form of light, temperature, motion, moisture or any other physical property. The sensor converts these physical changes into signal that can be measured. Sensors play an important role in IoT which will make an ecosystem for collecting, analysing, and processing data about a specific environment so that it can be monitored, managed, and controlled more easily and efficiently. Sensors bridge the gap between the physical world and the logical world.

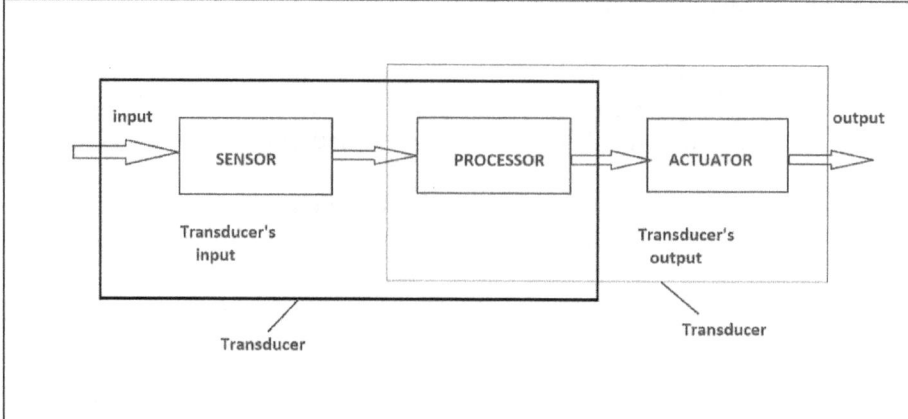

Transducer: It converts the signal from one physical form to another physical form. it is also called energy converter. For example, microphone converts sound to electrical signal. It is based on the principle of conservation of energy. The Sensor can be classified as

Based on Power Requirement

> **Active Sensors:** These Sensors require an external excitation signal or power source to work.

> **Passive Sensors**: These Sensors do not require any external power source and it can directly generate the output response.

Based on Means of Detection

The Sensors can be according to detection method they use such as electrical, biological, chemical, or radioactive detection.

Based on the Conversion Phenomenon

This classification is based on the input and output conversion

- ➤ **Photoelectric**: It Changes light to electrical signals.
- ➤ **Thermoelectric:** It Changes temperature difference to electrical voltage.
- ➤ **Electrochemical**: It Changes chemical reactions to electrical signals.
- ➤ **Electromagnetic**: It Changes magnetic fields to electrical signals.
- ➤ **Thermoptic**: It Changes temperature changes to electrical signals.

Based on Output Type

- ➤ **Analog Sensors:** It produce an output signal which is usually in the form of voltage, current, or resistance, proportional to the measured quantity.
- ➤ **Digital Sensors**: It provides discrete or digital data as output.

Types of Sensors

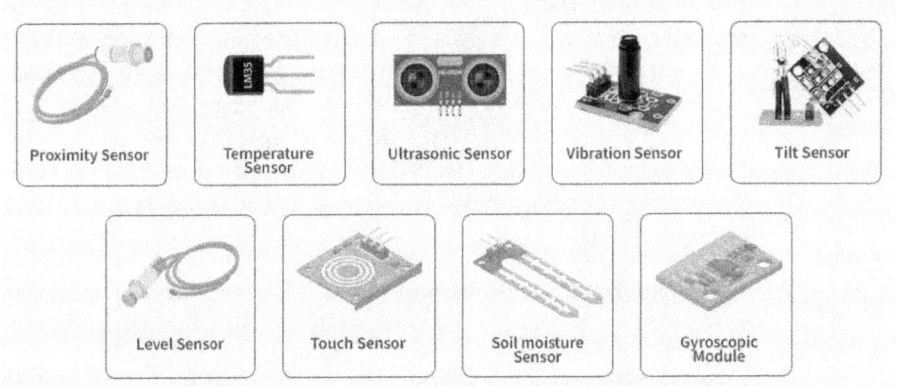

We live in the world of sensors, there are different types of sensors in our homes, offices, cars etc. by working to make our lives easier by turning on the lights by detecting our presence, adjusting the room temperature, detect smoke or fire, make us delicious coffee, and automatic door closing and so on. here we will discuss types of sensors one by one in detail:

- ➤ **Temperature sensors:** Monitoring temperature of used devices in industrial applications. it is used to measure temperature. this can be air temperature, liquid temperature or the temperature of solid. It can be analog or digital. In an **Analog Temperature Sensor**, the change in the Temperature correspond to change in its physical property like resistance or voltage. LM35 is a classic Analog Temperature Sensor. In Digital Temperature Sensor, the output is a discrete digital value, DS1621 is digital sensor which generates 9 bits temperature data.

- **Accelerometer sensors:** It measures the rate of change of velocity and this sensor generate magnitude and acceleration of the acceleration. Accelerometer sensor sensor ADXL335 provides 3 axes (X, Y, and Z) values in analog voltage. it is used in car electronics, ships, and agricultural machines.

- **Alcohol sensors:** as the name suggests it detects alcohol. Usually, alcohol sensors are used in breathalyzer devices, which determine whether the person is drunk or not. Law enforcement personnel use breathalyzers to catch drunk-and-drive culprits.

- **Radiation sensors:** Radiation Sensors/Detectors are electronic devices that sense the presence of alpha, beta, or gamma particles and provide signals to counters and display devices. Radiation detectors are used for surveys and sample counting.

- **Position sensors:** Position Sensors are electronic devices used to sense the positions of valves, doors, throttles, etc. and supply signals to the inputs of control or display devices. Key specifications include sensor type, sensor function, measurement range, and features that are specific to the sensor type. Position sensors are used wherever positional information is needed in a myriad of control applications. A common position transducer is a so-called string-pot, or string potentiometer.

- **Gas sensors:** It measures and detects concentration of different gases which is present in the atmosphere or any other environment.

- **Torque sensors:** This sensor is used for measuring the rotating torque and it is used to measure the speed of the rotation.

- **Optical sensors:** it is also called photosensors which can detect light waves at different points in the light spectrum including ultraviolet light, visible light, and infrared light. it is extensively used in smartphone, robotics and Blu-ray players.

- **Proximity sensors:** This sensor is used to detect the distance between two objects or detect the presence of an object. it is used in elevators, parking lots, automobiles, robotics, and numerous other environments.

- **Touch sensors:** Touch sensing devices detect physical contact on a monitored surface. Touch sensors are used extensively in electronic devices to support trackpad and touchscreen technologies. They're also used in many other systems, such as elevators, robotics and soap dispensers.

> **Image sensor:** it is used for distance measurement, pattern matching, colour checking, structured lighting, and motion capture and it is also used in different applications such as 3D imaging, video/broadcast, space, security, automotive, biometrics, medical, and machine vision.

1.4.4 Choosing The Right Sensor For Your IoT Project:

Sensors are critical to organizational success when it comes to the Internet of Things (IoT). They allow you to detect and measure the world around you, making it possible to collect data and control devices. The above list of sensors can be used in many applications based on different criteria and need, we have to choose the correct adaptable sensors for our projects.

1.4.5 Powering IoT Devices

The world is expeditiously moving towards a complete-digital age with the rise in the number of smart devices and advanced technologies like IoT. Modern digital equipment like smartphones, smart bulbs, smart thermostats, Alexa, Siri, etc., have gained significant prominence in the last couple of years. However, to your surprise, most smart devices need a low-voltage DC to run. This is because modern equipment has sophisticated integrated circuits that are designed to take DC power as their input. But, as we know, the power at our homes is distributed via AC power, so the devices need to convert the power from AC to DC to work efficiently. It is likely that the power needs for our digital systems will be more optimized and flexible in the future. Let us look at how power is supplied to IoT devices today.

Application of Power Supplies

The power application may differ depending on the devices and their design. The highest power consumption is done by devices with consistent operations and very little downtime. They utilize a high amount of energy to run. However, their high energy can be significantly lower than traditional equipment that needs massive energy inputs. So, devices that work extensively generally use lead-acid or lithium-ion batteries, which can stay charged for longer durations.

Apart from that, there are certain IoT devices, like smart thermostats, that consume significantly less power. As their operation is limited, they may take the room temperature, pass the information to the system, and go into sleep mode. This saves plenty of energy for the device. Such devices usually use alkaline galvanic cells that keep them running for extended periods.

Power Supply & IoT Device Operation

There is a significant impact on the operations of IoT devices with different power supplies. The following describes how the right power source for an IoT device can impact the system:

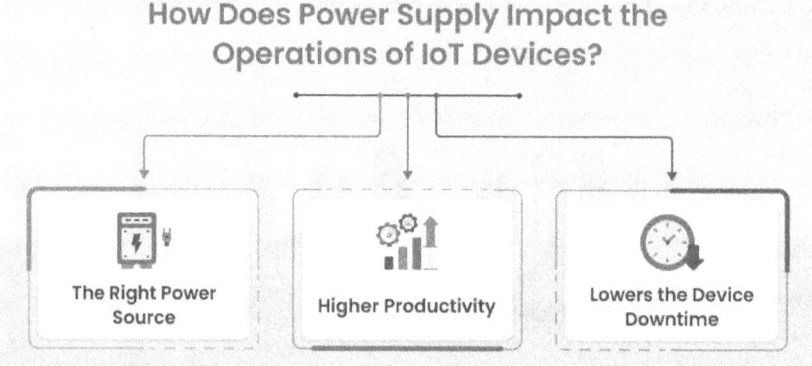

- ➤ **Better Efficiency**: Every digital device has set specifications of power requirements for its ideal use. When you always provide the device with company-specified power input, it performs with higher efficiency and delivers exceptional results with an increased lifespan.

- ➤ **Lowers Downtime**: As the device works more effectively with the right power supply, the maintenance needs for the device significantly lowers. This improves the working hours of the device, and it provides higher uptime to the process.

- ➤ **Higher Productivity**: It is natural with upgraded efficiency and performance, the device's productivity also increases. So supplying the manufacturer-specified power to your IoT devices can help you achieve higher work productivity.

Alternative Power Sources for IoT

Though chemical-based batteries provide greater performance and reliability to IoT systems, they are extremely harmful to the environment. Hence, the need for replacement is being substantially addressed, and more use of alternative power sources is being encouraged.

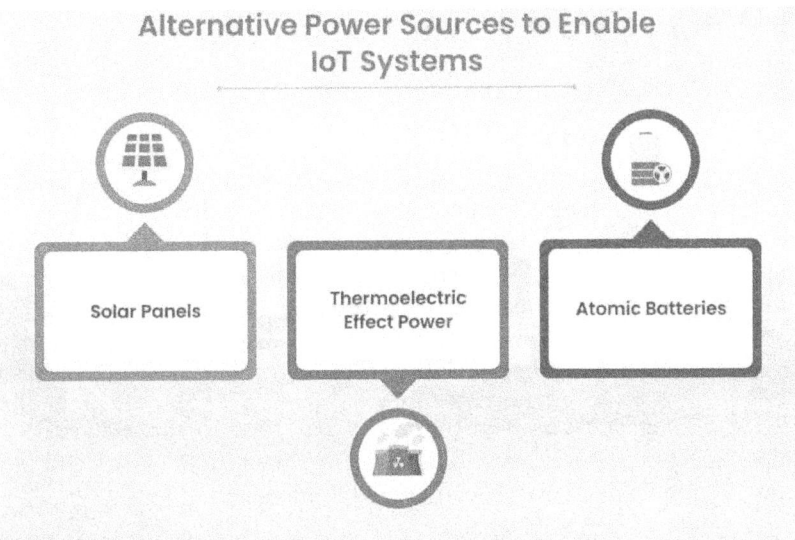

Solar Panels

This power source has gained immense popularity in recent years. It uses the photovoltaic effect in semiconductors to generate power for IoT devices. Solar panels have a simple operation. When a quantum of light hits the surface of a semiconductor, the electrons jump to a higher energy state, producing power that can be leveraged for multiple purposes.

Thermoelectric Effect Power

This is a powerful option that works on the concept of the Seebeck effect. In this method, a heterogeneous conductor is taken of which both sides have a substantial temperature difference. Due to the falling temperature on one side, the ions and electrons move to the colder side and generate sufficient electromotive force to power IoT electronic devices.

Atomic Batteries

This type of power source is very promising and is used in space programs to power satellites. In this method, the isotope batteries are designed with nanodiamonds, and the batteries can generate power for years. However, the limitation of this power source is that it only generates a small current and needs an accumulator to store and constantly draw power from the source.

1.5 History and Evolution of IoT Standards

1.5.1 Early Beginnings of IoT

The Internet of Things, commonly abbreviated as IoT, is a system of interconnected devices and sensors that share data with each other. While the term "Internet of Things" was coined in 1999 by Kevin Ashton, a British technology pioneer, the concept of connected devices dates back to the early days of radio and television. In this article, we'll take a look at the history of IoT and how it has evolved over time.

IoT has a long and complex history, dating back to the early days of computing. Here is a very simplified timeline of the history of IoT and some of the key events that have shaped the IoT landscape:

1970s: The first wireless networks are developed, laying the groundwork for IoT technologies.

1980s: The first commercial cellular networks are launched, opening up new possibilities for mobile devices and wireless data transmission.

1990s: The first internet-connected devices appear, including early versions of smart home devices and wearable computers.

2000s: The proliferation of broadband internet and wireless networks leads to an explosion in the number of connected devices. IoT technologies begin to be widely used in a variety of industries, from manufacturing to healthcare.

2010s: IoT becomes a major force in the consumer market, with products like Nest thermostats and Amazon Echo becoming popular household items. Businesses continue to find new ways to use IoT technologies to increase efficiency and gain insights into their operations.

2020s: The IoT landscape continues to evolve, with 5G networks beginning to be rolled out and new applications for IoT technologies emerging constantly.

IoT Device Management

IoT devices are usually equipped with sensors that collect data about their surroundings. This data is then transmitted over the internet to a central location where it can be analyzed and used to improve the performance of the device or the system as a whole.

One of the most important aspects of IoT is device management. IoT device management involves keeping track of all the devices on the network and ensuring that they are functioning properly. It also includes providing updates and security patches to keep the devices safe from hacking and other cyber threats.

Device management can be a challenge for large IoT networks due to the sheer number of devices involved. However, there are many software platforms available that can help simplify the process.

The future of IoT is shrouded in potential but there are still many challenges that need to be overcome before it can truly reach its full potential. However, with the right device management platform in place, anything is possible.

The Future of IoT

If the history of IoT has proven anything, it's that this network of connected devices has the potential to revolutionize the way we live, work, and play.

IoT devices are already making our lives more convenient and efficient. For example, smart thermostats can save homeowners money on their energy bills by automatically adjusting to temperature changes. And in the near future, IoT devices will become even more integrated into our everyday lives.

Some experts predict that there will be 50 billion IoT devices by 2020. With so many devices connected to the internet, there will be a vast amount of data generated that can be used to improve our lives in a variety of ways. For example, this data can be used to improve traffic flow, prevent crime, and even save lives.

The possibilities are endless when it comes to the future of IoT. We are only just beginning to scratch the surface of what is possible with this technology. As more and more devices become connected, we will continue to see new and innovative ways that IoT can make our lives better.

1.5.2 Role of Standardization

Standardization in IoT refers to the establishment of common protocols, guidelines, and frameworks that enable seamless communication and interaction between different devices and systems. It provides a foundation for the development of compatible IoT solutions, preventing fragmentation and ensuring a cohesive ecosystem.

Key Benefits of Standardization in IoT

- ➢ Interoperability: Standardization ensures that devices from different manufacturers can communicate and exchange data effectively, fostering a more connected and integrated IoT environment.

- ➢ Scalability: Standardized protocols and frameworks make it easier to scale IoT deployments, accommodating the growth of connected devices and data volumes.

- ➢ Security: Standardization can enhance security by promoting best practices for data protection and preventing vulnerabilities.

- ➢ Cost-Efficiency: By reducing development time and complexity, standardization can lead to cost savings for businesses and organizations.

- ➢ Innovation: A standardized IoT environment encourages innovation by providing a common foundation for developers to build upon.

Key IoT Standards and Organizations

- ➢ OneM2M: A global initiative focused on standardizing machine-to-machine (M2M) communication.

- ➢ OASIS: The Organization for the Advancement of Structured Information Standards, which develops and maintains various IoT standards.

- ➢ Bluetooth Special Interest Group (SIG): Responsible for the development of the Bluetooth standard, widely used in IoT applications.

- ➢ Wi-Fi Alliance: Promotes the adoption of Wi-Fi technology and develops related standards.

Challenges and Future Trends

While standardization is essential, it also presents challenges. Balancing the need for innovation with the desire for standardization can be complex. Additionally, the rapid pace of technological advancements may require frequent updates to existing standards.

In the future, we can expect to see a continued focus on standardization in IoT, with a particular emphasis on security, privacy, and interoperability. As the number of connected devices grows, the importance of standardization will only increase.

The Impact of Standardization on IoT Development

Standardization has a profound impact on IoT development in several ways:

- ➢ Reduced Development Costs: By providing a common framework, standardization can reduce development time and costs by eliminating the need for custom solutions.
- ➢ Enhanced Interoperability: Standardized protocols ensure that devices from different manufacturers can seamlessly communicate and exchange data, creating a more connected IoT ecosystem.
- ➢ Improved Security: Standardization can help improve IoT security by promoting best practices for data protection and preventing vulnerabilities.
- ➢ Accelerated Innovation: A standardized IoT environment encourages innovation by providing a common platform for developers to experiment and create new applications.
- ➢ Enhanced User Experience: Standardized IoT solutions can provide a more consistent and intuitive user experience, leading to greater adoption and satisfaction.

Case Studies of Successful Standardization in IoT

- ➢ Smart Cities: Standardization has played a crucial role in the development of smart cities, enabling the integration of various IoT devices and services.
- ➢ Industrial IoT: Standards like OPC UA have facilitated the adoption of IoT in industrial settings, improving efficiency and productivity.
- ➢ Consumer IoT: Standards such as Bluetooth and Wi-Fi have enabled the widespread adoption of consumer IoT devices like smart home appliances and wearables.

1.6. Internet Connectivity

1.6.1 IP Addressing

An IP address, or Internet Protocol address, is a unique string of numbers assigned to each device connected to a computer network that uses the Internet Protocol for communication. It serves as an identifier that allows devices to send and receive data over the network, ensuring that this data reaches the correct destination. i.e., Imagine every device on the internet as a house. For you to send a letter to a friend living in one of these houses, you need their home address. In the digital world, this home address is what we call an IP (Internet Protocol) Address. It's a unique string of numbers separated by periods (IPv4) or colons (IPv6) that identifies each device connected to the internet or a local network.

Types of IP Address

IP addresses can be classified in several ways based on their structure, purpose, and the type of network they are used in. Here's a breakdown of the different classifications of IP addresses:

1. Based on Addressing Scheme (IPv4 vs. IPv6)

IPv4:

This is the most common form of IP Address. It consists of four sets of numbers separated by dots. For example, 192.158.1.38. Each set of numbers can range from 0 to 255. This format can support over 4 billion unique addresses. Here's how the structure is broken down:

- Four Octets: Each octet represents eight bits, or a byte, and can take a value from 0 to 255. This range is derived from the possible combinations of eight bits ($2^8 = 256$ combinations).

- Example of IPv4 Address: 192.168.1.1
    - 192 is the first octet
    - 168 is the second octet
    - 1 is the third octet
    - 1 is the fourth octet

Each part of the IP address can indicate various aspects of the network configuration, from the network itself to the specific device within that network. In most cases, the network part of the address is represented by the first one to three octets, while the remaining section identifies the host (device).

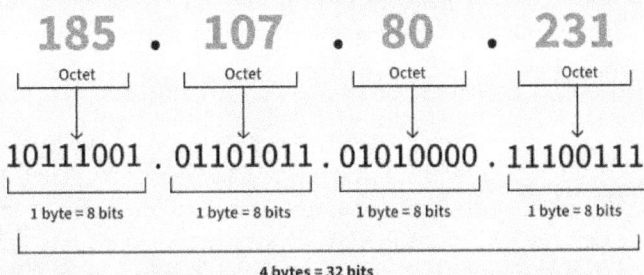

IPv6:

IPv6 addresses were created to deal with the shortage of IPv4 addresses. They use 128 bits instead of 32, offering a vastly greater number of possible addresses. These addresses are expressed as eight groups of four hexadecimal digits, each group representing 16 bits. The groups are separated by colons.

Example of IPv6 Address: 2001: 0db8: 85a3: 0000: 0000: 8a2e: 0370: 7334

Each group (like 2001, 0db8, 85a3, etc.) represents a 16-bit block of the address.

2. Based on Usage (Public vs. Private)

Public IP Addresses

A Public IP address is assigned to every device that directly accesses the internet. This address is unique across the entire internet. Here are the key characteristics and uses of public IP addresses:

- ➤ Uniqueness: Each public IP address is globally unique. No two devices on the internet can have the same public IP address at the same time.

- ➤ Accessibility: Devices with a public IP address can be accessed directly from anywhere on the internet, assuming no firewall or security settings block the access.

- ➤ Assigned by ISPs: Public IP addresses are assigned by Internet Service Providers (ISPs). When you connect to the internet through an ISP, your device or router receives a public IP address.

- ➤ Types: Public IP addresses can be static (permanently assigned to a device) or dynamic (temporarily assigned and can change over time).

Example Use: Public IP addresses are typically used for servers hosting websites, email servers, or any device that needs to be accessible from the internet. For instance, if you host a website on your own server at home, your ISP must assign a public IP address to your server so users around the world can access your site.

Private IP Addresses

Private IP addresses are used within private networks (such as home networks, office networks, etc.) and are not routable on the internet. This means that devices with private IP addresses cannot directly communicate with devices on the internet without a translating mechanism like a router performing Network Address Translation (NAT). Key features include:

> Not globally unique: Private IP addresses are only required to be unique within their own network. Different private networks can use the same range of IP addresses without conflict.

> Local communication: These addresses are used for communication between devices within the same network. They cannot be used to communicate directly with devices on the internet.

> Defined ranges: The Internet Assigned Numbers Authority (IANA) has reserved specific IP address ranges for private use:

   o IPv4: 10.0.0.0 to 10.255.255.255, 172.16.0.0 to 172.31.255.255, 192.168.0.0 to 192.168.255.255

   o IPv6: Addresses starting with FD or FC

Example Use: In a typical home network, the router assigns private IP addresses to each device (like smartphones, laptops, smart TVs) from the reserved ranges. These devices use their private IPs to communicate with each other and with the router. The router uses NAT to allow these devices to access the internet using its public IP address.

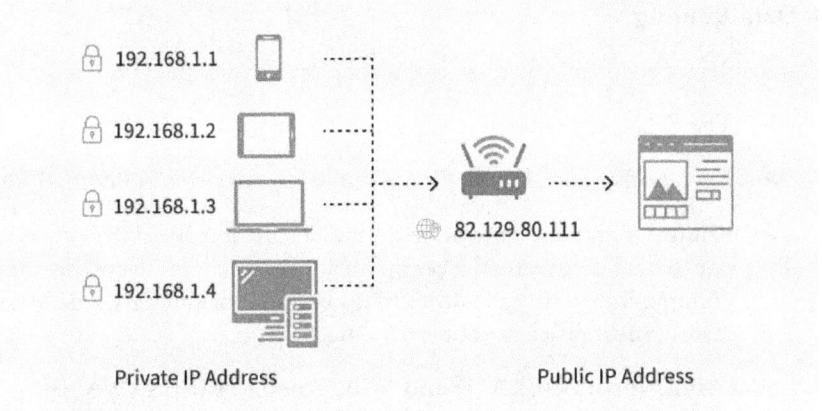

Private IP Address Public IP Address

3. Based on Assignment Method (Static vs. Dynamic)

Static IP Addresses:

➢ These are permanently assigned to a device, typically important for servers or devices that need a constant address.

➢ Reliable for network services that require regular access such as websites, remote management.

Dynamic IP Addresses:

➢ Temporarily assigned from a pool of available addresses by the Dynamic Host Configuration Protocol (DHCP).

➢ Cost-effective and efficient for providers, perfect for consumer devices that do not require permanent addresses.

How Do IP Addresses Work?

1. Unique Identification

Every device connected to a network, such as computers, smartphones, and servers, is assigned an IP address. This address is used to identify the device on the network, similar to how a home address identifies a specific location.

2. Communication Protocol

The Internet Protocol (IP), part of the broader suite of internet protocols, uses these addresses to facilitate the routing of data packets between devices. Each piece of data sent over a network is broken into smaller units called packets. Each packet includes both the sender's and the recipient's IP addresses.

3. Data Routing

When a device sends information to another device over the internet:

- The data is divided into packets.
- Each packet contains the IP address of the device it is destined for.
- Routers within the network read the destination IP address on each packet and determine the best path for the packet to travel. Routers communicate with each other to update and maintain records of the fastest, most efficient routes for data.

4. Local Area Networks (LAN) and Wide Area Networks (WAN)

- LAN: On local networks, IP addresses can be assigned manually by an administrator (static IP) or automatically by a DHCP server. Devices within the same network communicate directly using their local IP addresses.
- WAN: For devices on different networks, the data must travel through multiple routers across the internet. Each router makes independent decisions about the best route for the packets based on the destination IP address.

5. Network Address Translation (NAT)

Most devices on a home or small business network share a single public IP address when accessing the internet, even though each device has its own private IP address within the local network. NAT is a process where multiple local IP addresses are mapped to a single public IP address. This conserves IP addresses and adds a layer of security by hiding internal IP addresses from the external network.

1.6.2 Data Acquiring

A Data Acquisition System, often abbreviated as DAQ, consists of sensors, measuring instruments, and a computer. Its purpose is to gather and process essential data for

understanding electrical or physical phenomena. This system plays a crucial role in tasks like monitoring heating coil temperature to evaluate efficiency in achieving desired levels.

Data acquisition, also known as the process of collecting data, relies on specialized software that quickly captures, processes, and stores information.

It enables scientists and engineers to perform in-depth analysis for scientific or engineering purposes. Data acquisition systems are available in handheld and remote versions to cater to different measurement requirements. Handheld systems are suitable for direct interaction with subjects while remote systems excel at distant measurements, providing versatility in data collection.

Importance of Data Acquisition Systems

Data acquisition systems hold significant importance across various fields and industries for several reasons:

- ➤ Accurate Data Collection: The precise and consistent gathering of data from various sensors and sources is facilitated, resulting in reduced potential for human error and ensuring the integrity of the collected information.

- ➤ Real-Time Monitoring: Systems that acquire data provide real-time insights into processes. This enables prompt responses to changing conditions, leading to improved safety and enhanced operational efficiency.

Data acquisition systems are vital in quality control for manufacturing and industrial settings. They monitor parameters and ensure that products meet the required quality standards.

- ➤ Research and Development: They provide crucial data for experiments, simulations, and the creation of new technologies and products, supporting research endeavors effectively.

- ➤ Environmental Monitoring: The acquisition of data plays a crucial role in environmental studies. It aids in evaluating pollution levels, climate conditions, and the impact of human activities on ecosystems.

In the realm of medical applications, these systems play a vital role. They diligently monitor a patient's vital signs, aid in accurate diagnosis, and contribute to the advancement of medical devices and treatments. In automated systems, data collection plays a pivotal role as it enables machines and processes to operate efficiently without human intervention. This foundational aspect of automation ensures seamless functioning and optimal performance.

Data storage and retrieval play a crucial role in ensuring the availability of historical data for analysis, compliance, and auditing purposes. By facilitating seamless storage and easy access to information, this process enables organizations to effectively analyze past.

> Energy Management: In energy-related fields, systems for collecting data play a crucial role in monitoring the production, distribution, and consumption of electricity. This facilitates efficient energy management and promotes conservation practices.

Components of Data Acquisition System

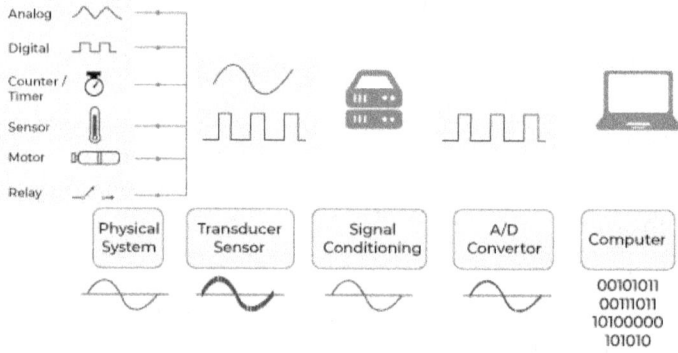

> Sensors: Devices that gather information about physical or environmental conditions, such as temperature, pressure, or light intensity.

> Signal Conditioning: To ensure accurate measurement, the raw sensor data undergoes preprocessing to filter out any noise and scale it appropriately.

> Data Logger: Hardware or software that records and stores the conditioned data over time.

> Analog-to-Digital Converter (ADC): Converts analog sensor signals into digital data that computers can process.

> Interface: Connects the data acquisition system to a computer or controller for data transfer and control.

> Power Supply: Provides the necessary electrical power to operate the system and sensors.

- ➤ Control Unit: The management of the data acquisition system involves overseeing its overall operation, which includes tasks such as triggering, timing, and synchronization.

- ➤ Software: Allows users to configure, monitor, and analyze the data collected by the system.

- ➤ Communication Protocols: The transmission and reception of data between a system and external devices or networks is known as data communication.

- ➤ Storage: For storing recorded data, there are a range of options available, including memory cards, hard drives, or cloud storage. These provide both temporary and permanent storage solutions.

- ➤ User Interface: This system allows users to interact with and control the data acquisition system effectively.

- ➤ Calibration and Calibration Standards: To ensure accuracy the sensors and system are periodically calibrated against known standards.

- ➤ Real-time Clock (RTC): Accurate timing is maintained to ensure synchronized data acquisition and timestamping.

- ➤ Triggering Mechanism: Data capture is initiated based on predefined events or specific conditions.

- ➤ Data Compression: Efforts are made to reduce the size of collected data for storage and transmission in remote or resource limited applications.

Basic Types of Data Acquisition Systems

There are some basic types of data acquisition systems given below:

1. Digital Data Acquisition Systems

Digital Data Acquisition Systems (DAS) are crucial for gathering and processing data from sensors, instruments and sources in a format. They offer benefits across industries. By digitizing analog signals these systems ensure accuracy. Minimize data loss during transmission and storage. Typically comprising components such as ADCs, microcontrollers and data storage units digital DAS provide real time data for analysis and control purposes. This enhances the efficiency and reliability of processes significantly.

Digital Data Acquisition Systems

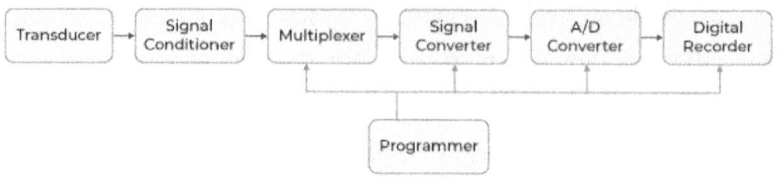

Moreover, digital DAS offer versatility in handling sensor types while seamlessly integrating into computer-based control and monitoring systems. Consequently, they have become tools, for research, industrial automation, medical monitoring, environmental studies among other fields. Their capacity to efficiently gather, analyze and share information plays a role, in making informed decisions and enhancing processes across different fields.

2. Analog Data Acquisition Systems

Analog Data Acquisition Systems (DAS) play a role, in fields as they enable the conversion of real-world analog signals into digital data for analysis and processing. These systems consist of sensors that capture analog data like voltage or current along with signal conditioning circuitry that filters, amplifies and preprocesses the signals. To facilitate storage and analysis by computers or microcontrollers analog to digital converters (ADCs) are used to convert these analog signals into a format.

Analog Data Acquisition Systems

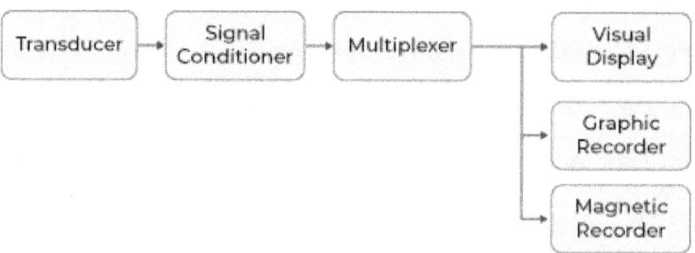

Analog DAS finds applications in fields like industrial automation, environmental monitoring, scientific research, and medical diagnostics. It ensures data accuracy, precision, and reliability, allowing organizations to make informed decisions, control processes, and monitor critical parameters. These systems are versatile tools that bridge the gap between the physical world and digital data analysis, facilitating advancements in various domains.

Data Acquisition Signal Used

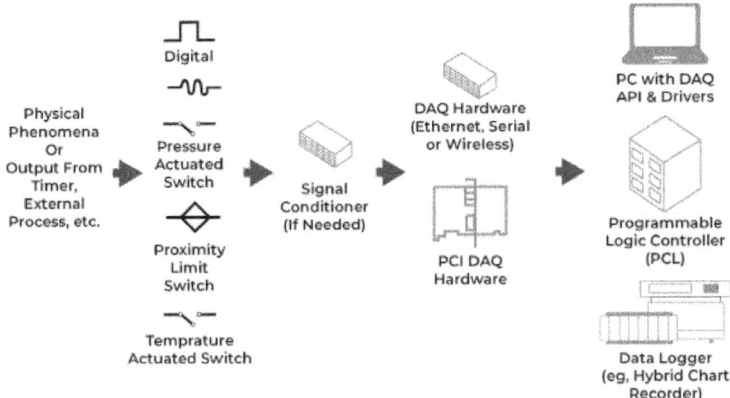

1. Voltage Signals

Voltage signals measure the potential difference between two points in a circuit. These electrical measurements are widely utilized to monitor analog quantities like voltage from sensors, transducers, or electronic devices. In various applications such as electronics testing, power monitoring, and environmental sensing, accurate electrical measurements are imperative, making voltage signals essential.

2. Current Signals

The current signals observed in a circuit are essential for measuring and monitoring electrical currents. They play a crucial role in applications like electric motor control, battery management, and ensuring electrical safety.

3. Power Signals

Power signals serve as valuable tools for efficiently managing energy consumption. They provide us with vital information about voltage, current, and other factors that enable us to monitor and optimize power usage across various settings such as industrial processes, buildings, and electrical grids.

4. Thermocouples

Thermocouples, the temperature sensors that operate by generating voltage based on temperature variations between two different metals, find extensive application in a wide range of sectors. These include industrial processes, scientific research endeavors, and climate monitoring activities.

5. Resistance

Resistance measurements involve the assessment of components or materials. This process holds significant importance in electronics as it verifies the integrity of electrical connections. In materials science, resistance measurements help in comprehending material properties such as conductivity and resistivity.

6. Strain Gauge Bridges

Strain gauges serve as sensors that measure the deformation or strain in objects experiencing mechanical stress. In engineering applications, strain gauge bridges are utilized to precisely detect changes in resistance caused by strain. This valuable tool facilitates structural analysis, load monitoring, and stress testing.

7. Digital Signals

Digital signals represent discrete states, typically binary. These states can be either on/off or high/low. They play a vital role in monitoring and controlling digital devices and systems, like microcontrollers, switches, and digital sensors. Moreover, digital signals are pervasive in computer systems, automation, and telecommunications.

Advantages of Data Acquisition Systems

- In situations where accuracy is of utmost importance, data acquisition systems prove to possess remarkable precision. These systems are capable of providing measurements that are exceedingly exact, making them suitable for circumstances that require high levels of accuracy.
- Real-time monitoring systems allow for the collection and monitoring of data in real-time. This enables quick identification of anomalies and facilitates prompt decision-making.
- Versatility: Data collection systems have the remarkable ability to be applied in a wide array of tasks. From scientific research endeavors to industrial process control operations, these systems demonstrate their adaptability and compatibility with an extensive range of sensors.
- Data storage often comprises tools for capturing and storing data, enabling users to reference previous data and observe patterns over time.

Disadvantages of Data Acquisition Systems

- Setting up a data acquisition system can be quite expensive as it requires the purchase of specialized hardware and software. The overall cost can be substantial due to these necessary components.

- These systems can be difficult to set up and maintain, requiring expertise in both hardware and software components. The configuration and maintenance processes are complex due to their intricate nature.

- Compatibility issues arise when ensuring the smooth integration of different sensors and equipment, posing a potential challenge.

- Data security becomes a concern when sensitive information is stored in these systems without implementing proper cybersecurity measures to mitigate potential risks.

- Maintenance requirements are an essential component to ensure optimal system operation, but they can increase the overall cost and effort of implementation.

1.6.3 Organizing the data

Data organization refers to the systematic arrangement of data in a structured format, making it easy to retrieve, analyze, and interpret. This process involves classifying data into various categories and organizing it into databases, spreadsheets, or other forms of storage systems. Key components of data organization include classification, categorization, and structuring. For example, in a business setting, customer data might be organized by demographics, purchase history, and engagement levels, allowing for targeted marketing efforts and personalized customer service.

For example, in a business setting, customer data might be organized by demographics, purchase history, and engagement levels, allowing for targeted marketing efforts and personalized customer service.

What is Data?

Data is nothing but systematically recorded values and facts about a quantity. When the data available to us is not systematic or organized, they are known as Raw Data. Mostly, the data given to us is in form of Raw data, and systematically Organizing them may be in form of either Bar Graph, Pictograph, Double Bar graph, or any other form of visual representation is called as Organization of Raw Data.

Example of Raw Data

15 people were asked about their favorite sports, these are the answers given by them,

Cricket, volleyball, tennis, cricket, cricket, tennis, badminton, volleyball, badminton, badminton, cricket, tennis, volleyball, cricket, tennis.

Methods of Organizing Data

There are numerous methods of Organizing data, from easy and simple methods like pictograph and Tally marks to methods that can be used for complex and large data like Histograms, bar graphs, and Double bar graphs. Let's learn about each of these methods in brief.

Organizing Raw Data in a Table Format

Sports	Number Of People
Cricket	5
Volleyball	3
Tennis	4
Badminton	3

The above table is hence, easier to interpret and analyze. The table is known as the Frequency Distribution Table, explaining how many times a particular data is selected.

Grouped Frequency Distribution

The term frequency in the frequency distribution table tells how many times a particular data has occurred or repeated. For example, In the example mentioned above, the number of people is the frequency, the frequency of choosing cricket as a sport is 5 while the frequency of choosing badminton as a sport is 3, and so on. Grouped frequency distribution is used when the data is extremely large and is complex to arrange the frequency of separate data.

For instance, there are 20 students in a class and all of them took a maths test out of 100. All of them passed the test, Following are the marks obtained by them,

35, 31, 80, 44, 50, 67, 89, 40, 45, 66, 71, 86, 56, 59, 69, 67, 82, 92, 43, 57.

Since forming the table for all the data will provide a very large table, It is better to group them separately and then write the frequency for the respective group. Let's make group of 10 marks starting from 30-40, 40-50, 50-60, 60-70, 70-80, 80-90, 90-100.

Marks in group	Number of students
30-40	3
40-50	4
50-60	3
60-70	3
70-80	2
80-90	4
90-100	1

Tally Marks

Tally is the easiest way of understanding numbers and simply marking them in groups. For 1 – 1 mark, for 2- 2marks, for 3- 3marks, for 4 – 4 marks, for 5- cross 4 marks to represent number 5, repeat the same for more numbers.

Below given table explains how tally marks are represented,

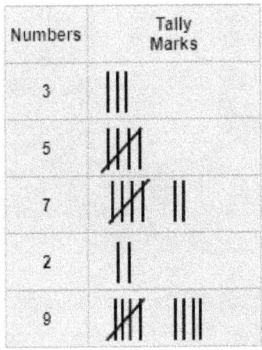

Pictograph

Representing given information in form of Pictures so that the data is in visual form and also easy to understand is a Pictograph. Pictographs can be called the earliest form of not only presenting certain data but also a way of communication when languages were not discovered, the only disadvantage of pictographs is that it is not advised to use when the information is too large and complex since explaining everything in pictures will be tedious.

Bar Graph

A graphical way of representing data with long bars, the length of the bars is decided by the frequency of each data. Bar graph are the most commonly used method of organizing data as it helps in identifying the relative size of the data easily and even large amount of data can be fitted in a bar graph with the help of scaling.

Example:

Represent the following table in form of a Bar Graph,

Sports	Number Of People
Cricket	5
Volleyball	3
Tennis	4
Badminton	3

Pie Chart

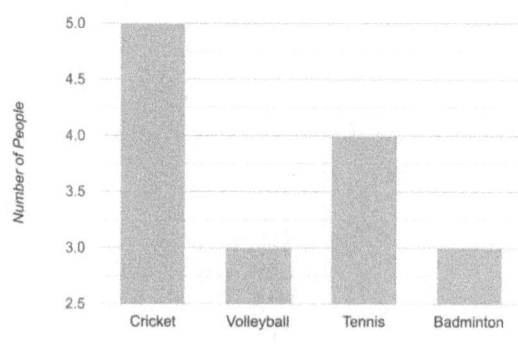

It is a pictorial representation of data on a circle, the circle disc is known as a Pie as it is in the same shape. The slices on the pie tell the amount of data for each category. The proportional or relative data is best represented on a pie chart as the entire data is easily comparable.

Example,

Represent the following data on a pie chart,

Sports	Number Of People
Cricket	5
Volleyball	3
Tennis	4
Badminton	3

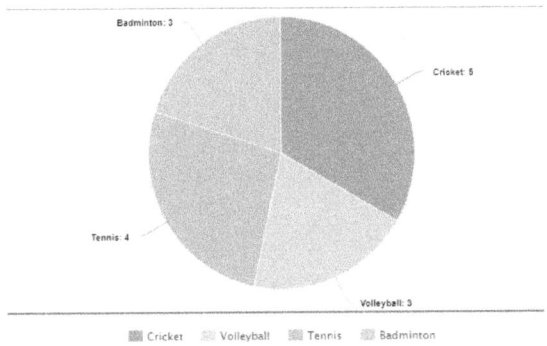

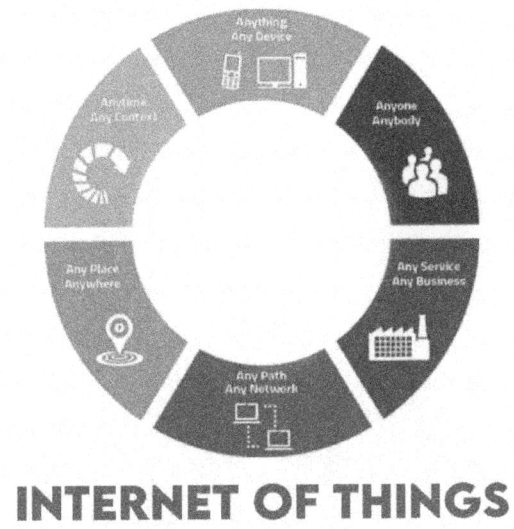

INTERNET OF THINGS

CHAPTER 2

INDEX

IOT DEVELOPMENT

2.1 Designing IoT Systems 121
    2.1.1 System Design and Architecture 121
    2.1.2 Hardware Design Considerations: 127
    2.1.3 Software Architecture for IoT Applications: 128
2.2 Embedded Systems in IoT 130
    2.2.1 Overview of Embedded Systems 130
    2.2.2 Microcontrollers for IoT 132
    2.2.3 Designing with Arduino and Raspberry Pi 137
    2.2.4 IOT Software Development Platforms 140
2.3 Data Collection and Storage 142
    2.3.1 IoT Data Collection Techniques 142
    2.3.2 Time Series Databases (TSDB) 149
    2.3.3 Data Integrity and Security 152
2.4 Cloud Computing and IoT 156
    2.4.1 Role of Cloud in IoT 156
    2.4.2 Cloud Services for IoT 159
    2.4.3 IoT Cloud Architecture 167
    2.4.4 Edge Computing and its Role in IoT 171
2.5 IoT Middleware 174
    2.5.1 Overview of Middleware in IoT 174
    2.5.2 Popular IoT Middleware Platforms 180

CHAPTER 2:

IOT DEVELOPMENT

2.1 Designing IoT Systems

2.1.1 System Design and Architecture

Systems Design is the process of defining the architecture, components, modules, interfaces, and data for a system to satisfy specified requirements. It involves translating user requirements into a detailed blueprint that guides the implementation phase. The goal is to create a well-organized and efficient structure that meets the intended purpose while considering factors like scalability, maintainability, and performance.

Why Learn System Design?

In any development process, be it Software or any other tech, the most important stage is Design. Without the designing phase, you cannot jump to the implementation or the testing part. The same is the case with the System as well. Systems Design not only is a vital step in the development of the system but also provides the backbone to handle exceptional scenarios because it represents the business logic of software.

Stage 1	Stage 2	Stage 3	Stage 4	Stage 5	Stage 6	Stage 7
Planning	Feasibility Study	System Design	Implementation	Testing	Deployment	Maintenance and Support
Define the project scope, goals, and resources.	Asses the practicality of the proposed system.	Develop a blueprint of the system architecture and components.	Transform the design into an operational system.	Verify that the system meets the specified requirements.	Introduce the system to its intended environment.	Ensure the ongoing functionality and address any issues that arise.

From the above SDLC steps, it is clear that system design acts as a backbone because no matter how good the coding part is executed, it, later on, becomes irrelevant if the corresponding design is not good. So here we get crucial vital information as to why it is been asked in every Product Based Company.

Below are the main 5 reasons why to learn system design:

> System Design is crucial in FAANG interviews.
> You need to have good expertise in System Design to be hired for Senior positions.
> System Design proficiency enhances job security.
> Understanding System Design will help you to have good communication.
> Learning System Design improves decision-making.

Objectives of Systems Design

Below are the main objectives of Systems Design:

Practicality: We need a system that should be targetting the set of audiences(users) corresponding to which they are designing.

Accuracy: Above system design should be designed in such a way it fulfills nearly all requirements around which it is designed be it functional o non-functional requirements.

Completeness: System design should meet all user requirements

Efficient: The system design should be such that it should not overuse surpassing the cost of resources nor under use as it will by now, we know will result in low thorough put (output) and less response time(latency).

Reliability: The system designed should be in proximity to a failure-free environment for a certain period of time.

Optimization: Time and space are just likely what we do for code chunks for individual components to work in a system.

Scalable(flexibility): System design should be adaptable with time as per different user needs of customers which we know will keep on changing on time.

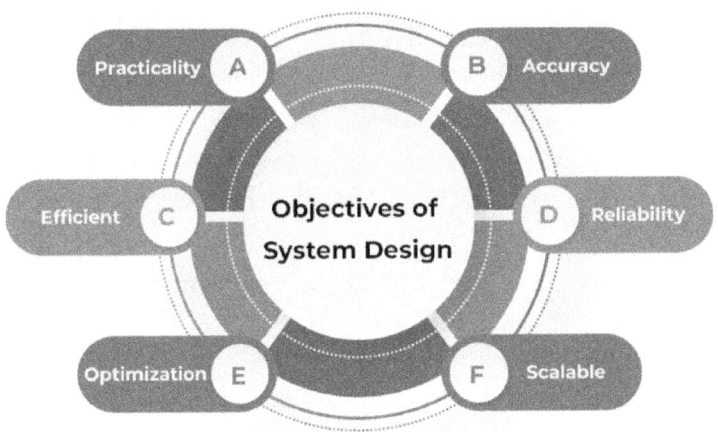

Components of System Design

Below are some of the major components of the System Design. discussed in brief. The detailed version of this will be discussed in different posts:

Load Balance: Distribute incoming traffic across multiple servers to optimize performance and ensure reliability.

Key-Value Stores: Storage systems that manage data as pairs of keys and values, often implemented using distributed hash tables.

Blob Storage: A service for storing large amounts of unstructured data, such as media files (e.g., YouTube, Netflix).

Databases: Organized collections of data that facilitate easy access, management, and modification.

Rate Limiters: Control the maximum number of requests a service can handle in a given timeframe to prevent overload.

Monitoring Systems: Tools that enable administrators to track and analyze infrastructure performance, including bandwidth and CPU usage.

- ➢ Distributed Messaging Queues: Mediums that facilitate communication between producers and consumers, ensuring reliable message delivery.0

- ➢ Distributed Unique ID Generators: Systems that generate unique identifiers for events or tasks in a distributed environment.

- ➢ Distributed Search: Mechanisms that allow users to search across multiple data sources or websites for relevant information.

- ➢ Distributed Logging Services: Systems that collect and trace logs across services to monitor and troubleshoot applications.

- ➢ Distributed Task Schedulers: Tools that manage and allocate computational resources for executing tasks across a distributed system.

COMPONENTS OF A SYSTEM

Load balancers	1	2	Key Value Stores
Blob Storage & Databases	3	4	Rate Limiters
Monitoring System	5	6	Distributed System Messaging Queue
Distributed Unique ID generator	7	8	Distributed Search
Distributed Logging Services	9	10	Distributed Task Scheduler

System architecture is a way in which we define how the components of a design are depicted design and deployment of software. It is basically the skeleton design of a software system depicting components, abstraction levels, and other aspects of a software system. In order to understand it in a layman's language, it is the aim or logic of a business should be crystal clear and laid out on a single sheet of paper. Here goals of big projects and further guides to scaling up are there for the existing system and upcoming systems to be scaled up.

System Architecture Patterns

There are various ways to organize the components in software or system architecture. And the different predefined organization of components in software architectures are known as software architecture patterns. A lot of patterns were tried and tested. Most of them have successfully solved various problems. In each pattern, the components are organized differently for solving a specific problem in software architectures.

Different types of System Architecture Patterns include:

Client-Server Architecture Pattern: Separates the system into two main components: clients that request services and servers that provide them.

Event-Driven Architecture Pattern: Uses events to trigger and communicate between decoupled components, enhancing responsiveness and scalability.

Microkernel Architecture Pattern: Centers around a core system (microkernel) with additional features and functionalities added as plugins or extensions.

Microservices Architecture Pattern: Breaks down applications into small, independent services that can be developed, deployed, and scaled independently.

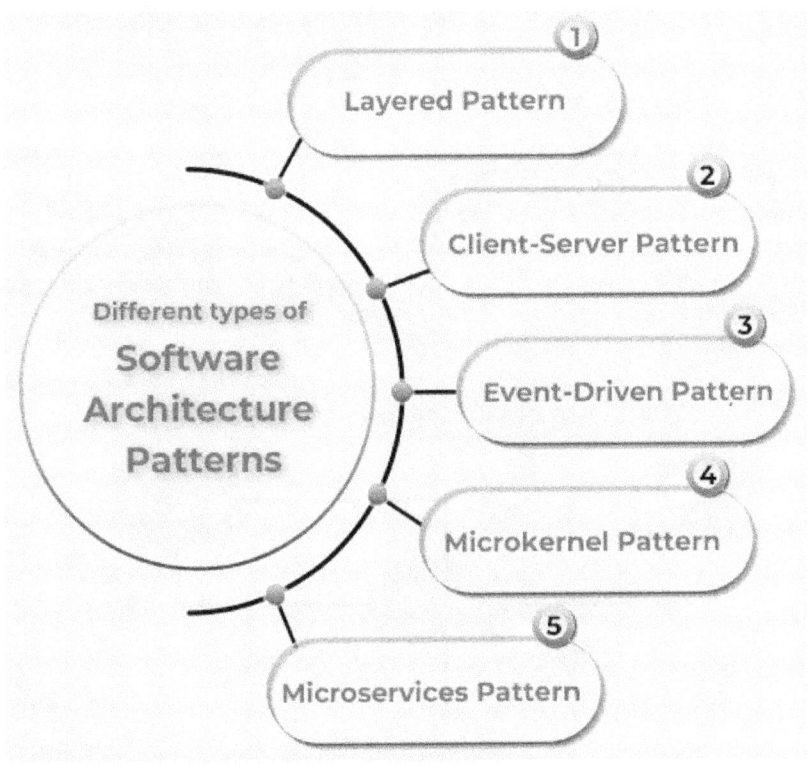

Modularity and Interfaces in Systems Design

Modularity and interfaces in systems design are essential concepts that enhance flexibility and usability by breaking down complex systems into manageable components and providing intuitive user interactions.

1. Modularity

Modular design involves breaking down complex products into smaller, independent components or modules. This allows each module (e.g., a car's engine or transmission) to be developed and tested separately, making the overall system more flexible and easier to manage. The final product is assembled by integrating these modules, enabling changes without affecting the entire system.

2. Interfaces

In systems design, interfaces are the points where users interact with the system. This includes navigation elements, data input forms, and report displays. Effective interfaces are intuitive and user-friendly, enhancing the overall user experience and ensuring efficient data collection and system navigation.

Example: Airline Reservation System

Having discussed the fundamentals of system design, we can now explore a practical example: the Airline Reservation System. This system will help illustrate the various components and design considerations involved. To better understand the Airline Reservation System, let's first examine its context-level flow diagram (DFD). In this diagram, key entities—Passenger, Travel Agent, and Airline—serve as the primary data sources and destinations.

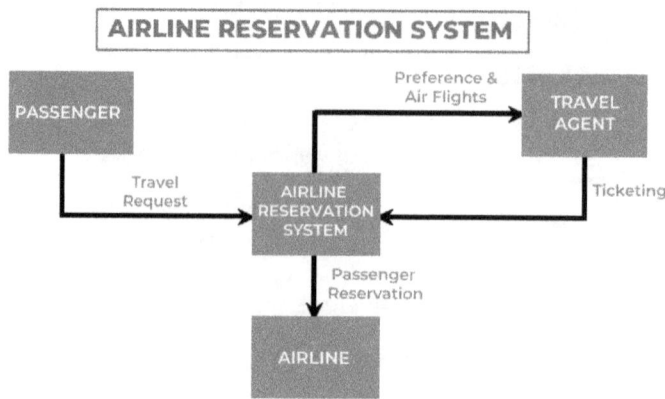

Data Flow: The flow diagram illustrates how data moves through the system. For instance, when a Passenger wants to book a flight, they initiate a travel request, which is represented by an arrow pointing towards the system.

Interaction with Travel Agent and Airline: The request is then transmitted to two main entities: the Travel Agent and the Airline. The Travel Agent checks seat availability and preferences, sending an air flight request to the Airline.

Ticketing Process: If a seat is available, the Travel Agent proceeds to issue a ticket based on the Passenger's request. This interaction is captured in the flow diagram as the ticketing process.

Handling Unavailability: If no tickets are available, the system generates a request for Passenger Reservation, indicating that the Airline must manage and inform the Passenger about their reservation options.

2.1.2 Hardware Design Considerations:

Key hardware design considerations for IoT devices include power efficiency, size and form factor, connectivity options, security, and scalability. For example, power efficiency is crucial for battery-powered devices, and size optimization is important for wearables. Connectivity options need to be chosen based on the application's requirements, and security features are essential to protect against cyber threats.

Here's a more detailed look at each consideration:

1. Power Efficiency and Battery Life:

Low-power components: Use microcontrollers and other components designed for low power consumption.

Efficient power management: Implement techniques like dynamic voltage scaling and sleep modes to conserve power.

Optimized software algorithms: Minimize energy usage by optimizing software algorithms.

Battery life: For battery-powered devices, battery life is a critical factor that needs to be carefully considered.

2. Size and Form Factor:

Compact design: Minimize the size of the device to make it more versatile and user-friendly.

Durability: Ensure that the device is durable enough to withstand the intended environment.

Form factor: Consider the shape and dimensions of the device to fit various applications, such as wearables.

3. Connectivity Options:

Communication protocols: Choose appropriate protocols like Wi-Fi, Bluetooth, Zigbee, or LoRa based on range, power, and data requirements.

Wireless communication: For remote or wireless devices, wireless communication is essential.

Network infrastructure: Consider the existing network infrastructure when choosing connectivity options.

4. Security Features:

Encryption and authentication: Implement robust security measures like encryption and authentication to protect data and prevent unauthorized access.

Secure boot: Use secure boot mechanisms to ensure that the device starts up with a known secure state.

Cybersecurity: Protect against various cyber threats by implementing appropriate security measures.

5. Scalability and Future-Proofing:

Future-proofing: Design the hardware to be easily adaptable to future updates and new technologies without major redesigns.

Scalability: Ensure that the hardware can accommodate future expansions and growth without significant changes.

Modularity: Design the hardware with modular components to allow for easier upgrades and maintenance.

2.1.3 Software Architecture for IoT Applications:

IoT software architecture typically employs a layered approach to organize various components and functions, facilitating communication and data processing between connected devices and applications. This architecture often includes layers for sensing, network communication, data processing, and application-specific functionalities.

Here's a breakdown of common IoT software architecture layers:

1. Sensing/Perception Layer:

This layer is responsible for collecting data from the physical world using sensors and actuators.

Sensors gather information like temperature, humidity, pressure, and more, while actuators control physical actions.

This layer connects the physical environment with the digital world.

2. Network Layer:

This layer enables communication between devices and the wider network, including the cloud.

It uses various communication protocols like Wi-Fi, Bluetooth, Zigbee, and cellular networks.

This layer ensures seamless connectivity and data transfer.

3. Data Processing/Middleware Layer:

This layer handles data processing, analytics, and storage.

It can involve cloud-based platforms, edge computing solutions, or a combination of both.

This layer provides insights from the collected data, enabling decision-making and automation.

4. Application Layer:

This layer provides user interfaces and applications that allow users to interact with the IoT system.

It can be accessed through mobile apps, web interfaces, or other platforms.

This layer enables users to monitor, control, and access the data and functionalities of the IoT system.

2.2 Embedded Systems in IoT

2.2.1 Overview of Embedded Systems

Embedded system is a computational system that is developed based on an integration of both hardware and software in order to perform a given task. It can be said as a dedicated computer system has been developed for some particular reason. But it is not our traditional computer system or general-purpose computers, these are the Embedded systems that may work independently or attached to a larger system to work on a few specific functions. These embedded systems can work without human intervention or with little human intervention.

Components of Embedded Systems

1. Hardware **2.** Software **3.** Firmware

Block Structure of Embedded System

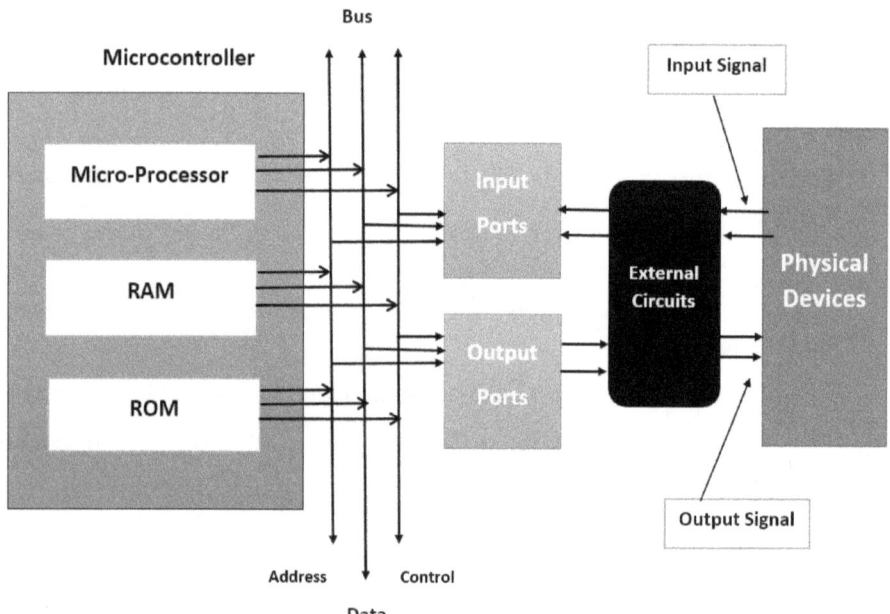

How does an Embedded System Work?

Embedded systems operate from the combination of hardware and software that focuses on certain operations. An embedded system at its heart has microcontroller or microprocessor hardware on which user writes the code in form of software for control of the system. Here is how it generally works:

Hardware Layer: Some of the hardware elements that are incorporated in an embedded system include the sensor, actuator, memory, current I/O interfaces as well as power supply. These components are interfaced with the micro controller or micro processor depending up on the input signals accepted.

Input/Output (I/O) Interfaces: They to give the system input in form of data from sensors or inputs made by the users and the microcontroller processes the data received. The processed data is then utilized to coordinate the output devices such as displays, motors or communication modules.

Firmware: _Firmware which is integrated within a system's hardware comprises of certain instructions to accomplish a task. Such software is often used for real time processing and is tuned to work in the most optimal manner on the system hardware.

Processing: Depending on the given software and the input data received from the system's inputs the microcontroller calculates the appropriate output or response and manages the system's components.

Real-time Operation: Some of the most common systems are real time, this implies that they have the ability to process events or inputs at given time. This real time capability makes sure that the system accomplishes its intended function within stated time demands.

Advantages of Embedded System

- Small size.
- Enhanced real-time performance.
- Easily customizable for a specific application.

Disadvantages of Embedded System

- High development cost.
- Time-consuming design process.
- As it is application-specific less market available.

2.2.2 Microcontrollers for IoT

A microcontroller (MCU) is a small computer on a single integrated circuit that is designed to control specific tasks within electronic systems. It combines the functions of a central processing unit (CPU), memory, and input/output interfaces, all on a single chip.Microcontrollers are widely used in embedded systems, such as home appliances, automotive systems, medical devices, and industrial control systems. They are also used in consumer electronics products, such as gaming systems, digital cameras, and audio players.A typical microcontroller consists of a processor core, volatile and non-volatile memory, input/output peripherals, and various communication interfaces. The processor core is responsible for executing instructions and controlling the other components of the microcontroller. The memory is used to store data and program code, while the input/output peripherals are used to interact with the external environment.

Microcontrollers are programmable, which means that they can be customized to perform specific tasks. The programming languages used to write code for microcontrollers vary depending on the manufacturer and the type of microcontroller. Some of the commonly used programming languages include C, C++, and assembly language.A microcontroller is a self-contained desktop that can be utilized in an embedded system. A few microcontrollers may run at clock rate rates and use four-bit expressions. Because many of the devices they control are battery-operated, microcontrollers must often be low-power. Microcontrollers are found in a wide range of products, including consumer electronics, automobile engines, computer peripherals, and test and measurement equipment. These are also well-suited to long-term battery usage. The vast majority of microcontrollers in use today are embedded in other devices.

The microcontroller used in Embedded System. for example:

- ➢ Security Systems
- ➢ Laser Printers
- ➢ Automation System
- ➢ Robotics

Working of Microcontroller:

The microcontroller chip is a high-speed device, yet it is slow when compared to a computer. As a result, each command will be executed quickly within the microcontroller. The quartz oscillator is enabled and through control logic register once the supply is powered on. Parasite capacitors will be recharged for a few seconds while the early preparation is taking place. Once the voltage level reaches its maximum value and the oscillator's frequency stabilizes, the operation of writing bits through special function registers becomes stable. Everything is controlled by the oscillator's CLK, and the whole electronics will begin to function. All of this happens in a matter of nanoseconds. A microcontroller's major role is that it can be thought of as a self-contained system with a processor memory. Its peripherals can be used in the same way that an 8051 microcontroller can. The bulk of microcontrollers in use today are embedded in other types of machinery such as telephones, appliances, vehicles, and computer system peripherals.

Types of Microcontroller:

Here are some of the most common types of microcontrollers:

8-bit Microcontrollers: These are the most basic type of microcontrollers, typically used in simple applications such as toys, small appliances, and remote controls. They have a limited processing power and memory capacity, but they are easy to use and cost-effective.

16-bit Microcontrollers: These are more advanced than 8-bit microcontrollers and are capable of performing more complex tasks. They are commonly used in applications such as medical devices, automotive systems, and industrial control systems.

32-bit Microcontrollers: These are the most powerful and feature-rich microcontrollers, capable of handling large amounts of data and performing high-speed processing. They are used in applications such as gaming systems, multimedia devices, and high-end industrial automation.

ARM Microcontrollers: These microcontrollers are based on the ARM architecture and are widely used in a variety of applications, including mobile devices, automotive systems, and industrial control systems.

PIC Microcontrollers: These microcontrollers are manufactured by Microchip Technology and are commonly used in a wide range of applications, including home appliances, automotive systems, and medical devices.

AVR Microcontrollers: These microcontrollers are manufactured by Atmel Corporation and are commonly used in applications such as robotics, industrial control systems, and consumer electronics.

FPGA-based Microcontrollers: These microcontrollers use field-programmable gate arrays (FPGAs) to provide highly customizable and flexible processing capabilities. They are commonly used in applications such as digital signal processing, video processing, and high-speed networking.

CPU: The microcontroller is referred to as a CPU device since it is utilized to carry and decode data before effectively completing the assigned duty. All microcontroller components are connected to a specific system utilizing a central processing unit. The CPU can decode instructions retrieved from the programmable memory.

Memory: The memory chip of a microcontroller functions similarly to a microprocessor in that it stores all of the data as well as programming. Microcontrollers have a limited quantity of RAM/ROM/flash memory for storing program source code.

Input and Output ports: In general, these ports are used to interface or otherwise drive various appliances like LEDs, LCDs, printers, and so on.

Serial Ports: Serial ports are used to offer serial interfaces between the microcontroller and a range of additional peripherals, such as the parallel port.

Timers: Timers and counters are included in a microcontroller. In a microcontroller, they are used to manage all timing and counting activities. The fundamental function of a counter is to count external pulses, whereas timers conduct clock tasks, pulse production, modulations, frequency measurement, and oscillations, among other things.

ADC (Analog to Digital Converter): ADC is an acronym for Automated Data Collection (Analog to Digital Converter). Analog to digital converter is abbreviated as ADC. The primary function of an ADC is to convert analog signals to digital signals. The required input signals for ADC are analog, and the resulting digital signal is employed in a variety of digital applications such as measurement equipment.

Control Interpretation: This controller is used to provide delayed control to a running application, with internal or external interpretation.

Block with Special Functions: A specific function block is included in some special microcontrollers built for particular devices such as robots and space systems. This block has additional ports for doing specific tasks.

Microcontroller Applications:

In contrast to microprocessors, which are used in personal computers and other devices, microcontrollers are mostly employed in embedded devices. These are mostly utilized in a variety of products such as implantable medical devices, machine tools, automotive engine control systems, office equipment, remote-controlled appliances, and so on. The following are some of the most common uses for microcontrollers.

Microcontroller Properties:

- Microcontroller devices are capable of having words longer than 64 bits.
- Microcontroller consist of RAM, ROM, Timer, I/O Ports.
- Microcontroller ROM is used for program storage and RAM is used for data storage.
- It is designed by using CISC architecture.
- The power consumption of modern microcontrollers is significantly lower and have operating voltage range from 1.8V to 5.5V
- The latest feature of microcontroller is flash memory like EPROM and EEPROM.
- The most recent feature of a microcontroller is flash memory, such as EPROM and EEPROM.

Uses of Microcontroller:

Microcontrollers are used in a wide range of electronic devices and systems, including:

- Home Appliances: Many home appliances, such as washing machines, refrigerators, and air conditioners, use microcontrollers to perform various functions, such as temperature control, timing, and monitoring.
- Automotive Systems: Microcontrollers are used in automotive systems, such as engine control units, anti-lock braking systems, and airbag systems, to control various functions and ensure safe and efficient operation.
- Medical Devices: Medical devices, such as insulin pumps, heart monitors, and blood glucose meters, use microcontrollers to perform various functions and provide accurate and reliable results.
- Industrial Control Systems: Microcontrollers are used in industrial control systems, such as robotics, process control systems, and manufacturing equipment, to control and monitor various processes and operations.

- Consumer Electronics: Many consumer electronics devices, such as digital cameras, gaming systems, and audio players, use microcontrollers to perform various functions and provide advanced features and capabilities.

- IoT Devices: Internet of Things (IoT) devices, such as smart home systems, wearables, and environmental sensors, use microcontrollers to connect to the internet and perform various functions.

- Aerospace and Defense Systems: Microcontrollers are used in aerospace and defense systems, such as satellites, avionics, and missiles, to control and monitor various functions and ensure safe and efficient operation.

Issues in Microcontroller:

some of the most common issues that can arise with microcontrollers:

- Timing Issues: Microcontrollers rely on precise timing to execute instructions and perform tasks. Any issues with timing can cause errors and malfunctions, which can be difficult to diagnose and fix.

- Power Issues: Microcontrollers require a stable and consistent power supply to operate correctly. Any fluctuations or disruptions in the power supply can cause the microcontroller to malfunction or fail.

- Heat Issues: Microcontrollers generate heat during operation, and excessive heat can damage the device or cause it to malfunction. Heat issues can be caused by poor design, inadequate cooling, or high ambient temperatures.

- Noise Issues: Microcontrollers can be affected by electromagnetic interference (EMI) and radio frequency interference (RFI) from other electronic devices, which can cause errors and malfunctions.

- Code Issues: The programming code used to control the microcontroller can contain errors and bugs, which can cause the device to malfunction or fail.

- Security Issues: Microcontrollers can be vulnerable to security breaches, including unauthorized access, data theft, and malware attacks.

- Compatibility Issues: Microcontrollers may not be compatible with other electronic components or devices, which can cause errors and malfunctions.

2.2.3 Designing with Arduino and Raspberry Pi

There are a wide variety of controller boards that we can use for our hardware projects. The two most popular among them are: Arduino and Raspberry Pi. Arduino is based on the ATmega family and has a relatively simple design and software structure. Raspberry Pi, basically is a single-board computer. Both of them have a CPU which executes the instructions, timers, memory and I/O pins. The key distinction between the two is that Arduino tends to have a strong I/O capability which drives external hardware directly. Whereas Raspberry Pi has a weak I/O which requires transistors to drive the hardware.

What is Arduino?

Arduino is an open-source, cross-platform, very simple hardware and software environment intended for interactive projects. It could be an electronic board having a microcontroller—a computer in one chip—besides a development environment within which one writes, compiles, and ultimately downloads code onto the microcontroller. The Arduino boards were designed to make simple engagements with an electronic system easy for both supporters and audiences: beginners, enthusiasts, and learners.

Advantages of Arduino

- **User Friendly**: Arduino IDE is so user-friendly that even a complete beginner finds it very easy to learn.
- **Above all**: Open-source, Arduino has an enormous community providing a huge number of tutorials, libraries, and other resources.
- **variety of shields:** There exist a variety of shields that can give extended capabilities to an Arduino for wireless, motor control, and even Internet connectivity.
- **Economical**: Arduino boards are much cheaper in price than most other microcontrollers or development boards.
- **Platform Independent**: The Arduino Software runs on Windows, Mac OS X and Linux.

Disadvantages of Arduino

- **Limited Computational Power**: The processing and memory resources of the Arduino boards are actually quite limited, so they cannot be used for higher operations, such as an operating system workable through intensive computation.

- **Absence of Multitasking**: Arduino boards are fundamentally designed for single-task execution, signifying their inability to manage several tasks concurrently.
- **Connectivity is limited**: While shields can absolutely extend the connective selection, the basic model of an Arduino does have its features lacking, such as Wi-Fi and Ethernet.

What is Raspberry Pi?

The Raspberry Pi is a low-cost, small-sized, single-board computer developed by the Raspberry Pi Foundation. On the contrary, Raspberry Pi is a complete computer with an installed operating system—a form of Linux on most versions. It does all tasks that would normally be performed on a regular desktop; it browses the internet, it plays videos, and it runs software programs.

Advantages of Raspberry Pi

Full-Fledged Computer: Raspberry Pi is running on a full-fledged operating system, which can perform tasks like running a desktop computer, including multitasking.

Versatile: Means that the Raspberry Pi is useful for a wide range of uses — from simple projects like home automation to complex applications in artificial intelligence and machine learning.

Extensive Connectivity: Raspberry Pi has numerous options for connectivity, such as HDMI, USB, Ethernet, Wi-Fi, and Bluetooth, making the system ideal for networked projects.

Strong Community Support: Besides Arduino, the Raspberry Pi is also developed on a Dynamite-sized community that boasts very active forums, tutorials, and resources.

GPIO Pins: The Raspberry Pi makes it possible to interface with electronic components by the use of General-Purpose Input/Output GPIO Pins, this is by far sophisticated compared to Arduino inputs.

Disadvantages of Raspberry Pi

Complexity: Setting up and using the Raspberry Pi is a bit more complicated compared to Arduino, because it requires some knowledge of operating systems and possibly command-line interfaces.

High Power Consumption: The Raspberry Pi has high power consumption compared to an Arduino, which could become a problem for battery-powered projects.

Cost: Raspberry Pi is pretty cheap, though becomes rather expensive with the designing of the SD cards, power supplies, and cases in comparison to Arduino boards. Overkill for Simple Projects: For simple electronics projects, Raspberry Pi might be overpowered and unnecessary, making Arduino a considerably better option.

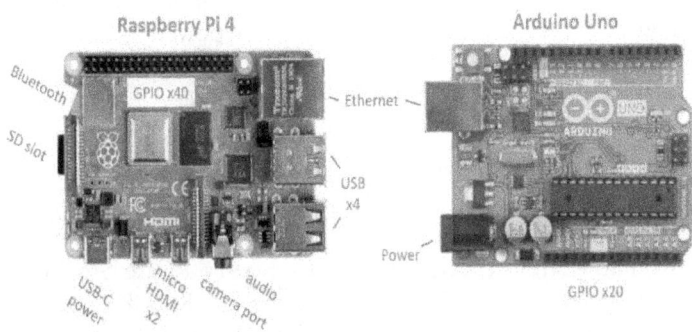

S No.	Arduino	Raspberry Pi
1	In the year 2005, the classrooms of the Interactive Design Institute in Ivrea, Italy, first introduced the Arduino board.	In the year 2012, Eben Upton first introduced the Raspberry Pi device in February.
2	Control unit of the Arduino is from the at mega family.	The control unit of Raspberry Pi is from the ARM family.
3	Arduino is based on a microcontroller.	While Raspberry Pi is based on a microprocessor.
4	It is designed to control the electrical components connected to the circuit board in a system.	While Raspberry Pi computes data and produces valuable outputs, and controls components in a system based on the outcome of its computation.
5	Arduino boards have a simple hardware and software structure.	While Raspberry Pi boards have a complex architecture of hardware and software.

6	CPU architecture: 8 bit.	CPU architecture: 64 bit.
7	It uses very little RAM, 2 kB.	While Raspberry Pi requires more RAM, 1 GB.
8	It clocks a processing speed of 16 MHz.	While Raspberry Pi clocks a processing speed of 1.4 GHz.
9	It is cheaper in cost.	While Raspberry Pi is expensive.
10	It has a higher I/O current drive strength.	While Raspberry Pi has a lower I/O current drive strength.
11	It consumes about 200 MW of power.	While it consumes about 700 MW of power.
12	Its logic level is 5V.	Its logic level is 3V.
13	It does not have internet support.	It has inbuilt Ethernet port and WiFi support.
14	It has higher current drive strength.	It has lower current drive strength.
15	Some of the applications of Arduino are traffic light countdown timer, Weighing machines, etc.	Some of the applications of Raspberry Pi are Stop motion cameras, Robot Controllers, Game Servers.
16	Operating systems are required in Arduino.	Operating System is required in Raspberry Pi.
17	Two tiny cores Arduino with 32 MHz	Single core and 700 MHz

2.2.4 IOT Software Development Platforms

What is an IoT Platform?

Simply put, an IoT platform is a tool for managing IoT systems.

IoT systems consist of four primary components: the hardware, the software, the user interface, and the network. Say, for example, you have an army of IoT robots. The hardware consists of the robots and their sensors; the software tells them how to march in a single file; a network is what allows them to communicate with each other and you; and the user interface is how you tell them which direction to march in.

The problem with managing an IoT system like this army of robots is that the four components making up the system are dependent on one another but managed independently. There's no overarching system in control of these four elements, ensuring that they're communicating the way they're meant to, checking for issues with your bots, or organising the data being gathered.

An IoT platform is what connects the four components into a cohesive, manageable, and interpretable system. These platforms help make data ingestion, communication, device management, and application operations a smooth, unified process.

Not only that, but IoT platforms give you a framework to build upon, rather than having to create your robot army from the ground up. It makes developing your IoT system faster, easier, and much more practical.

The 5 types of IoT Platforms

There are five types of IoT platforms:

IoT Connectivity Management Platforms

IoT Connectivity Management platforms are, as the name suggests, centred around the networking component of IoT systems. They provide users with the software, connectivity hardware, and data directing necessary for keeping their devices online. Their networks generally rely on existing carrier services and Wi-Fi, configuring the connection in a way that allows for easy IoT setup.

IoT Device Management Platforms

IoT Device management platforms specialise in the grunt work involved with IoT devices. They ensure that everything is connected and secure, and keep you updated on the status of your devices. Device management platforms update the firmware, notify you of changes in your devices, report metrics, and patch security. This kind of IoT platform will help you with the routine tasks associated with your devices, no matter how many you have.

IoT Cloud Platforms

IoT Cloud platforms provide users with the infrastructure required to create a cohesive IoT system. They're a central location for all of your backend processes and data to exist and operate. One of the biggest benefits of cloud platforms is their scalability; regardless of how small you start; a cloud platform can grow with you and your IoT system.

IoT Application Enablement Platforms

IoT Application enablement platforms are a one-size-fits-all approach that offers users everything they need to get an IoT system off the ground. They provide you with the devices, software, development, and deployment of IoT systems. They're a one-stop shop for kickstarting your system, saving you from having to manage developers, network configuration, and hardware engineering yourself.

IoT Advanced Analytics Platforms

IoT Advanced analytics platforms are a great solution for data-driven IoT systems. Users looking for sophisticated IoT systems that utilise machine learning, artificial intelligence, statistical modeling, and mass data harvesting can use this kind of platform to interpret and act upon the gathered data. IoT systems that primarily work to ingest data, rather than perform tasks, will benefit the most from these platforms.

2.3 Data Collection and Storage

2.3.1 IoT Data Collection Techniques

IoT data collection is the process of gathering data from a network of interconnected devices and sensors that communicate with each other over the internet. These devices, often embedded in objects, monitor and measure real-time data on various parameters, such as movement, humidity, temperature, usage patterns, etc.

The collected IoT data is transmitted to central systems where it can be processed and analyzed to extract actionable insights. This data can be stored and retrieved at any moment in time.

Types of IoT data collection

Automation data

Automation IoT data collection entails gathering information from processes and systems that operate autonomously (without human intervention. This type of data is important in industrial settings where automated machinery and production lines are monitored to ensure optimal performance. By collecting IoT data on machine status, operational parameters, and performance metrics, organizations can identify inefficiencies, predict maintenance needs, optimize, and prevent downtime.

Equipment data

Equipment IoT data collection entails the collections of data from various types of IoT devices, machinery, and equipment. This data includes metrics such as usage patterns, operational status, and performance benchmarks. The equipment IoT data is collected in real time to facilitate predictive maintenance, ensuring that machines operate efficiently and reducing downtime.

Environmental data

Environmental data collection entails gathering information IoT data about physical conditions, such as temperature, humidity, air quality, and light levels. This type of IoT data collection is vital in sectors like smart agriculture, where soil moisture and weather conditions need to be monitored, and in smart buildings to maintain optimal living conditions.

Location data

Location data collection entails gathering of IoT data from devices and sensors equipped with GPS or other positional technologies. This IoT data provides real-time insights into the geographical location, movement of individuals or assets, employee monitoring, and other management tasks. Location IoT data collection is widely used in logistics, asset management and asset tracking, supply chain management, and navigating systems.

Benefits of IoT data collection

Proper IoT data collection can deliver numerous benefits to organizations:

- **Improved operational efficiency:** IoT data collection systems boost operation efficiency and productivity by automating sensor data collection.
- **Accurate real-time insights:** IoT data collection allows real-time monitoring and instant issue resolution for organization.
- **Better decision-making:** IoT data collection allows organizations to gain insights into operational performance, market trends, and customer behavior. This is vital in strategic planning, **predictive maintenance**, and decision making.

- **Saved costs:** IoT data collection will identify inefficiencies in processes, which improves profitability, reduce costs, and optimize operations.
- **Improved user experience:** Automated IoT data collection will help you understand the user's habits, needs, preference, and behavior. This is essential in improving customer experience.

Challenges of IoT data collection

Despite its benefits, IoT data collection presents several challenges, including the following:

Data security and privacy concerns

Ensuring data security and privacy is a major concern in IoT data collection because of the sensitive nature of the data generated by IoT devices and smart sensors. Therefore, you must implement robust data governance practices, access controls, and encryption protocols to protect IoT from unauthorized access, cyber threats, and data breaches.

Moreover, compliance with data protection regulations like CCPA and GDPR is critical in safeguarding user privacy and maintaining trust in IoT data collection systems.

Scalability challenges with large data volumes

Managing the scalability issues related with huge volumes of IoT data is another critical challenge in IoT data collection. As the number of data sources and connected IoT devices grows, organizations should scale their data analytics, data processing, and data storage infrastructure to handle the increasing data loads.

Implementing edge computing technologies, distributed computing framework, and scalable storage solutions can assist address scalability challenges and ensure optimal performance in IoT data collection systems.

How IoT data collection works

The working of IoT data collection entails the following stages:

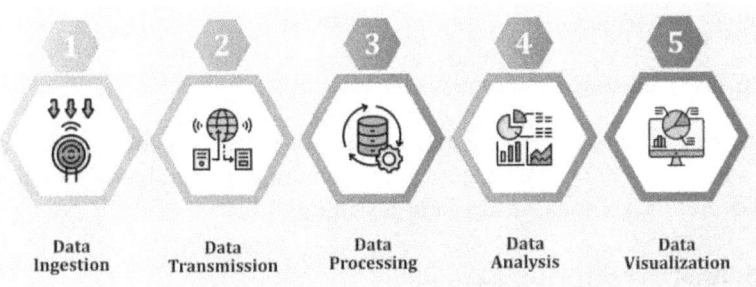

Stage 1: Data generation

The first stage in IoT data collection entails collecting data from machines, devices, and sensors installed in various environments. This data include location information, device status updates, sensor readings, and other relevant metrics.

Stage 2: Data transmission

Once IoT data is gathered, it needs to be transmitted to a central system or cloud server for further processing and analysis. This transmission is done using special translators, known as IoT gateways. For instance, the gateways receives all the information and messages from smart sensors, performs preliminary data filtering and processing, and then transmits the data through wired or wireless networks ((LoRaWAN, Zigbee, Bluetooth, cellular networks).

The IoT gateway also ensures data security through encryption and provides efficient transmission protocol. This protects data confidentiality and integrity during transmission.

Organizations can use on-premise servers, edge computing solutions, and cloud platforms to receive and store the collected IoT data for subsequent processing and analysis.

For example, ThingsBoard is an open-source IoT platform for data collection, processing, visualization, and device management.

Stage 3: Data processing

The received data is processed and analyzed to extract meaningful insights. The processing includes data cleaning, organizing data insights, adding metadata to IoT data, etc.

Stage 4: Data storage

The processed data is then stored in data lakes, and databases for analysis and visualization. Your chosen data storage solution must be capable of handling huge volumes of IoT data, secure, and scalable.

Stage 5: Analysis and visualization

Analysis techniques like predictive analytics, machine learning, and data mining can be leveraged to derive actionable insights from the collected and stored IoT data. Moreover, visualization dashboards and tools allow organizations to interpret and communicate the findings of IoT data analysis.

Methods of IoT data collection

Telemetry data collection

Telemetry IoT data collection entails the continuous remote monitoring and transmission of data from IoT sensors/devices in real time. This method captures data about environmental conditions, operational status, and device performance.

The telemetry data is essential in enabling predictive maintenance, detecting anomalies, and monitoring device health in industrial IoT solutions.

IoT Data collection architecture and technology

Device Layer

This is the primary layer of the IoT ecosystem, consisting of devices that communicate with each other and collect data from the physical environment. These devices range from simple sensors monitoring physical conditions to complex machines monitoring industrial processes.

Communication Layer

The Communication Layer ensures data transfer between the Device Layer and subsequent layers. Within this layer, IoT Gateways play a critical role.

These gateways act as intermediaries, aggregating data from multiple devices and ensuring efficient communication with the IT Edge Layer.

The IoT gateways in this layer handle various communication technologies and protocols (HTTP/HTTPS, MQTT, and CoAP, Wi-Fi, Bluetooth, Zigbee, and cellular networks). They also provide necessary security measures, such as data encryption and authentication, to ensure data integrity, efficiency, and reliability during transmission.

IT Edge Layer

The IT Edge Layer processes data closer to the data source, reducing latency and bandwidth use. It is made up of the firmware, hardware systems, and operating system of the IoT devices.

IoT Gateways are again crucial in this layer. They perform preliminary data filtering and aggregation. Also, it sometimes performs edge analytics before forwarding the data to the central processing systems.

This layer's proximity to data sources allows for real-time data processing, which is essential for applications requiring immediate response, such as industrial automation..

Event Processing Layer

The event processing layer is responsible for processing and storing data from IoT devices to detect patterns, anomalies, and significant events. The processing that happens in this layer include data cleaning, organizing data insights, and adding metadata to IoT data.

This layer uses advanced analytics and machine learning algorithms to derive and to provide immediate insights and trigger automated responses.

Client Communication Layer

The client communication layer manages interactions between the IoT system and end-users or applications. This includes dashboards, mobile apps, and APIs that allow users to access data, monitor, and analyze IoT data. It ensures that the right information is delivered to the right users or stakeholders.

Future trends in IoT data collection

Advancements in real-time data visualization

The advancements in real-time data visualization technologies will play a key role in advancing IoT data collection. For example, innovations in interactive dashboards, augmented reality, and data visualization tools will allow organizations to gain deeper insights from the collected IoT data in real time.

Moreover, enhanced visualization capabilities will allow for improved situation awareness in diverse IoT applications, proactive monitoring, and faster decision-making.

Integration of machine learning and AI for data analysis

The future trends in IoT data collection will focus on the integration of machine learning and artificial intelligence in advancing IoT data collection and analysis. This will drive innovation in the data collection process and empower organizations to extract actionable insights from the collected IoT data.

AI-powered analytics tools will predict future trends, detect patterns, and automate data processing based on IoT data. Similarly, machine learning models will enable predictive maintenance in IoT systems, enhance anomaly detection, and optimize IoT data collection strategies.

Sensor data collection

Sensor data collection involves gathering information from different sensors embedded in IoT devices. These sensors collect physical parameters, like motion sensor, pressure, humidity, temperature, etc.

The sensor data offers valuable insights into the equipment performance, user behavior, and surrounding environment.

By aggregating and analyzing sensor data, organizations can enhance user experience, improve efficiency, and optimize processes.

Historical data storage

The historical data storage entails retaining and archiving IoT data for regulatory compliance, trend analysis, and future analysis. This method of IoT data collection allows organizations to identify patterns, track performance over time, and make data-driven decisions according to historical trends.

2.3.2 Time Series Databases (TSDB)

A Time-Series Database (TSDB) is a software system specifically designed to handle time-series data, sequences of data points indexed by time. These data points typically consist of successive measurements made over a time interval and are used to track and analyze patterns of change over time.

The main difference between time-series data and other data types is that time information is an integral part of the data. For instance, think about monitoring the stock market. The value of a particular stock is only meaningful at a specific point in time. As such, time-series data often consists of timestamps and corresponding values, making it different from traditional relational data.

TSDBs are optimized for handling this type of data, providing functionalities that are not available in other database systems. They are designed to efficiently ingest, store, and query large amounts of time-stamped data. This makes them ideal for many applications—first and foremost, data streaming from IoT devices.

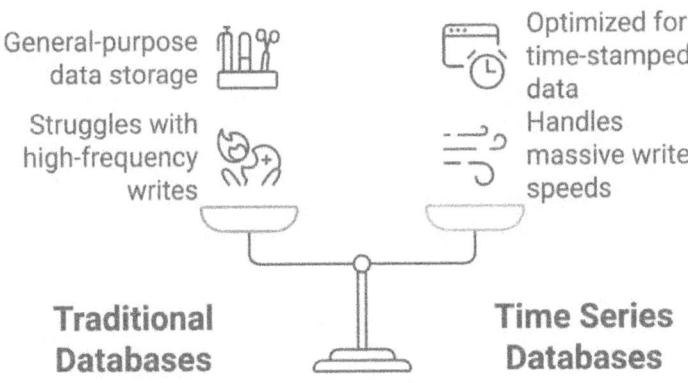

Characteristics of Time Series Databases

There are a few things that TSDBs do differently than traditional databases.

Optimized for time-stamped data: At their core, TSDBs are built to handle data with timestamps as a fundamental attribute. Every data point in a TSDB includes a timestamp, which serves as its primary index. This allows these databases to efficiently store and retrieve time-ordered sequences and provide quick access to historical trends or recent events. Most TSDBs use *time-based partitioning*, meaning the data is stored in partitions based on time intervals (e.g., hourly, daily). This enables efficient pruning, where queries ignore irrelevant partitions altogether.

High ingestion rates: Time series data is often generated at a rapid pace—think of IoT devices sending thousands of data points per second or a server monitoring tool capturing system metrics in real time. TSDBs are optimized for these high write rates and can ingest vast amounts of data without slowing down or losing information. This is usually achieved using append-only data storage models and in-memory buffers to prevent locks or transactional bottlenecks.

Efficient queries for time ranges: Analyzing time series data often involves querying specific time intervals or windows, such as "last 24 hours" or "this year compared to last year." TSDBs are built with this in mind, offering specialized query capabilities that allow users to quickly retrieve data over defined time ranges. They also support aggregations like averages, sums, or trends to offer valuable analytics without complex query logic.

The query optimization techniques include:

Pre-aggregated data: TSDBs often pre-calculate summaries for common time intervals (e.g., hourly or daily averages).

Sliding window algorithms: These help efficiently compute metrics over moving time windows, such as rolling averages.

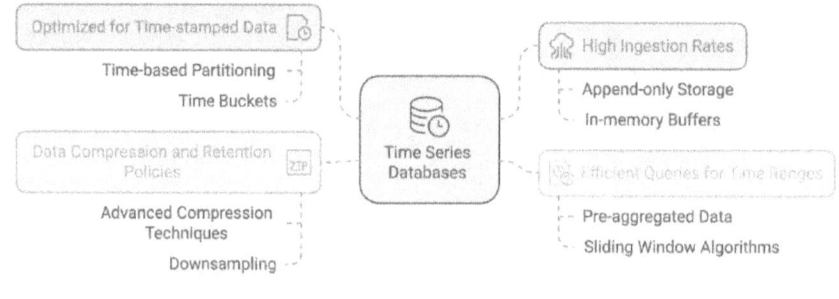

Use Cases for Time Series Databases

Time series databases are used in many modern data-driven applications and across diverse industries. Let's explore the main use cases.

1. Internet of Things (IoT)

IoT devices, like smart thermostats, industrial sensors, and environmental monitors, generate continuous streams of time-stamped data. TSDBs are used to store and analyze this data, and power applications like:

Smart homes: Monitoring and controlling appliances based on time-sensitive data.

Industrial automation: Tracking machine performance and detecting anomalies in real time to minimize downtime.

Environmental monitoring: Collecting data from sensors to track air quality, weather patterns, or water levels over time.

2. DevOps and system monitoring

In DevOps, TSDBs are widely used to monitor IT infrastructure and applications by collecting metrics like CPU usage, memory consumption, and network throughput. They enable:

Performance monitoring: Visualizing system health and performance metrics in real time.

Anomaly detection: Identifying unusual patterns, such as spikes in server load or network latency.

Capacity planning: Using historical trends to predict and allocate future resource needs.

Tools like Prometheus and Grafana often integrate with TSDBs to provide visualization and alerting capabilities for DevOps teams.

3. Financial markets

TSDBs are critical for processing and analyzing the vast amounts of high-frequency data generated in financial markets. They are used for:

Algorithmic trading: Storing and analyzing market data in milliseconds to execute trades based on real-time trends.

Risk management: Monitoring financial metrics over time to assess and mitigate risks.

Market analysis: Analyzing historical data to identify patterns, trends, and anomalies in market behaviour.

4. Other applications

While the three use cases above are very common, time series databases can also find applications in a variety of other fields:

Healthcare: Monitoring patient vitals in real time and analyzing medical device data.

Scientific research: Collecting and analyzing data for climate modelling, astronomical observations, and other time-dependent phenomena.

Business analytics: Tracking customer behaviour **analysing sales trends**, and monitoring key performance indicators over time.

Exploring Time Series Database Applications

- **Other Applications** — Includes healthcare, scientific research, and business analytics
- **Financial Markets** — Supports algorithmic trading, risk management, and market analysis
- **DevOps** — Monitors IT infrastructure for performance, anomaly detection, and capacity planning
- **IoT** — Used for smart homes, industrial automation, and environmental monitoring

2.3.3 Data Integrity and Security

Data protection and integrity have become very important in this modern world for organizations, companies, and even for the people. Unique, basic, and important to the theme here are two concepts Data Security and Data Integrity. Although both oversee separate ideas in the sector of data management they are commonly referred to. Out of these two, it is vital to have a clear distinction between Data security and Data integrity to avoid confusion on the appropriate measures to be taken when protecting the information and maintaining the integrity of the information systems.

What is Data Security?

Data security refers to the prevention of data from unauthorized users. It is only allowed to access the data to the authorized users. In the database, the DBA or head of the department can access all the data. Some users are only allowed to retrieve data, whereas others are allowed to retrieve and modify the data.

Advantages of Data Security

Protection Against Breaches: It controls access to save data as it has firewalls as well as Data encryption to avoid breaches of sensitive information.

Compliance with Regulations: To ensure that an organization monitors data security measures and proactively adheres to pertinent data protection laws, such as GDPR, and HIPAA among others, strong Data Security measures are to be put in place.

Preservation of Reputation: Protecting the data, then will help the organizations minimize the losses due to cases like hacker attacks and or data leaks while at the same time avoiding any bad reputation that may be resulting from such incidents.

Disadvantages of Data Security

Cost: About Data Security, it can go a long way in protecting an organization's data and information; however, it can be very costly since it involves the procurement of more hardware and software, personnel to monitor and update the system and time to ensure that every possible loophole is closed.

Complexity: The management and maintenance of data security can be intricate and rather challenging, more so in large organizations where data is constantly flowing through the organization both internally and externally and through a huge number of entry points that are potential targets to intruders.

Potential for Reduced Accessibility: While most types of security measures focus on the ways of preventing unauthorized access, they can create problems for gaining access to data for other legitimate purposes within a business.

What is Data Integrity?

Data integrity is defined as the data contained in the database is both correct and consistent. For this purpose, the data stored in the database must satisfy certain procedures (rules). The data in a database must be correct and consistent. DBMS provides different ways to implement such types of constraints (rules).

It can be implemented by rules i.e., Primary Key, Secondary Key, Foreign Key. This improves data integrity in a database.

Advantages of Data Integrity

Accurate Decision-Making: Ensuring data integrity enables people to make excellent decisions by using factual information hence promoting success.

Consistency Across Systems: Data Integrity stabilizes data in the chain so that whenever it is accessed it has not transformed or been impaired in any way.

Compliance and Auditability: As a rule, keeping data unalterable is mandatory to meet the requirements, while it helps auditors along with compliance personnel greatly while investigating stuff.

Disadvantages of Data Integrity

Vulnerability to Human Error: It may be also affected through human interference through wrong data entry in the computer, or through alteration of data by a human being, which results in wrong information.

Complexity in Management: Data Integrity must be protected with the means of data handling management and often, it is a challenging task in large and evolving organizations.

Dependence on Technology: Data Integrity is accomplished with the help of various technological tools and systems and hence exposes the data integrity to problems related to failure or misconfiguration.

Difference Between Data Security and Data Integrity

Data Security	Data Integrity
Data security refers to the prevention of data corruption through the use of controlled access mechanisms.	Data integrity refers to the quality of data, which assures the data is complete and has a whole structure.
Its motive is the protection of data.	Its motive is the validity of data.
Its work is to only the people who should have access to the data are the only ones who can access the data.	Its work is to check the data is correct and not corrupt.
It refers to making sure that data is accessed by its intended users, thus ensuring the privacy and protection of data.	It refers to the structure of the data and how it matches the schema of the database.
Some of the popular means of data security are authentication/authorization, masking, and encryptions.	Some of the means to preserve integrity are backing up, error detection, designing a suitable user interface, and correcting data.
It relates to the physical form of data against accidental or intentional loss or misuse and destruction.	It relates to the logical protection (correct, complete, and consistent) of data.

Data Security	Data Integrity
It avoids unauthorized access to data.	It avoids human error when data is entered.
It can be implemented through: user accounts (passwords) authentication schemes	It can be implemented by following the rules: • Primary Key • Foreign Key • Relationship

2.4 Cloud Computing and IoT

2.4.1 Role of Cloud in IoT

One component that improves the success of the **Internet of Things** is **Cloud Computing**. Cloud computing enables users to perform computing tasks using services provided over the Internet. The use of the Internet of Things in conjunction with cloud technologies has become a kind of catalyst: the Internet of Things and cloud computing are now related to each other. These are true technologies of the future that will bring many benefits.

Due to the rapid growth of technology, the problem of storing, processing, and accessing large amounts of data has arisen. Great innovation relates to the mutual use of the Internet of Things and cloud technologies. In combination, it will be possible to use powerful processing of sensory data streams and new monitoring services. As an example, sensor data can be uploaded and saved using cloud computing for later use as intelligent monitoring and activation using other devices. The goal is to transform data into insights and thus drive cost-effective and productive action.

BenefitsAnd Functions of IoT Cloud:

There are many benefits of combining these services –

- IoT Cloud Computing provides many connectivity options, implying large network access. People use a wide range of devices to gain access to cloud computing resources: mobile devices, tablets, laptops. This is convenient for users but creates the problem of the need for network access points.

- Developers can use IoT cloud computing on-demand. In other words, it is a web service accessed without special permission or any help. The only requirement is Internet access.

- Based on the request, users can scale the service according to their needs. Fast and flexible means you can expand storage space, edit software settings, and work with the number of users. Due to this characteristic, it is possible to provide deep computing power and storage.

- Cloud Computing implies the pooling of resources. It influences increased collaboration and builds close connections between users.

- As the number of IoT devices and automation in use grows, security concerns emerge. Cloud solutions provide companies with reliable authentication and encryption protocols.

- Finally, IoT cloud computing is convenient because you get exactly as much from the service as you pay. This means that costs vary depending on use: the provider measures your usage statistics. A growing network of objects with IP addresses is needed to connect to the Internet and exchange data between the components of the network.

It is important to note that cloud architecture must be well-designed since reliability, security, economy, and performance optimization depends upon it. Using well-designed CI/CD pipelines, structured services, and sandboxed environments results in a secure environment and agile development.

Comparison of Internet of Things and Cloud Computing:

Cloud is a centralized system helping to transfer and deliver data and files to data centers over the Internet. A variety of data and programs are easy to access from a centralized cloud system.

The Internet of Things refers to devices connected to the Internet. In the IoT, data is stored in real-time, as well as historical data. The IoT can analyze and instruct devices to make effective decisions, as well as track how certain actions function.

Cloud computing encompasses the delivery of data to datacenters over the Internet. IBM divides cloud computing into six different categories:

Platform as a Service (PaaS) – The cloud contains everything you need to build and deliver cloud applications so there is no need to maintain and buy equipment, software, etc.

Software as a Service (SaaS) – In this case, applications run in the cloud and other companies operate devices that connect to users' computers through a web browser.

Infrastructure as a Service (IaaS) – IaaS is an option providing companies with storage, servers, networks and hubs processing data for each use.

Public cloud – Companies manage spaces and provide users with quick access through the public network.

Private cloud – The same as a public cloud, but only one person has access here, which can be an organization, an individual company, or a user.

Hybrid cloud – Based on a private cloud, but provides access to a public cloud.

Now, the Internet of Things refers to connecting devices to the Internet. Everyday devices such as cars and household appliances may have an Internet connection, and with the advancement of the Internet of Things, more and more devices will join this list.

Pairing with edge computing:

Data processing at the network edge or edge computing is used with IoT solutions and enables faster processing and response times. To get a better understanding of how this works, consider a large factory with many implemented IoT sensors. In this situation, it makes sense, before sending data to the cloud for processing, to aggregate it close to the border to prevent cloud overload by reducing direct connections.

Data centers with this approach make data processing much faster. Yet, an approach that is only based on the edge will never provide a complete view of business operations. If there is no cloud solution, then the factory only controls each unit individually. Also, it has no way of imagining how these units work in relation to each other. This is why only the combination of the edge and the cloud will enable businesses to benefit from IoT developments.

The Role of Cloud Computing on the Internet of Things:

Cloud computing works to improve the efficiency of daily tasks in conjunction with the Internet of Things. Cloud computing is about providing a path for data to reach its destination while the Internet of Things generates a huge amount of data.

According to Amazon Web Services, there are four benefits of cloud computing:

- No need to pre-guess infrastructure capacity needs
- Saves money, because you only need to pay for those resources that you use, the larger the scale, the more savings
- In a few minutes, platforms can be deployed around the world
- Flexibility and speed in providing resources to developers

2.4.2 Cloud Services for IoT

IoT cloud platforms combine the capabilities of IoT devices with cloud computing to provide an end-to-end service. Other names for them are Cloud Service IoT Platform. Nowadays, when billions of devices are connected to the Internet, we see an expanding opportunity to tap massive data generated from these devices and process it efficiently through various apps. IoT devices have several sensors linked to the cloud, often via gateways. Multiple IoT Cloud Platforms are available on the market today, provided by various service providers and hosting a diverse range of applications. These can also be expanded to services that use powerful machine learning algorithms for predictive analysis, such as disaster prevention and recovery planning, which use data from edge devices.

Features of IoT Cloud Platform

An IoT cloud platform can be created on top of generic clouds from Microsoft, Amazon, and Google, or IBM. Network operators AT&T, Vodafone, and Verizon, may offer their IoT platforms that emphasize network connectivity. Vertically integrated platforms could be developed for specific industries such as oil and gas, logistics and transportation, etc. Device makers such as Samsung (ARTIK Cloud) have their own IoT cloud platforms.

Connectivity and network administration, device management, data collecting, processing analysis and visualization, application enablement, integration, and storage are all common aspects. The cloud for IoT can be used in three ways: Infrastructure-as-a-Service (IaaS), Platform-as-a-Service (PaaS), or Software-as-a-Service (SaaS) are all terms for cloud computing (SaaS). PaaS examples include GE Predix, Honeywell Sentience, Siemens MindSphere, Cumulocity, Bosch IoT, and Carriots. PaaS allows developers to deploy, configure, and manage their apps. The prefix is developed on the Microsoft Azure platform (PaaS). Similarly, MindSphere is built on SAP Cloud (PaaS). Siemens' Industrial Machinery Catalyst on the Cloud is an example of SaaS, which is a ready-to-use app that requires very little maintenance.

Various Cloud IoT Platforms

Thingworx 8 IoT Platform

Thingworx is a major IoT platform for industrial organizations that enables device connectivity. It allows for the experience of today's connected world. Thingworx 8 is a smarter, quicker, and easier platform that allows you to design, distribute, and enhance industrial projects and apps. PTC Thingworx is an IoT platform designed for enterprise app development. It includes fundamental features such as:

- ➢ Simple interconnection with electronic equipment such as sensors and RFIDs

- ➢ Once you've completed the setup, you'll be able to work remotely.

- ➢ Pre-built widgets for the dashboard

- ➢ Remove the project's complexity.

- ➢ Machine learning that is integrated

Advantages:

- ➢ Customers might benefit from simple web page designs.

- ➢ Devices that are simple to manage

> Solutions for simple connectivity

Disadvantages:

> Difficult to utilize with C# custom programs.

> Complex systems are difficult to handle.

> The inability to deploy the edge application on a customized platform.

Amazon Web Services IoT Platform

Amazon has a monopoly on the consumer cloud market. Back in 2004, they were the first to commercialize cloud computing truly. Since then, they've made significant investments in innovation and feature development, and they now have the most comprehensive set of tools that are accessible. It's a massively scalable platform that claims to be capable of supporting billions of devices and trillions of interactions between them. AWS IoT charges are dependent on the basis of the number of messages delivered and received. Each IoT transaction can be viewed as a message exchanged between a device and a server. Amazon charges a fee based on the number of messages transmitted or received between the endpoints. Amazon has made it easier for developers to acquire data from sensors and Internet-connected devices. They assist you in collecting and sending data to the cloud and analyzing that data to provide the capacity to manage devices. Even if the gadgets are not connected to the Internet, you can easily communicate with them.

The following are the primary characteristics of the AWS IoT platform:

> Device administration

> Device security gateway

> Encryption and authentication

> Shadow of a device

Advantages:

> Excellent integration with the Laas product.

> Over the period of the last six years, the price has decreased.

> Open and adaptable

Disadvantages:

- ➤ AWS has a steep learning curve.
- ➤ Three outages have occurred in the last two years.
- ➤ It is not safe to host important enterprise applications on this server.

Microsoft Azure IoT Suite

Microsoft Azure offers a variety of services for developing IoT solutions. It boosts your profitability and productivity by utilizing pre-built connected solutions. It examines untapped data to help businesses transform. This provides answers for a tiny Proof of Concept (PoC) for rolling out your ideas. Azure Suite can easily analyze and act on new data. It takes its cloud services for the Internet of Things very seriously. They offer services such as cloud storage, machine learning, and Internet of Things (IoT) services and have even created their operating system for IoT devices. This implies that they aspire to become a full-service provider of IoT solutions. Pricing is divided into four tiers based on the amount of IoT data generated by your devices. Less than 8,000 SMS per unit per day are free. Things start getting a little more complicated when you start integrating with other Microsoft services, but they have a great cost calculator to help you out. Like Amazon, Google, Oracle, and IBM, Microsoft has several more fascinating services that you can use on their cloud platforms. These include machine learning data analytics, allowing you to create some genuinely cutting-edge apps.

Azure IoT Suite includes capabilities such as:

- ➤ Simple Device Registration.
- ➤ Integration with SAP, Salesforce, Oracle, WebSphere, and other systems is extensive.
- ➤ Visualization and dashboards
- ➤ Streaming in real-time

Advantages:

- ➤ Provides third-party services
- ➤ Scalable and secure

- High level of availability

Disadvantages:

- Management is required.
- Expensive
- There is no bug support.

Google Cloud's IoT Platform

Google, the search engine titan, also takes the Internet of Things very seriously. They claim that the "Google Cloud IoT Platform is the perfect place to launch IoT initiatives, using Google's heritage of web-scale computing, analytics, and machine intelligence." Google's platform is one of the greatest we have right now. Google offers a complete platform for Internet-of-Things solutions. It makes it simple to connect, store, and manage IoT data. This platform assists us in growing our business. Their primary goal is to make things quick and straightforward. Google Cloud pricing is done per minute, which is less expensive than competing platforms.

Google Cloud's IoT platform includes the following features:

- It offers a lot of storage
- Reduces server maintenance costs by utilizing a completely secure, intelligent, and responsive IoT data platform.
- Scalable and efficient
- Examine large amounts of data

Advantages:

- The most rapid input/output
- Access time is reduced.
- Integrates with other Google services.

Disadvantage:

- Most of the components are Google technologies, with only a few programming languages available.

IBM Watson IoT Platform

IBM is yet another IT giant attempting to establish itself as an IoT platform authority. They are trying to make their cloud services as user-friendly as possible by using simple apps and interfaces. IBM Watson is a sophisticated platform supported by IBM's Bluemix and hybrid cloud PaaS (platform as a service) development platforms. They make IoT services more accessible to beginners by providing simple sample apps and interfaces. Because you can quickly try out their sample to see how it works, it distinguishes itself from other platforms.

The following functionalities are available to users:

- Data exchange in real-time
- Secure communication
- Cognitive systems
- Data sensor and weather data service was recently added.

Advantages:

- Utilize untapped data
- Handle massive amounts of data and
- Improve customer service

Disadvantages:

- A lot of upkeep is required.
- Allow enough time for Watson integration.
- Switching costs are high.

Salesforce IoT Cloud

Salesforce is a company that is specialized in customer relationship management. Thunder is focused on high-speed, real-time decision-making in the cloud, which powers the Salesforce IoT cloud platform. The goal is to develop more meaningful encounters with customers. Their simple point-and-click interface is intended to link you with your clients successfully.

Salesforce IoT Cloud's key features include:

- Improved data collecting
- Enhanced customer involvement
- Event processing in real-time
- Improvements in technology

Advantages:

- Increase the number of connecting devices and messages to billions.
- Simple user interface designs for connecting with customers.

Disadvantages:

- Liability for security
- Flexibility constraints

Cisco IoT Cloud Connect

Cisco Internet of Things accelerates digital transformation and data-driven actions. Cisco IoT Cloud Connect is a cloud-based mobile suite. It provides solutions for mobile operators to create an outstanding IoT experience. It allows you to deploy your devices in a variety of ways. Popular Cisco IoT Cloud Connect use cases include home security, healthcare, predictive maintenance, payment solutions, etc.

The Cisco Cloud Connect's key feature is:

- Connectivity for data and voice
- Report on device and IP session
- The billing system is adaptable.
- Options for flexible deployment

Advantages:

- Operational savings are driven by data that reduce inventory, downtime, and time to market.

- It has increased the ability to support company evolution based on a dependable, transparent technology foundation compatible with future technology releases.

- New revenue streams and business opportunities

- Risk is reduced due to a more holistic, easily managed security approach to both physical and cyber risks.

- Through informed prioritization, you can make faster and better decisions.

Disadvantages:

- Complex systems are difficult to handle.

- The inability to deploy the edge application on a customized platform.

Thingspeak IoT Platform

Thingspeak is an open-source platform for collecting and storing sensor data in the cloud. It includes an app for analyzing and visualizing data in Matlab. Sensor data can be sent via Arduino, Raspberry Pi, and Beaglebone. You can save data in a different channel.

Thingspeak has the following characteristics:

- Data should be collected using private means.

- App integration Event planning

- Analytics and visualization in MATLAB

Advantages:

- Channel hosting is provided for free.

- Simple visualization

➤ Added new functionality to Ruby, Node.js, and Python.

Disadvantages:

➤ API data posting is restricted.

➤ ThingSpeak API can be complex for newcomers.

2.4.3 IoT Cloud Architecture

- Cloud computing architecture is a combination of **service-oriented architecture** and **event-driven architecture**. **Cloud computing architecture** refers to the components and subcomponents required for cloud computing. These components typically consist of a front-end platform (fat client, thin client, mobile device), back-end platforms (servers, storage), a cloud-based delivery, and a network (Internet, Intranet, Intercloud). Combined, these components make up cloud computing architecture. Cloud computing architecture is divided into the following two parts –

➤ Front End

➤ Back End

The below diagram shows the architecture of cloud computing -

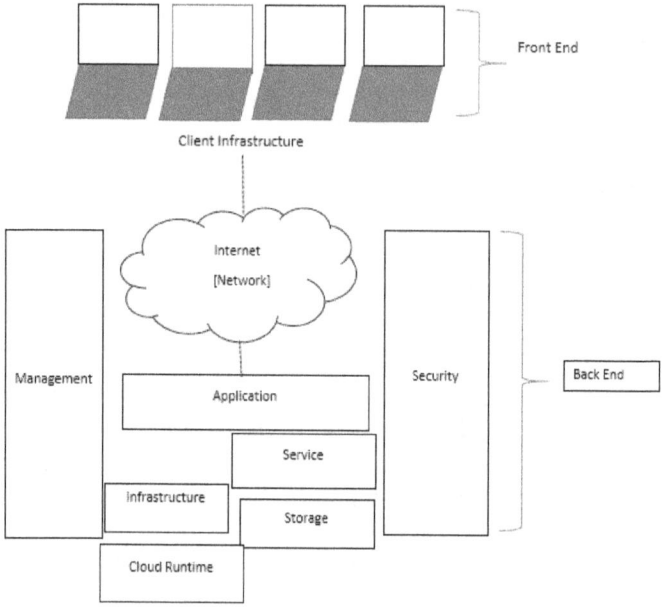

Front End

The front end is used by the client. It contains client-side interfaces and applications that are required to access the cloud computing platforms. The front end includes web servers (including Chrome, Firefox, internet explorer, etc.), thin & fat clients, tablets, and mobile devices

Front-end is the side that is visible to the client, customer, or user. Front-end pieces include the user interface and the client's computer system or network that is used for accessing the cloud system. You have probably noticed that different cloud computing systems use different user interfaces — for example, not only can you choose from a variety of web browsers (including Chrome, Safari, Firefox, etc.), but the Google Docs user interface is different than that of Salesforce.

Back End

The back end is used by the service provider. It manages all the resources that are required to provide cloud computing services. It includes a huge amount of data storage, security mechanism, virtual machines, deploying models, servers, traffic control mechanisms, etc.

On the other hand, the back-end pieces are on the side used by the service provider. These include various servers, computers, data storage systems, virtual machines, and programs that together constitute the cloud of computing services. The back-end side also is responsible for providing security mechanisms, traffic control, and protocols that connect networked computers for communication.

Components of Cloud Computing Architecture

There are the following components of cloud computing architecture -

1. Client Infrastructure: Client Infrastructure is a Front end component. It provides GUI (Graphical User Interface) to interact with the cloud.

2. Application: The application may be any software or platform that a client wants to access.

3. Service: A Cloud Services manages that which type of service you access according to the client's requirement.

Cloud computing offers the following three types of services:

i. Software as a Service (SaaS)

It is also known as **cloud application services**. Mostly, SaaS applications run directly through the web browser means we do not require to download and install these applications.

Consumers interact with the top layer of the cloud, SaaS.

Whereas users view IaaS and PaaS as raw infrastructure and platform building tools/environments, the SaaS layer of the cloud is the finished product as seen through mobile applications, enterprise-level business solutions, and every single app held within the Apple App Store and the Google Play store. Some important example of SaaS is given below –

Example: Google Apps, Salesforce Dropbox, Slack, Hubspot, Cisco WebEx.

ii. Platform as a Service (PaaS)

It is also known as **cloud platform services**. It is quite similar to SaaS, but the difference is that PaaS provides a platform for software creation, but using SaaS, we can access software over the internet without the need for any platform.

PaaS is the second layer of the cloud providing developers with the tools needed to build applications/software and the development environment required to build, stage, edit and launch applications. Much like the IaaS layer of the cloud, PaaS answers a specific need, dev tools, and environments, enabling companies and individual developers to build the products and services they eventually bring to market. PaaS is built on top of the IaaS layer as it requires RAM, bandwidth, CPU to operate.

Traditional providers of PaaS are Amazon, Cloud Foundry, Long Jump, Rackspace, and Google. PaaS is the middle layer of the cloud which leverages IaaS resources to build SaaS applications.

Example: Windows Azure, Force.com, Magento Commerce Cloud, OpenShift.

iii. Infrastructure as a Service (IaaS)

It is also known as **cloud infrastructure services**. It is responsible for managing applications data, middleware, and runtime environments.

IaaS is the primary layer of the cloud providing data center hardware (e.g. servers, nodes, hypervisors) to consumers and companies for a low monthly price. IaaS enables companies to lease servers packed with computing resources like RAM, bandwidth, CPU, and IP, hosted in a remote data center.

Traditional providers of IaaS are Digital Ocean, Amazon, Google, Microsoft, and Rackspace. IaaS is the foundation for PaaS and SaaS.

Example: Amazon Web Services (AWS) EC2, Google Compute Engine (GCE), Cisco Metapod.

4. Runtime Cloud: Runtime Cloud provides the **execution and runtime environment** to the virtual machines.

5. Storage: Storage is one of the most important components of cloud computing. It provides a huge amount of storage capacity in the cloud to store and manage data.

6. Infrastructure: It provides services on the **host level, application level,** and **network level**. Cloud infrastructure includes hardware and software components such as servers, storage, network devices, virtualization software, and other storage resources that are needed to support the cloud computing model.

7. Management: Management is used to manage components such as application, service, runtime cloud, storage, infrastructure, and other security issues in the backend and establish coordination between them.

8. Security: Security is an in-built back-end component of cloud computing. It implements a security mechanism in the back end.

9. Internet: The Internet is a medium through which the front end and back end can interact and communicate with each other.

2.4.4 Edge Computing and its Role in IoT

This technology increases the efficient usage of bandwidth by analyzing the data at the edges itself, unlike the cloud which requires the transfer of data from the IOT requiring large bandwidth, making it useful to be used in remote locations with minimum cost. It allows smart applications and devices to respond to data almost at the same time which is important in terms of business and self-driving cars. It has the ability to process data without even putting it on a public cloud, this ensures full security. Data might get corrupt while on an extended network thus affecting the data reliability for the industries to use. Edge computation of data provides a limitation to the use of cloud.

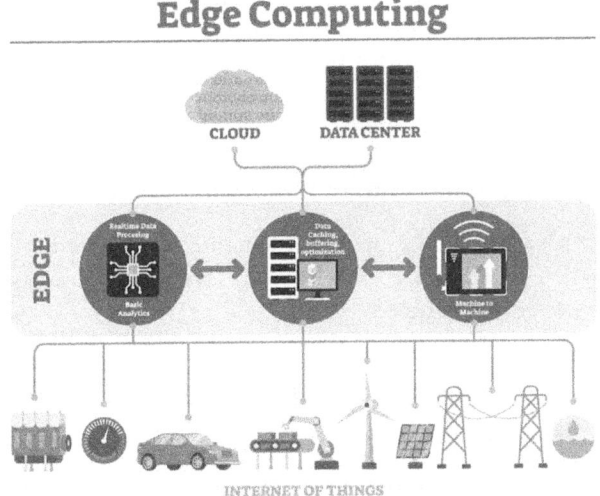

Edge vs Fog Computing: Edge is more specific towards computational processes for edge devices. So, fog includes edge computing, but would also include the network for the processed data to its final destination. **Real Life Application Of Edge Technology:**

1. **Autonomous Vehicles** – GE Digital partner, Intel, estimates that autonomous cars, with hundreds of on-vehicle sensors, will generate 40 TB of data for every eight hours of driving. Therefore, wheels—edge computing plays a dominant role. Sending all the data to cloud is unsafe and impractical. The car immediately response to the events which has valuable data when coupled into digital twin and performance of other cars of its class.

2. **Fleet Management** – Let's example considering a trucking company, the main goal is to combine and send data from multiple operational data points like wheels, brakes, batteries, etc to the cloud. Health key operational components are analysed by the cloud. Thus, essentially a fleet management solution encourages the vehicle to lower the cost.

5 Key Benefits Of Edge Computing:

- Faster response time.

- Security and Compliance.

- Cost-effective Solution.

- Reliable Operation With Intermittent Connectivity.

- Reduced latency

Limitation Of Edge Computing:

1. **Complexity:** Setting up and maintaining edge computing systems can be challenging, especially if there are many devices or a vast geographic region involved.

2. **Limited resources:** Edge devices frequently have constrained processing, storage, and bandwidth, which can restrict their capacity to carry out specific activities.

3. **Dependence on connectivity:** In order for edge computing to work correctly, connectivity is required. If the connection is lost, the system may not be able to work.

4. **Security Concern:** Edge devices may be susceptible to security risks such malware, hacking, and physical interference.

Edge Cloud Computing Services:

- IOT (Internet Of Things)

- Gaming

- Health Care

- Smart City

- Intelligent Transportation
- Enterprise Security

Edge Computing enables data to be analysed, processed, and transferred at the edge of a network. Meaning, the data is analysed locally, closer to where it is stored, in real-time without latency. Edge computing allow data from Internet of things device to be analysed edge of network before being send to a data center or cloud.

Advantages:

- It offers high speed, reduced latency better reliability which allows for quicker data processing and content delivery.
- It offers better security by distributing processing, storage, and applications across a wide range of devices and data centers, which makes it difficult for any single disruption to take down the network.
- It offers a far less expensive route to scalability and versatility, allowing companies to expand their computing capacity through a combination of IoT devices and edge data centers.
- Since the data is processed locally, less time and resources are needed for data to be transmitted among the millions of connected devices.
- It guarantees data privacy and security while sending the data over networks across international borders because a sizable amount of raw data is processed close to the protected edge devices.
- In cases of intermittent connectivity and constrained bandwidth brought on by remote places, such as forests or sailing vessels, edge computing is beneficial.

Disadvantages:

- It requires more storage capacity.
- Security challenges in edge computing is high due to huge amount of data.
- It only analyse the data.

> Cost of edge computing is very high.

> It requires advanced infrastructure.

2.5 IoT Middleware

2.5.1 Overview of Middleware in IoT

IoT middleware is software that sits between the hardware and applications layers in an Internet of Things (IoT) system, providing a set of services and functionalities to manage the communication and interaction between different IoT devices, platforms, and applications. IoT middleware is essentially the glue that connects different components of an IoT system, enabling them to work together seamlessly.

Importance of IoT Middleware in IoT Application

IoT middleware plays a crucial role in the development and deployment of IoT applications. It provides a range of services and functionalities that enable the integration, interoperability, and management of diverse IoT devices, platforms, and applications. Without IoT middleware, it would be difficult to manage the vast amount of data generated by IoT devices, and to enable the communication and coordination of different IoT devices and systems.

IoT middleware enables developers to build modular and reusable IoT applications, reducing the time and cost involved in creating custom solutions from scratch. It also helps to ensure the scalability, security, and reliability of IoT applications, enabling them to be deployed in a variety of environments and use cases. In addition, IoT middleware enables the development of IoT applications that can leverage multiple data sources and platforms, enhancing the richness and usefulness of the data generated by IoT devices.

How IoT Middleware Works?

IoT middleware works by providing a layer of software between the hardware and applications layers in an IoT system. The middleware layer provides a range of services and functionalities that enable the communication, coordination, and management of different IoT devices, platforms, and applications.

IoT middleware typically includes the following components

Communication middleware – This middleware layer is responsible for managing the communication between different IoT devices and platforms. It provides a set of protocols and standards for data exchange, and enables the translation of data between different formats and protocols.

Data management middleware – This middleware layer is responsible for managing the data generated by IoT devices. It provides a set of tools for collecting, storing, and processing data, and enables the integration of data from multiple sources.

Device management middleware – This middleware layer is responsible for managing the configuration, monitoring, and control of IoT devices. It provides a set of tools for device registration, provisioning, and firmware updates, and enables remote management of IoT devices.

Security middleware – This middleware layer is responsible for providing security and privacy services to IoT applications. It provides a set of tools for authentication, authorization, and encryption, and enables secure communication between IoT devices and applications.

Types of IoT Middleware and Their Functionalities

There are several types of IoT middleware, each with its own set of functionalities and use cases. Some of the most common types of IoT middleware include –

Application enablement platforms (AEPs) – AEPs provide a set of tools and services for building, deploying, and managing IoT applications. They typically include a range of data management, device management, and security features, as well as tools for creating custom dashboards, analytics, and visualizations.

Integration middleware – Integration middleware provides a set of tools for integrating different IoT devices and platforms. It enables the translation of data between different formats and protocols, and provides a set of APIs for accessing and managing IoT data.

Gateway middleware – Gateway middleware provides a layer of software between IoT devices and the cloud, enabling local processing and analysis of IoT data. It also enables communication between devices that use different protocols, and provides a set of tools for managing device connectivity and data transfer.

Message-oriented middleware (MOM) – MOM provides a set of tools for managing message-based communication between different IoT devices and platforms. It enables reliable and efficient delivery of messages between devices, and supports features such as publish/subscribe, point-to-point messaging, and message queuing.

Advantages of Using IoT Middleware

There are several advantages to using IoT middleware in the development and deployment of IoT applications. Here are some of the key benefits −

Integration and interoperability − IoT middleware provides a layer of abstraction that enables different IoT devices, platforms, and applications to communicate and interact with each other. This makes it easier to integrate disparate systems and devices, and enables seamless interoperability between them.

Scalability − IoT middleware enables the development of modular and reusable IoT applications that can be easily scaled up or down as needed. This makes it easier to manage and maintain large-scale IoT deployments, and enables organizations to quickly adapt to changing business needs and requirements.

Security − IoT middleware provides a range of security tools and services that help to protect IoT devices and data from unauthorized access and attack. This includes features such as authentication, authorization, encryption, and access control, which help to ensure the confidentiality, integrity, and availability of IoT data.

Reduced development time and cost − IoT middleware provides a range of pre-built modules, libraries, and APIs that can be used to quickly and easily build IoT applications. This reduces the time and cost involved in developing custom solutions from scratch, and enables developers to focus on building value-added features and functionality.

IoT Middleware Layers and Benefits

IoT middleware is a software layer that sits between the IoT devices (sensors, actuators, and controllers) and the application layer (user interfaces, dashboards, analytics tools). It acts as an intermediary that handles communication, data processing, integration, and management of devices and networks, simplifying the development and deployment of IoT solutions. Middleware abstracts the details of device interactions and offers standardized services such as communication management, data storage, processing, security, and orchestration, making it easier to integrate diverse IoT systems.

IoT Middleware Layers

1. Device Layer: This layer consists of IoT devices such as sensors, actuators, and smart devices. Middleware interacts with these devices by collecting data and sending control commands.

2. Network Layer: This layer manages communication between devices and the middleware, including handling different communication protocols like Wi-Fi, Zigbee, LoRaWAN, and 5G. The network layer ensures that data from devices can be sent securely and reliably to the middleware.

3. Middleware Layer: The core layer, which is responsible for integrating devices, managing data, providing security services, and offering APIs for applications. This layer is responsible for:

   ➢ Data Management: Collecting, filtering, and storing data from IoT devices.

   ➢ Interoperability: Ensuring devices from different manufacturers can work together seamlessly.

   ➢ Security: Handling authentication, encryption, and ensuring data integrity.

   ➢ Application Integration: Offering APIs that developers can use to build IoT applications on top of the middleware.

4. Application Layer: This layer includes applications that leverage IoT data and insights to provide services such as dashboards, control systems, and analytics. The middleware layer abstracts the complexity of device management, allowing the application layer to focus on business logic.

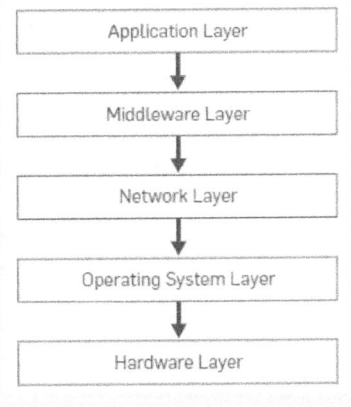

Key Features of IoT Middleware

IoT middleware provides a wide range of services to ensure efficient device management, data processing, and secure communication. Some key features include:

1. Device Management: IoT middleware simplifies the management of a diverse set of devices, including:

Device Registration: Automatically registering and provisioning new devices.

Monitoring: Continuously monitoring the status and performance of connected devices.

Firmware Updates: Providing secure and automated over-the-air (OTA) updates for device firmware.

Device Configuration: Remotely configuring and updating device settings.

2. Interoperability: One of the biggest challenges in IoT is dealing with the variety of devices, communication protocols, and data formats. Middleware provides:

Protocol Translation: Converts data between different communication protocols (e.g., MQTT, CoAP, HTTP).

Standardized APIs: Offers a unified API that abstracts device-specific details, making it easier for applications to interact with heterogeneous devices.

3. Data Management and Analytics: IoT systems generate massive amounts of data in real-time. Middleware plays a critical role in managing and processing this data:

Data Collection: Collects data from connected devices and sensors.

Data Filtering and Aggregation: Filters out redundant or irrelevant data and aggregates data from multiple sources.

Data Storage: Stores data locally or on the cloud for further analysis.

Real-Time Data Processing: Provides edge analytics or cloud-based processing capabilities to enable real-time decision-making.

4. Security and Privacy: IoT middleware is responsible for ensuring the security of devices, data, and communications:

Authentication and Authorization: Implements user and device authentication, ensuring that only authorized entities can access the system.

Encryption: Encrypts data during transmission and at rest to protect it from unauthorized access.

Anomaly Detection: Monitors network and device behavior to detect security threats or anomalies.

5. Scalability and Flexibility: IoT systems often need to scale to accommodate thousands or millions of connected devices. Middleware offers:

Horizontal Scalability: The ability to add new devices and services without significant changes to the underlying infrastructure.

Modularity: Middleware is often designed to be modular, enabling organizations to add or remove specific services as needed.

6. Integration with Cloud and Edge Computing: IoT middleware integrates seamlessly with cloud and edge computing platforms to enable:

Cloud Integration: Allows data storage and analytics on cloud platforms like AWS IoT, Microsoft Azure, or Google Cloud IoT.

Edge Computing Support: Supports processing data at the edge of the network, reducing latency and bandwidth usage, and enabling real-time decision-making closer to the source of data generation.

Benefits of IoT Middleware

IoT middleware provides numerous advantages to IoT developers and organizations:

1. Simplifies Development: Middleware abstracts the complexity of device interactions and protocols, making it easier for developers to build IoT applications. Developers can focus on application logic and user experience instead of dealing with low-level device management.

2. Improves Interoperability: By supporting multiple communication protocols and offering APIs, middleware enables devices from different manufacturers to work together, promoting interoperability within an IoT ecosystem.

3. Enables Scalability: Middleware platforms are designed to scale horizontally, allowing businesses to expand their IoT infrastructure as needed without overhauling the system.

4. Enhances Security: With built-in security features like authentication, encryption, and anomaly detection, middleware ensures that the IoT system is secure from cyberattacks and data breaches.

5. Optimizes Data Management: Middleware helps in managing the massive volumes of data generated by IoT devices, offering tools for data filtering, aggregation, storage, and real-time analytics.

6. Enables Rapid Integration: Middleware platforms provide APIs that make it easy to integrate IoT systems with third-party applications, cloud services, and enterprise systems.

2.5.2 Popular IoT Middleware Platforms

There are several IoT middleware platforms available in the market, including:

AWS IoT Core: Provides a managed cloud platform to connect devices, manage data, and perform analytics.

Google Cloud IoT: Offers device management, data processing, and analytics capabilities with tight integration into Google's cloud services.

Microsoft Azure IoT Hub: Provides secure communication, device management, and integration with other Azure services for cloud-based IoT systems.

ThingWorx: A powerful IoT platform that offers device connectivity, data management, and analytics with a focus on industrial IoT.

Kaa IoT: An open-source IoT middleware that provides tools for device management, data collection, and integration with third-party applications.

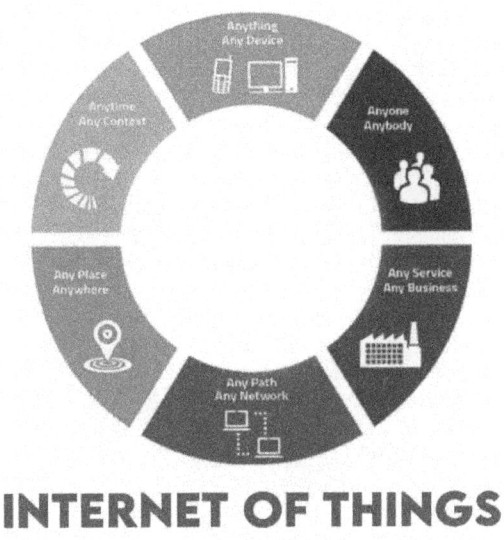

INTERNET OF THINGS

CHAPTER 3

INDEX

IOT SECURITY AND PRIVACY

3.1 Security Challenges in IoT 185
    3.1.1 IoT Security Threats and Risks 185
    3.1.2 Security Tips for IoT Devices 187
3.2 Privacy in IoT 190
    3.2.1 Privacy Risks in IoT Environments 190
    3.2.2 IoT Security Solutions 191
3.3 IoT Authentication and Authorization 193
    3.3.1 Authentication Mechanisms for IoT Devices 193
    3.3.2 Secure Communication Protocols 198
3.4 Cryptographic Techniques for IoT Security 203
    3.4.1 Lightweight Cryptographic Algorithms for IoT: 203
    3.4.2 Public Key Infrastructure (PKI) in IoT 206
3.5 Threat Modelling in IoT 207
    3.5.1 Identifying and Assessing Risks in IoT Systems: 207
    3.5.2 Common Attack Scenarios 208
3.6 Incident response in IoT 211
    3.6.1 Detecting and mitigating iot breaches 213
    3.6.2 Role of machine learning in threat detection 214

CHAPTER 3:

IOT SECURITY AND PRIVACY

3.1 Security Challenges in IoT

3.1.1 IoT Security Threats and Risks

Anything that has connection to Internet is prone to threats. As per the saying, "There are two types of parties one that has been hacked and another that doesn't know it has been hacked." This statement throws light on the fact that we are always prone to vulnerabilities. It depends upon who is least vulnerable. Unless we don't identify these threats over the internet then won't be able to take steps to protect our computer system against these threats. Any threat on IoT is backed by a purpose. The purpose may differ depending upon intruder's target:

Since IoT enabled devices are used and operated by humans, an intruder may try to gain unauthorized access to the device.By gaining access to wireless IoT devices, the intruder may get hold of confidential information.IoT devices require low power and less computational capability. Due to this, they cannot afford to have complex protocols. Therefore it becomes an easy target for intruders.

Vulnerability of IoT Devices: The easiest way to pick threat to IoT device is its vulnerability. Companies that provide IoT based solutions begin with addressing this issue first before commemorating on the underlying software. There are two types of vulnerability: hardware and software. A hardware vulnerability is difficult to detect. However, it is more difficult to repair the damage. Software vulnerability points towards a poorly written algorithm with a back door. Thus providing access to intruders for spying at such moments.

Easy Exposure of IoT Devices: This is one of the most essential issues faced by IoT industry. Any device that is not attended or exposed to troublemakers is an open invitation for threats. In majority cases, IoT devices are not are prone to third-party exposure – they either lay open or accessible to anyone. Which means that an intruder can easily steal the device and connect it with another device containing harmful data. Thus extracting cryptographic secrets, modifying programming and replacing devices with a malicious one.

1. Weak Credentials: Generally, large manufactures ship their products with a username of "admin" and with the password "0000" or "1234" and the consumers of these devices don't change them until they were forced to that by security executive. These kinds of acts make a path for hackers to hack consumer's privacy and let them control the consumer's device. In 2016, the Mirai botnet Attack as a result of using weak credentials.

2. Complex Structure of IoT Devices: IoT devices have a very complex structure that makes it difficult to find the fault in devices. Even if a device is hacked the owner of that device will be unaware of that fact. Hackers can force the device to join any malicious botnets or the device may get infected by any virus. We can not directly say that the device was hacked because of its complex structure. A few years ago, a security agency has proved that a smart refrigerator was found sent thousand plus spam mails. The interesting fact was that the owner of that refrigerator even did not know about that.

3. Outdated Software and Hardware: It has been seen that IoT devices are secured when they are shipped. But the issues come here when these devices do not get regular updates. When a company manufactures its device, it makes the devices secure from all the threats of that time but as we discussed earlier, the Internet and technologies are growing at a very fast rate. So after a year or two, it becomes very easy for hackers to find the weakness of old devices with modern technologies. That's why security updates are the most important ones.

4. Rapid increase in Ransomwar: With the advancement of the internet, hackers are also getting advanced. In the past few years, there is a rapid increase in malicious software or ransomware. This is causing a big challenge for IoT device manufacturers to secure their devices.

5. Small Scale Attacks: IoT devices are attacked on a very small scale. Manufacturing companies are trying to secure their devices for large scale attacks but no company is paying to attention small attacks. Hackers do small attacks on IoT devices such as baby monitoring devices or open wireless connections and then forced to join botnets.

6. Insecure Data Transfer: It is very difficult to transmit data securely in such a large amount as there are billions of IoT enabled devices. There is always a risk of data leaking or get infected or corrupted.

7. Smart Objects: Smart objects are the main building block of any device. These smart objects should able to communicate with another object or device or a sensor in any infrastructure securely. Even while these devices or objects are not aware of each other's network status. This is also an important issue. Hackers can hack these devices in open wireless networks.

Human Attacks on IoT Devices:

Cyber Reconnaissance: Here intruder uses cracking techniques and malicious software to conduct espionage on the targeted user to gain access to secret information on the existing systems.

Brute Force Attack: Here the intruders make an attempt to guess user's password with help of automated software, which makes several attempts unless it gets the right password to grant access.

Tracking: User's each move is captured using UID of IoT device. Tracking a user gives away precise location in time where they wish to live.

3.1.2 Security Tips for IoT Devices

With the increasing technology in today's world the use of IoT devices is preferred the most. IoT device is also called the double-edged sword. Along with making the lifestyle easy it also brings a threat in terms of security and safety. Hackers all over the world take advantage of this IoT device and threaten you and misuse your system for the wrong purpose. But this does not mean we stop using such a device but the solution is we should take some of the precautions which help users to fall under such threats.

1. Get Familiar With the Network and with the Connected Device

When an IoT device is connected to the internet it makes the network vulnerable with several possible malicious threats and thus the attackers takes advantage of it and jump into the system. If more such number of devices are connected than it equipped actually than it becomes more vulnerable and hence your information is very much prone to be leaked or at least accessible all over the wire. To reduce this threat we need to know our network and the device connected on it along with its susceptibility to disclose the information running over it. Cybercriminals use your location, your personal details to use against you.

2. Providing IoT Device Access on Your Network

Once the device is connected to your internet understand the device and kind of network it is actually using or running on. IoT device comes with some security patches or features (sometimes hidden ones) which are to be known before using it. Before installing it or purchasing it check the security manner of that device along with a priority. Always go for newer models that have fewer threats and many safety measures. Check the setting of the device before using it. You might want to change the default privacy settings.

3. Use a Unique and Strong Password for all Device and Account

Make use of a strong and unique password for all your accounts and device. Avoid using the default password like the device name or the company name of the product. If you find difficulty remembering all the passwords of the different devices than take the help of a password manager. Also keep on changing the password periodically. These measures help us even when somebody has accessed any of your accounts as they won't be able to use it if your password is changed. Also set the limit on the wrong password attempt and lockout your account for privacy.

4. Make use of the Separate Network for Your Smart Device

Utilizing a separate network for your house and office is the best way to stay away from threats. This way you can segment your network. Avoid using the public Wi-Fi network since the administrator or even person using the same network may try to access the data even without your permission or consent. This is not generally a good idea. By this it becomes easy to temper your device and account. Especially no transactions for bank and any other monetary issue is done by the public network.

5. Configure Your Device Setting

Before using the device you should never forget to change the default setting of the device because many times device while shipping with the insecure network and security settings which can be dangerous. Weak credential, permission, and many more setting should be changed according to your requirements. Configuring always helps to make the accessibility, integrity as well working functioning more stronger and enhances to one more level than previous one.

6. Install Firewalls and Other Security Solution for Vulnerability

It is always recommended to install the extra firewalls which are used to avoid the unauthorized traffic over network and detection systems/intrusion prevention systems (IDS/IPS). You can use a different kind of scanner to avoid threats like the vulnerability scanners to uncover security weaknesses within your network and the port scanner to discover the ports in the network. Check whether this port is necessary or not and then fix it.

7. Make Use of Strong Encryption

Whenever you use the WI-FI make sure you use the secure network that is encrypted. Do not use the public Wi-Fi at all because your information could be easily found by the attackers. Ensure your own network that you are working on is well updated and not WEP or WPA instead of WPA2. WPA2 is itself vulnerable to reinstallation attacks and install and update the patches for reducing the risk level to the user. Also make sure you add some settings like two-way authentication in the system so that the risk level is reduced and also you add one more layer of safety to your device.

8. Disable device features that you don't need

Always make a habit of reading the privacy policy of the app before using it. Make sure you know how the app management uses the information you share. Also try to use as much as less feature of the app. For example try to avoid the location permission or voice control permission unless you need it. Also you can enable them when needed so avoid putting them on all the time. Also make sure you disconnect your device proper after the use.

9. Keep Universal Plug and Play off (UPnP)

While the universal plug is designed seamlessly for the IoT device but it also helps the hackers outside to access your network vulnerably using UPnP protocol. Many devices have the UPnP protocol enable default so before using the device make sure you disable it unless you want your access to put at risk.

10. Implement Physical Security

Please avoid losing your phone especially when you have all the apps loaded that control IoT devices. Make sure you have pin, password or another secure method to open it and also make sure you have the ability to wipe it's data remotely. One way of doing it is setting up automatic backup or selective backups for any device data.

3.2 Privacy in IoT

3.2.1 Privacy Risks in IoT Environments

Internet-enabled devices pose a number of security challenges. But while the Internet of Things has brought connectivity to new devices, the general cybersecurity issues aren't really new. We've been dealing with hackers for as long as we've enjoyed the benefits of the Internet.

Weak authentication: Passwords are one of the first lines of defense against hacking attempts. But **if your password isn't strong, your device isn't secure.** Most default passwords are relatively weak—because they're intended to be changed—and in some cases they may be publicly accessible or stored in the application's source code. (That's extremely risky.) End users may also set the password to something that's easy to remember. But if it's easy to remember, it's probably easy to penetrate.

Many IoT devices have little or no authentication at all. Even if there's no important data stored on the device itself, a vulnerable IoT device can be a gateway to an entire network, or it can be assimilated into a botnet, where hackers can use its processing power to distribute malware and distributed denial of service (DDoS) attacks. Weak authentication is a serious IoT security concern. Manufacturers can help make authentication more secure by requiring multiple steps, using strong default passwords, and setting parameters that lead to secure user-generated passwords.

Low processing power: Most IoT applications use very little data. This reduces costs and extends battery life, but it can make them difficult to update Over-the-Air (OTA), and prevents the device from using cybersecurity features like firewalls, virus scanners, and end-to-end encryption. This ultimately leaves them more vulnerable to hacking.

This is where it's crucial that the network itself has built-in security features.

Legacy assets: If an application wasn't originally designed for cloud connectivity, it's probably ill-equipped to combat modern cyber attacks. For example, these older assets may not be compatible with newer encryption standards. It's risky to make outdated applications Internet-enabled without making significant changes—but that's not always possible with legacy assets. They've been cobbled together over years (possibly even decades), which turns even small security improvements into a monumental undertaking.

Shared network access: It's easier for IoT device to use the same network as the end user's other devices—such as their WiFi or LAN—but it also makes the entire network more vulnerable. Someone can hack an IoT device to get their foot in the door and gain access to more sensitive data stored on the network or other connected devices. Likewise, another device on the network could be used to hack the IoT device. In either of those scenarios, customers and manufacturers wind up pointing fingers at each other. Every IoT application should use a separate network and/or have a security gateway or firewall—so if there's a security breach on the device, it remains isolated to the device. (This is one of the advantages of cellular IoT.) A Virtual Private Network (VPN) helps protect your devices from outside the network, but if your application shares a connection with other devices, it's still vulnerable to attacks from them if they become corrupted.

Inconsistent security standards: Within IoT, there's a bit of a free-for-all when it comes to security standards. There's no universal, industry-wide standard, which means companies and niches all have to develop their own protocols and guidelines. The lack of standardization makes it harder to secure IoT devices, and it also makes it harder to enable machine-to-machine (M2M) communication without increasing risk.

Lack of encryption: One of the greatest threats to IoT security is the lack of encryption on regular transmissions. Many IoT devices don't encrypt the data they send, which means if someone penetrates the network, they can intercept credentials and other important information transmitted to and from the device.

Missing firmware updates: Another of the biggest IoT security risks is if devices go out in the field with a bug that creates vulnerabilities. Whether they come from your own developed code or a third party, manufacturers need the ability to issue firmware updates to eliminate these security risks. Ideally, this should happen remotely, but that's not always feasible. If a network's data transfer rates are too low or it has limited messaging capabilities, you may have to physically access the device to issue the update.

3.2.2 IoT Security Solutions

Security is imperative. For IoT businesses and vendors, the introduction of new technology and the increase in global deployments bring a myriad of new security issues that need to be considered when deploying M2M devices.

1. Physical security: Since IoT applications are often remote, physical security is crucial for preventing unauthorized access to a device. This is where it's valuable to use resilient components and specialized hardware that makes your data more difficult to access.

For example, in cellular IoT devices, lots of critical information is stored on the SIM card. Most form factors for SIMs are removable, which makes this data more vulnerable. An eSIM, however, is soldered directly onto the circuit board. They're harder to physically access, and they're also more resistant to changes in temperature and shock damage, which are sometimes used in attempts to sabotage or hack a device.

2. Remote access security: Moreover, a robust remote-access security protocol is needed that allows

- SIM functionality to be locked to specific devices
- The ability to remotely disable connections if there's a physical security breach

3. Private networks: Sending and receiving messages through remotely deployed devices is in itself a security risk. Connecting devices and enabling this communication using public-access networks, such as WiFi, opens up those messages for interception. Encrypting messages is a step in the right direction but using public networks to send sensitive data demands more precautions. We recommend building private networks on top of existing security mechanisms to ensure that data never crosses the public Internet.Emnify helps IoT manufacturers create Virtual Private Networks (VPNs) using OpenVPN, a versatile open standard that gives you secure remote access to your devices from anywhere.

4. Abnormality detection: The moment someone attempts to breach your device or there's abnormal network activity, you need to know. With aemnify's cloud communication platform, we forward the relevant connectivity information to your operational dashboards, where you can evaluate whether there was an employee error or a serious threat.

5. IMEI lock: An International Mobile Station Equipment Identity (IMEI) is the unique ID number found on most mobile devices. An IMEI lock will enable you to configure a SIMs functionality to a specific IMEI in real time to prevent the SIM being removed and used in any other device.

6. Encrypted data transfer: To securely transport data to and from your devices, you need to encrypt data transfers within the network. There are a variety of protocols developers can use to secure a device's communication, the most common of which is Transport Layer Security (TLS). But while your application and network may be secure, there's a gap between them where your data can be intercepted. Using an X.509 certificate and/or a single VPN/IPSec connection between the mobile network and the application server, you can close this security gap. Alternatively, emnify also enables you

to use <u>intra-cloud connect</u> to establish a secure VPN for your entire deployment, so there's no need for public IPs.

7. Network-based firewall: Typically, small M2M devices have limited processing power. This prevents them from establishing firewalls. A *network-based* firewall, however, protects your data the moment it enters the network. This takes the labor-intensive process of packet filtering away from the device, ensuring malicious traffic is never transmitted to the device or even able to enter the network in the first place.Network-based firewalls allow businesses to monitor and block traffic outside of your VPN, or simply block specific communications. It can also detect intrusions or hacking attempts that do not align with pre-configured policies.

8. Limited connectivity profile: Your IoT application was designed for a specific purpose. The more you can isolate your device's network connectivity to its core functions, the more secure it will be. Does it need access to voice capabilities? Does it need to receive external SMS messages? If not, that functionality should be restricted.

3.3 IoT Authentication and Authorization

3.3.1 Authentication Mechanisms for IoT Devices

Authentication mechanisms for Internet of Things (IoT) devices are critical for ensuring secure access, data integrity, and privacy within IoT networks. Since IoT devices often operate in environments with limited resources (such as processing power, memory, and battery life), traditional authentication methods need to be adapted for these constraints. Below are common authentication mechanisms used in IoT devices:

1. Password-based Authentication

Description: The device and server authenticate based on a shared secret, such as a password or PIN.

Benefits: Simple and easy to implement.

Challenges: Vulnerable to brute-force attacks, especially if the password is weak. Managing passwords for large numbers of devices is challenging.

Use cases: Typically used in less critical applications, often combined with other methods for added security.

2. Public Key Infrastructure (PKI)

Description: Devices use asymmetric cryptography with a public/private key pair. The device stores the private key securely, and the public key is used by the server to authenticate the device.

Benefits: Strong security with encryption. Private keys are not shared, reducing risk.

Challenges: Key management is complex. Devices need to securely store private keys.

Use cases: Suitable for enterprise-level deployments and secure communications in IoT.

3. Certificate-based Authentication

Description: Devices are issued certificates from a trusted authority (e.g., a Certificate Authority, CA). These certificates contain the public key and the device's identity.

Benefits: Strong security; certificates are difficult to forge.

Challenges: Requires a Public Key Infrastructure (PKI) for managing certificates. Key storage can be difficult for resource-constrained devices.

Use cases: Common in secure IoT networks like **smart cities** or **healthcare systems**.

4. Token-based Authentication (e.g., JWT, OAuth)

Description: Devices authenticate using time-limited tokens, such as a JSON Web Token (JWT) or OAuth token, typically issued after an initial authentication process.

Benefits: Ideal for cloud-connected IoT systems, tokens can be limited in scope, reducing access risks.

Challenges: Secure management of token issuance, expiration, and renewal is necessary.

Use cases: Cloud-based IoT services, such as **smart home hubs** or **remote monitoring systems**.

5. Biometric Authentication

Description: Devices use biometric data (e.g., fingerprints, facial recognition) to authenticate users or devices.

Benefits: User-friendly, difficult for attackers to replicate.

Challenges: Requires specialized hardware, and raises privacy concerns.

Use cases: Common in consumer IoT devices like **smartphones** or **wearable devices**.

6. Multi-factor Authentication (MFA)

Description: Combines two or more factors (something the device knows, something the device has, and something the device is) for authentication.

Benefits: Adds an extra layer of security, reducing unauthorized access.

Challenges: Can increase complexity and may not be feasible for resource-constrained devices.

Use cases: Used in **critical IoT applications**, such as **enterprise IoT systems** or **smart security devices**.

7. Device Fingerprinting

Description: Devices are identified based on unique hardware or software characteristics (e.g., MAC address, IP address, or hardware ID).

Benefits: Passive authentication, no need for user interaction.

Challenges: Can be spoofed if hardware characteristics are manipulated. Privacy concerns due to device tracking.

Use cases: Common in **device management systems** and **network monitoring** for **IoT security**.

8. One-Time Passwords (OTP)

Description: A time-sensitive, single-use password (e.g., sent via SMS or email) is used for authentication.

Benefits: Reduces the risk of password reuse or theft.

Challenges: Vulnerable to interception if not transmitted securely. User inconvenience if not implemented smoothly.

Use cases: Often used in **financial IoT applications** or **remote access systems**.

9. Challenge-Response Authentication

Description: The device and server exchange a challenge-response pair to verify authenticity. The device signs or encrypts the challenge with its private key and sends it back.

Benefits: Prevents replay attacks; secure communication between devices.

Challenges: If not securely generated, challenges can be vulnerable to interception.

Use cases: Used in **secure communication** systems between **IoT devices** and **servers**.

10. Lightweight Cryptographic Protocols (for Constrained Devices)

Description: Protocols like **Elliptic Curve Cryptography (ECC)** or **Advanced Encryption Standard (AES)** are optimized for devices with limited resources.

Benefits: Low computational overhead and energy efficiency, ideal for battery-powered IoT devices.

Challenges: Implementation complexity; could still pose challenges for extremely resource-constrained devices.

Use cases: **Low-power IoT devices**, such as **smart sensors** or **wearables**.

11. OAuth 2.0 (Authorization Framework)

Description: OAuth 2.0 is a protocol that allows devices to access resources without sharing user credentials. It uses tokens for secure access.

Benefits: Delegates access control, allowing devices to authenticate using access tokens without sharing credentials.

Challenges: Token management and secure transport are crucial for preventing token theft or misuse.

Use cases: Used in **cloud-connected IoT systems**, where devices need to access external services or data.

12. Device-to-Device Authentication (D2D)

Description: Devices authenticate each other directly, using shared secrets or public/private keys.

Benefits: No reliance on central servers, faster authentication in some cases.

Challenges: Devices need secure key storage, which may be difficult for resource-limited devices.

Use cases: **Peer-to-peer IoT systems**, like **smart home networks** where devices communicate directly.

13. Mutual Authentication

Description: Both the device and the server authenticate each other, usually using certificates or cryptographic keys.

Benefits: Provides two-way trust and prevents unauthorized access.

Challenges: Key management and secure storage are required for both the device and the server.

Use cases: **Critical IoT applications** like **industrial control systems** or **healthcare devices**.

14. Zero Trust Authentication

Description: Assumes that threats may exist both inside and outside the network, requiring continuous authentication at every point in the network.

Benefits: Continuous authentication reduces the risk of unauthorized access even if a device is compromised.

Challenges: Complex to implement and may introduce latency due to constant checks.

Use cases: **High-security IoT environments**, such as **industrial IoT**, **smart city infrastructure**, or **critical healthcare systems**.

15. Blockchain-based Authentication

Description: Blockchain can be used to securely and decentralize authentication and identity management for IoT devices.

Benefits: Immutable, decentralized record of authentication events, reducing the risk of tampering.

Challenges: Scalability issues as the number of devices grows, and resource consumption required to write to the blockchain.

Use cases: **Critical IoT systems** requiring high levels of security and traceability, such as **supply chain** and **autonomous vehicles**.

16. Attribute-based Authentication (ABAC)

Description: Authentication is based on attributes (e.g., device type, location, ownership), and access is granted based on policies that combine these attributes.

Benefits: Provides fine-grained access control and dynamic security based on the context.

Challenges: Managing complex policies can be challenging, especially as the system grows.

Use cases: Smart cities, enterprise networks, and **smart buildings**, where device context and access policies change frequently.

17. Side-channel Authentication

Description: This technique leverages side-channel data (e.g., power consumption, electromagnetic emissions, or timing characteristics) to authenticate devices.

Benefits: Very difficult for attackers to replicate the side-channel signals, providing robust security.

Challenges: Collecting and analyzing side-channel data is complex and can lead to false positives.

Use cases: High-security IoT systems like **military IoT, critical infrastructure** requiring extra security.

3.3.2 Secure Communication Protocols

TLS (Transport Layer Security) and **SSL (Secure Sockets Layer)** are cryptographic protocols designed to provide secure communication over a computer network, including the Internet. These protocols are widely used in **IoT systems** to ensure the security, confidentiality, and integrity of data transmitted between devices, servers, or other components in a network.

What is SSL (Secure Sockets Layer)?

SSL was the first widely adopted protocol for securing communications on the internet. It was developed by Netscape in the mid-1990s to secure web traffic. SSL provides encryption, data integrity, and authentication.

SSL Versions:

SSL 1.0: Never released due to severe security flaws.

SSL 2.0: Released in 1995, but soon deprecated due to security vulnerabilities.

SSL 3.0: Introduced in 1996, but eventually deprecated due to vulnerabilities (e.g., POODLE attack).

What is TLS (Transport Layer Security)?

TLS is the successor to SSL, offering stronger encryption and better security. TLS was introduced in 1999 as a more secure replacement for SSL. While **TLS and SSL** share similarities, TLS provides improvements in encryption algorithms and fixes many of SSL's security issues.

TLS Versions:

TLS 1.0: Released in 1999.

TLS 1.1: Released in 2006 (deprecated due to security vulnerabilities).

TLS 1.2: Released in 2008 and is still widely used today.

TLS 1.3: Released in 2018, with better performance and security features, and more streamlined encryption methods.

Differences Between SSL and TLS:

Feature	SSL	TLS
Release Year	1995 (SSL 2.0), 1996 (SSL 3.0)	1999 (TLS 1.0)
Encryption	Less efficient and less secure	Improved encryption algorithms
Security	Vulnerable to certain attacks (e.g., POODLE)	Stronger security and resistance to attacks
Handshake	SSL handshake is less efficient	TLS handshake is more efficient and secure
Performance	Slower performance	Faster due to fewer handshake steps
Compatibility	Deprecated and no longer secure	Modern systems widely use TLS 1.2 and 1.3

How TLS and SSL Work:

The primary role of **TLS** and **SSL** is to establish a secure connection between two devices (client-server or device-to-device) over a potentially insecure network like the internet. This is achieved through a series of steps:

1. Handshake Process:

The handshake process is the critical part where the devices agree on how to communicate securely. Here's an overview:

Step 1: ClientHello

The client (IoT device or server) sends a "ClientHello" message, proposing a list of supported cryptographic algorithms (e.g., encryption and hash functions).

Step 2: ServerHello

The server responds with a "ServerHello" message, selecting a cipher suite (the combination of encryption and hash algorithms) from the list provided by the client.

Step 3: Server Certificate

The server sends its digital certificate to the client. This certificate is issued by a trusted Certificate Authority (CA) and contains the server's public key.

Step 4: Key Exchange

The client validates the server's certificate. The client and server exchange a shared secret (pre-master secret), which is used to derive session keys. In TLS, this exchange happens using **public key cryptography**.

Step 5: Session Key Creation

Both the client and server use the agreed-upon algorithms and the pre-master secret to generate session keys for encrypting and decrypting the actual data.

Step 6: Secure Communication

Once the session key is generated, both devices switch to encrypted communication using symmetric encryption (AES or similar) for better performance. All subsequent data exchanged between the devices is encrypted.

Benefits of TLS and SSL for IoT:

Data Encryption: TLS and SSL ensure that data transmitted between devices (or between devices and servers) is encrypted. This means that even if a third party intercepts the data, they cannot read it without the proper decryption key.

Authentication: These protocols use **digital certificates** issued by trusted Certificate Authorities (CAs) to authenticate the identity of the server (and optionally, the client). This prevents man-in-the-middle attacks and ensures that the devices are communicating with trusted parties.

Data Integrity: Both protocols use **message authentication codes (MACs)** to ensure that the data has not been altered during transmission. If the data is tampered with, the receiver can detect it and reject the data.

Forward Secrecy: In modern versions of TLS (particularly TLS 1.2 and TLS 1.3), forward secrecy is supported, which means that session keys are never reused. Even if the server's private key is compromised in the future, past communications remain secure.

Examples of TLS/SSL Use Cases in IoT:

Smart Home Devices: **Smart thermostats, smart locks, security cameras**, and other IoT devices use TLS to secure communication between the device and a cloud server or mobile app. This ensures that user commands and sensitive data (e.g., security footage or temperature settings) are protected from unauthorized access.

Wearable Health Devices: Devices like **fitness trackers, smartwatches**, and **medical sensors** transmit personal health data (e.g., heart rate, blood pressure) to mobile apps or healthcare providers. Using TLS, this data is securely transmitted, protecting the privacy of users' health information.

Industrial IoT (IIoT): In industrial environments, **sensors, controllers**, and **machines** exchange sensitive data related to system performance and operations. TLS is used to ensure that this data remains private and secure, preventing malicious interference or data breaches in critical infrastructure.

Cloud-based IoT Platforms: IoT platforms, which aggregate and analyze data from multiple devices, use SSL/TLS to secure communication between edge devices (like gateways or sensors) and the cloud. This prevents unauthorized users from accessing or tampering with device data during transmission.

3.3.3 Role-based access control (RBAC) in IoT

Role-based access control (RBAC) in IoT is **a security mechanism that restricts access to IoT devices, data, and systems based on the roles of users within an organization**. It grants permissions to specific job roles rather than individual users, ensuring that employees only access the information and resources they need for their responsibilities. This helps protect sensitive data, reduces the risk of unauthorized access, and improves security in IoT environments.

Here's a more detailed explanation:

How RBAC Works in IoT:

- **Define Roles:** An organization defines different roles based on job functions, such as administrator, technician, user, etc.
- **Assign Permissions to Roles:** Each role is assigned specific permissions, such as reading, writing, deleting, or executing commands on IoT devices or data.
- **Assign Users to Roles:** Users are assigned to the roles that match their job responsibilities.
- **Access Control:** When a user attempts to access a resource (device, data, etc.), the system checks their role and associated permissions. If they have the necessary permissions, they gain access; otherwise, access is denied.

Benefits of RBAC in IoT:

- **Enhanced Security:** By limiting access to authorized users only, RBAC significantly reduces the risk of unauthorized access and potential security breaches.
- **Simplified Access Management:** RBAC provides a structured and manageable approach to access control, making it easier to administer and maintain.
- **Improved Compliance:** RBAC helps organizations meet regulatory requirements and industry standards that mandate access control mechanisms.
- **Reduced Complexity:** RBAC simplifies access control compared to individually granting permissions to each user, reducing the administrative burden and complexity.
- **Enhanced Data Protection:** RBAC helps protect sensitive IoT data from unauthorized access, modification, or deletion.
- **Improved Efficiency:** By ensuring users only have access to the information they need, RBAC can improve efficiency and productivity.

3.4 Cryptographic Techniques for IoT Security

3.4.1 Lightweight Cryptographic Algorithms for IoT:

Cryptography is the key factor that prevents anyone from directly accessing information regarding any encrypted data. Lightweight cryptography refers to all those algorithms which are designed to consume fewer resources and make them more powerful. These lightweight cryptography algorithms can be applied to various IoT devices, securing the connection and ensuring safe data transfer. But how can such algorithms increase the security factor, and how can they be applicable to IoT devices? First, let us see how cryptography works.

What Is Cryptography?

Cryptography is the technique of converting plain text or normal information into a non-readable format that has no language format and cannot be read by anyone. Only the machines can convert such non-readable text into an original message using reverse cryptography. This helps to transfer the information to the network without worrying about the misuse of information. The confidentiality of the information is maintained when passed through the network using encryption.

How does Cryptography work?

Good cryptography refers to such non-breachable algorithms that cannot be cracked by any hacker. The cryptography method includes encryption of information, generating a key, hashing, passing through different servers and again decrypting the encrypted information to its original form. The steps are mentioned below

Encryption ? Normal text is converted into the non-readable format by changing the positions of letters and each character, using a specific unique key that is the cypher text. It is all mathematically calculated according to a unique key.

Key ? The key generated using random numbers are then passed through the internet along with the encrypted message.

Hashing ? Hashing algorithms help to create a digital fingerprint. It helps to maintain the ritghteousness of the original data even if the original data is changed.

Decryption ? The message generated is then decrypted using the same key so that each and every character can be arranged in its original position.

Lightweight Cryptography Used In IoT Devices

Lightweight cryptography focuses on the efficient use of computational resources required to encrypt the data. Nowadays, there are many powerful cryptography algorithms such as RSA public-key encryption, Diffie-Hellman exchange algorithm, Elliptic Curve Cryptography, Twofish, Blowfish and Advanced Encryption Standard (AES). But these algorithms perform many mathematical operations at once and can be difficult for a longer input text. Hence research is carried out in lightweight cryptography, which uses less computational power but generates powerful cypher text.

This lightweight cryptography can be used especially in IoT devices because IoT devices must run on low power. Technological advancement has given us smaller transmitters, microchips, advanced low-power Bluetooth, and faster internet, and this all made IoT sensors smaller in size. Small IoT sensors fit easily on devices and consume low power. Hence there is a need for lightweight cryptography to encrypt the data with low power consumption.

Which Are Different Lightweight Cryptography Methods?

There are many popular lightweight cryptography methods that can ensure the secure transfer of data between IoT devices. Some of the famous lightweight cryptography methods are ?

- ➢ **PRESENT** ? Present is a lightweight block cypher algorithm that runs on limited resources and provides powerful encryption. It operates on data blocks of only 64 bits and has a key size of 80 bits. It is simple and reduces the complexity of implementation, mainly used in IoT devices and smart cards.

- ➢ **LED** ?LLIghtweight Encryption and Decryption (LED) is another lightweight block cypher algorithm that uses a data block of 64 bits and a key size of 128 bits. Mainly used in wearable devices, smart cards and other IoT embedded systems.

- ➢ **SPONGENET** ? Mainly used in IoT devices for a large variety of applications and data integrity checks. A good alternative to other lightweight algorithms, such as SHA-3 and Keccak.

- **ECC** ? Another public-key cryptography is Elliptic Curve Cryptography (ECC) that uses a mathematical form of elliptic curves to generate secure encryption keys. It is lightweight and used in digital signatures, key agreements and different cryptographic applications for IoT devices.

- **Grain-128a** ? A lightweight steam cipher algorithm having a 128-bit key, known for its strong encryption with no vulnerabilities. It is used in wireless communications, smart devices, and low-power operated IoT devices.

How Lightweight Cryptography Benefits IoT Devices?

There are many factors affecting IoT devices when a hacker tries to break a connection or steal information from the IoT grid, increasing vulnerability. Encryption at low power consumption can help to maintain a secure connection in the network and provides confidentiality. IoT devices boost up with lightweight cryptography.

- **Efficient Resource Optimization** ? Low resource requirement is the first priority in making a good IoT device. Consuming low power, IoT devices can be maintained for a longer time period with a secure connection.

- **Simplified Algorithm** ? Lightweight cryptography provides simpler and faster encryption and decryption unless traditional cryptography methods.

- **Key Management** ? Generally, follows single key management, which is simple and efficient for smaller IoT devices.

- **Security trade-offs** ? If we compare both the traditional and lightweight cryptography methods, lightweight uses simpler algorithms. Hence it may have lesser security strengths but is still much more powerful for smaller low-power operating IoT devices, making communication secure.

- **Authentication** ? Authentication always requires an ID and password, and it must have to be passed securely through the network grid. Hence at lower connectivity areas, such as login using a smartwatch or any other IoT device authentication, lightweight cryptography helps the most.

3.4.2 Public Key Infrastructure (PKI) in IoT

Public key infrastructure or PKI is the governing body behind issuing digital certificates. It helps to protect confidential data and gives unique identities to users and systems. Thus, it ensures security in communications.The public key infrastructure uses a pair of keys: the public key and the private key to achieve security. The public keys are prone to attacks and thus an intact infrastructure is needed to maintain them.The security of a cryptosystem relies on its keys. Thus, it is important that we have a solid key management system in place.

It involves managing the key life cycle which is as follows:

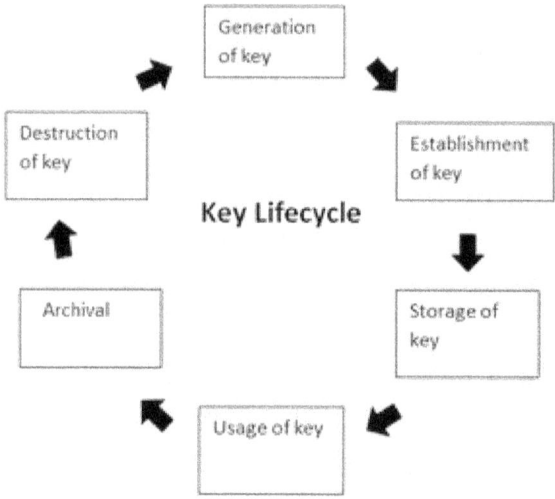

Public key management further requires:

Keeping the private key secret: Only the owner of a private key is authorized to use a private key. It should thus remain out of reach of any other person.Assuring the public key: Public keys are in the open domain and can be publicly accessed. When this extent of public accessibility, it becomes hard to know if a key is correct and what it will be used for. The purpose of a public key must be explicitly defined.PKI or public key infrastructure aims at achieving the assurance of public key.

Public Key Infrastructure:

Public key infrastructure affirms the usage of a public key. PKI identifies a public key along with its purpose. It usually consists of the following components:

- ➢ A digital certificate also called a public key certificate
- ➢ Private Key tokens
- ➢ Registration authority
- ➢ Certification authority
- ➢ CMS or Certification management system

Disadvantages of PKI:

Speed: Since PKI uses super complex algorithms to create a secure key pair. So it eventually slows down the process and data transfer.

Private Key Compromise: Even though PKI can't be hacked very easily but a private key can be hacked by a professional hacker, since PKI uses Public and Private key to encrypt and decrypt data so with user's private key in hand and public key which is easily available the information can be decrypted easily.

3.5 Threat Modelling in IoT

3.5.1 Identifying and Assessing Risks in IoT Systems:

1. Identify IoT Assets and Associated Risks:

Asset Identification: Begin by mapping out all IoT devices, data, and systems within the scope of the assessment.

Vulnerability Assessment: Identify potential weaknesses in the identified assets, including hardware, software, firmware, and configurations.

Threat Identification: Catalog potential threats, such as hacking attempts, malware, insider threats, and natural disasters.

2. Analyze and Assess Risks:

Impact Assessment: Determine the potential consequences of each identified risk, considering data breaches, operational disruptions, and financial losses.

Likelihood Assessment: Evaluate the probability of each risk occurring, considering factors like the availability of exploit information, attacker motivation, and existing security controls.

Risk Ranking: Prioritize risks based on the combination of impact and likelihood, focusing on the most critical threats.

3. Develop Mitigation Strategies and Plans:

Risk Mitigation: Develop and implement measures to reduce the likelihood or impact of identified risks.

Security Controls: Implement security controls such as strong authentication, access controls, encryption, and firewalls.

Incident Response: Develop and test incident response plans to address potential security breaches.

Monitoring and Maintenance: Continuously monitor IoT devices and networks for threats and vulnerabilities, and regularly update firmware and software.

4. Key Considerations for IoT Risk Assessment:

Complexity: IoT systems often involve a wide range of devices and network protocols, making it essential to have a comprehensive and systematic assessment process.

Dynamic Environment: IoT devices are constantly evolving, and new vulnerabilities are being discovered regularly, requiring ongoing monitoring and updates.

Regulatory Compliance: IoT deployments may be subject to various regulations and standards, requiring compliance with specific security requirements.

Human Factors: Educate employees about IoT security risks and best practices to minimize the risk of human error.

3.5.2 Common Attack Scenarios

Common Attack Scenarios in IoT refer to the various methods that attackers can use to exploit vulnerabilities in Internet of Things (IoT) devices and networks. As IoT devices become increasingly interconnected, they can present significant security risks if not properly protected. Here are some of the most common attack scenarios in IoT:

1. Botnet Attacks (e.g., Mirai Botnet)

Description: Attackers take control of a large number of compromised IoT devices and form a botnet. These devices are then used to launch Distributed Denial of Service (DDoS) attacks on websites or networks, overwhelming them with traffic and causing service disruptions.

Example: The **Mirai botnet** took control of thousands of IoT devices (such as cameras and routers) to launch massive DDoS attacks.

Impact: Disruption of services, website outages, and potential data breaches.

2. Man-in-the-Middle (MITM) Attacks

Description: In a MITM attack, an attacker intercepts communication between two parties (e.g., between an IoT device and its server) and can alter or capture the data being exchanged.

Example: An attacker could intercept the communication between a smart thermostat and the control server, potentially altering temperature settings or gaining access to sensitive data.

Impact: Data theft, device manipulation, and unauthorized access.

3. Physical Attacks on IoT Devices

Description: IoT devices can be physically tampered with by attackers to gain access to the device, extract data, or modify its functionality.

Example: An attacker could access an IoT device like a security camera or smart lock by physically tampering with it and obtaining sensitive information such as passwords or encryption keys.

Impact: Loss of confidentiality, integrity, and availability of data.

4. Device Hijacking

Description: Attackers can hijack IoT devices and take control of their operations, making them perform actions or collect data without the owner's consent.

Example: An attacker could hijack a smart home device like a camera or lock to spy on users or gain unauthorized access to a home.

Impact: Privacy breaches, unauthorized access to physical spaces, and potential damage to the device's functionality.

5. Firmware Exploits

Description: Many IoT devices rely on firmware (software that runs directly on the hardware) to function. Attackers can exploit vulnerabilities in this firmware to gain control of the device or modify its behavior.

Example: An attacker could exploit a known vulnerability in a smart speaker's firmware to turn on the microphone and listen to private conversations.

Impact: Device compromise, unauthorized access to sensitive data, and loss of user trust.

6. Unauthorized Device Access (Backdoor)

Description: Some IoT devices may have **backdoors** (hidden access points) that allow unauthorized users to access the device, bypassing normal authentication mechanisms.

Example: A device like a smart camera could have a backdoor that an attacker uses to remotely access the video feed without authorization.

Impact: Compromise of user privacy, unauthorized data access, and control over the device.

7. Data Interception and Eavesdropping

Description: Attackers can intercept data transmitted over the network between IoT devices and cloud servers or other devices. This can lead to the exposure of sensitive information.

Example: In a **smart home**, an attacker could intercept communication between a smart lock and the mobile app, potentially gaining unauthorized access.

Impact: Loss of confidentiality, privacy violations, and data theft.

8. Privilege Escalation

Description: Attackers exploit vulnerabilities to escalate their privileges, granting them more access than intended by the system's design. This can allow them to perform unauthorized actions on IoT devices.

Example: A user with limited access to an IoT device (like a smart thermostat) may escalate privileges to gain full administrative control, changing device settings or disabling security features.

Impact: Unauthorized changes to device settings, loss of control over IoT systems.

9. Side-Channel Attacks

Description: Attackers can gain information about the internal workings of a device by observing side-channel signals such as power consumption, electromagnetic emissions, or timing behavior.

Example: A side-channel attack could be used on an IoT device to extract cryptographic keys used for encrypting data without directly breaking the encryption.

Impact: Data theft, cryptographic key compromise, and device manipulation.

10. Denial of Service (DoS) and Distributed Denial of Service (DDoS)

Description: Attackers may flood IoT devices or networks with excessive requests to overload them, causing a disruption or complete service outage.

Example: A DDoS attack could target an IoT-enabled industrial control system, disrupting production or causing a factory to shut down.

Impact: Service outages, system downtime, and potential physical damage to equipment.

11. Firmware and Software Updates Exploits

Description: Attackers may exploit vulnerabilities in the update process of IoT devices by pushing malicious or corrupted firmware updates to devices, often without the user's knowledge.

Example: An attacker could exploit a vulnerability in an IoT device's firmware update mechanism to install malicious software or backdoors on the device.

Impact: Device compromise, remote control, and potential data theft.

12. Rogue IoT Devices

Description: Attackers may introduce rogue IoT devices into a network to gain unauthorized access, collect data, or control other devices.

Example: A hacker could install a rogue IoT sensor on a corporate network to intercept sensitive information or launch further attacks on the network.

Impact: Unauthorized access, data breaches, and network infiltration.

3.6 Incident response in IoT

Incident response in IoT refers to the processes and procedures an organization uses to detect, respond to, and recover from security incidents involving IoT devices and networks. This includes planning for potential incidents, detecting and analyzing them, containing and eradicating the threat, and restoring affected systems to normal operation.

Key aspects of IoT incident response:

- Planning: Developing a comprehensive incident response plan that includes roles, responsibilities, escalation paths, and procedures for handling various incident types.

- Detection and Analysis: Implementing monitoring tools and techniques to detect suspicious activity or anomalies on IoT devices and networks. This may involve analyzing log files, network traffic, and device behavior.

- Containment, Eradication, and Recovery: Taking steps to isolate the affected devices or systems, remove the threat, and restore them to their original state or a safe working condition.

- Post-Incident Activity: Conducting a thorough review of the incident to identify lessons learned, improve security practices, and ensure that similar incidents can be prevented in the future.

Challenges in IoT Incident Response:

- Diverse and Scalable: The wide variety of IoT devices and their distributed nature can make it difficult to monitor and manage them effectively.

- Resource Constraints: Many IoT devices have limited processing power, memory, and storage, making it difficult to install and run comprehensive security software.

- Communication and Network Issues: IoT devices may use different communication protocols and network infrastructures, which can complicate incident detection and response efforts.

- Lack of Standardization: The lack of standardized security protocols and practices in the IoT space can make it challenging to develop consistent incident response procedure.

Tools and Technologies:

- Security Information and Event Management (SIEM) systems: These systems collect and analyze data from various IoT devices and systems to detect potential security threats.

- Intrusion Detection and Prevention Systems (IDS/IPS): These systems can detect and prevent malicious traffic from entering or exiting IoT networks.

- Packet Capture Tools: These tools can capture network traffic from IoT devices to help analyze the nature of an incident.
- Automated Incident Response Platforms: These platforms can automate some of the incident response steps, such as containment and eradication, to speed up the response process.

3.6.1 Detecting and mitigating iot breaches

Detecting and mitigating IoT breaches involves a multi-layered approach, including robust security protocols, regular updates, and proactive monitoring. Key strategies include implementing strong authentication, encryption, and firewalls. Network segmentation and intrusion detection systems are also crucial for isolating potential threats and preventing them from spreading. Additionally, AI and machine learning can be used to analyze network traffic and identify abnormal activity that may indicate a breach.

Detection:

- Network Scanning: Regularly scan the network for unauthorized devices to identify potential vulnerabilities.
- Intrusion Detection Systems (IDS): Utilize IDS to detect and alert on suspicious network activity.
- SNMP Monitoring: Employ Simple Network Management Protocol (SNMP) to monitor and manage IoT devices, which can help detect DDoS attacks.
- AI/ML for Anomaly Detection: Use AI and ML algorithms to analyze network traffic and identify patterns that may indicate a breach.
- Honeypots: Deploy honeypots to attract and analyze attacks, gathering information on attacker behavior and potential vulnerabilities.

Mitigation:

- Strong Authentication: Require strong credentials, TLS encryption, and PKI-based authentication for all IoT devices.
- Regular Firmware Updates: Implement regular firmware updates (manually or via over-the-air patching) to address known vulnerabilities.

- Firewalls and Network Segmentation: Restrict network access via firewalls and implement network segmentation to isolate IoT devices from critical business systems.

- Encryption: Encrypt sensitive data both during transmission and storage.

- Access Control Lists (ACLs): Utilize ACLs to restrict access to IoT devices and resources.

- Moving Target Defense: Implement moving target defense techniques to make it harder for attackers to exploit vulnerabilities.

- Data Visibility Solutions: Use data visibility solutions to monitor traffic to and from IoT equipment and proactively identify security fixes.

- Unified IT/OT/IoT Security: Break down silos between IT and OT teams to create a unified security strategy.

3.6.2 Role of machine learning in threat detection

Machine learning (ML) plays a crucial role in threat detection by automating and enhancing the identification of malicious activities. ML algorithms can analyze vast datasets, identify patterns, and predict potential threats, improving the accuracy and speed of detection compared to traditional methods. This includes detecting known threats, identifying emerging threats, and even anticipating future attacks.

Here's a more detailed look at the role of ML in threat detection:

1. Identifying Anomalies and Patterns:

ML models can learn normal network behavior and identify deviations or anomalies that might indicate a threat.

- This can include detecting unusual login patterns, network traffic, or file access.

2. Predicting Potential Threats:

- ML can analyze historical data and trends to predict future threats and vulnerabilities, enabling proactive security measures.

- This includes identifying potential attack vectors and vulnerabilities in systems.

3. Detecting Malware and Phishing: [ML algorithms can detect new and previously unseen malware by analyzing their behavior and characteristics.

> They can also identify phishing attempts by analyzing email content and website behavior.

4. Detecting Insider Threats:

> ML can be used to analyze user behavior and identify deviations from established patterns that might indicate insider threats.

> This can include detecting unusual logins, data access, or file transfers.

5. Enhancing Security Operations:

> ML can automate tasks like threat hunting and security analysis, freeing up human analysts to focus on more complex issues.

> It can also provide real-time alerts and insights to security teams, allowing them to respond to threats faster.

6. Adapting to Evolving Threats:

> ML models can learn and adapt to new threat patterns as they emerge, ensuring ongoing protection against evolving cyber risks.

> This allows security systems to stay ahead of attackers who are constantly developing new techniques.

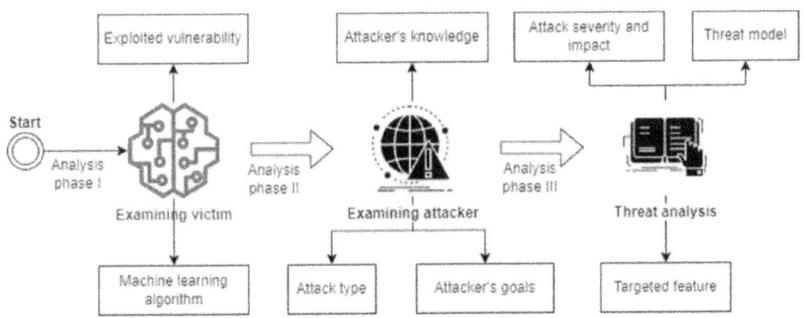

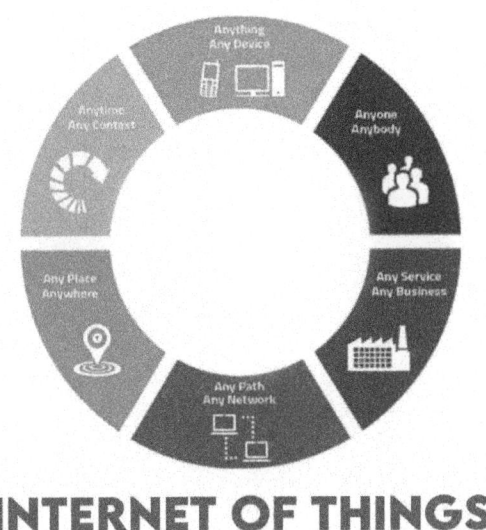

INTERNET OF THINGS

CHAPTER 4

INDEX

IOT APPLICATIONS AND USE CASES

4.1 Smart Homes and Buildings 221
    4.1.1 IoT for Home Automation 221
    4.1.2 Smart Lighting 225
    4.1.3 Security and surveillance system 228
4.2 Industrial IoT (IIoT) 230
    4.2.1 IoT in Manufacturing 230
    4.2.2 Predictive Maintenance with IoT 232
    4.2.3 Industrial automation and robotics 236
    4.2.4 Supply Chain Management 238
4.3 Healthcare and Wearables 241
    4.3.1 IoT in Healthcare Systems 241
    4.3.2 Remote Patient Monitoring and Telemedicine 245
    4.3.3 Health and wearables IoT: 247
    4.3.4 Challenges in IoT healthcare Applications 250
4.4 Smart Cities and Infrastructure: 253
    4.4.1 Smart Transportation System 253
    4.4.2 IoT in Urban Planning 258
    4.4.3 Waste and water management 259
    4.4.4 Environmental monitoring 261

4.5 IoT in Agriculture and Environment 264
    4.5.1 Precision Agriculture with IoT 264
    4.5.2 Smart Irrigation Systems 266
    4.5.3 IoT for Livestock Monitoring 269
    4.5.4 Environment and Climate Monitoring 271
4.6 IoT in Retail 274
    4.6.1 Inventory Management with IoT 274
    4.6.2 Strategies to Enhance Customer Experience Through IoT 278
4.7 IoT in Energy Management 282
    4.7.1 Smart Grids and Energy Distribution 282
    4.7.2 Renewable Energy Integration 285

CHAPTER 4:

IOT APPLICATIONS AND USE CASES

4.1 Smart Homes and Buildings

4.1.1 IoT for Home Automation

Smart Home: A smart home is a residence that uses internet-connected devices to enable the remote monitoring and management of appliances and systems, such as lighting and heating.

Smart home technology -- also often referred to as home automation or domotics from the Latin word *domus*, meaning home -- provides homeowners security, comfort, convenience and energy efficiency by letting them control smart devices, often using a smart home app on their smartphone or another networked device.

A part of the internet of things (IoT), smart home systems and devices often operate together, sharing consumer usage data among themselves and automating actions based on the homeowners' preferences.

How does smart home technology work?

A smart home isn't a collection of disparate smart devices and appliances, but rather ones that work together to create a remotely controllable network.

All devices -- such as lights, thermostats, security systems and appliances -- are controlled by a master home automation controller, often called a smart home hub. This hub is a hardware device that acts as the central point of the smart home system and can sense, process data and communicate wirelessly. It combines all the disparate apps into a single smart home app that homeowners can control remotely. Examples of smart home hubs include Amazon Echo, Google Home and Wink Hub. While many smart home products use Wi-Fi and Bluetooth to connect to the smart home network, others depend on wireless protocols such as Zigbee or Z-Wave.

Smart home devices can be either programmed to follow specific schedules or commands or they can be set to respond to voice commands through home assistants such as Amazon Alexa or Google Assistant. For example, a smart thermostat can learn the homeowner's habits and automatically adjust the temperature based on their specific schedule.

Examples of smart home technologies

Nearly every aspect of life where technology has entered the domestic space -- including lightbulbs, dishwashers and other appliances -- has seen the introduction of a smart home alternative:

Smart TVs. These TVs connect to the internet to access content through applications, such as on-demand video and music. Some smart TVs also include voice or gesture recognition.

Smart lighting systems. In addition to being able to be controlled remotely and customized, smart lighting systems can detect when occupants are in the room and adjust lighting as needed. Smart lightbulbs can also regulate themselves based on daylight availability.

Smart thermostats. Smart thermostats, such as Google Nest, come with integrated Wi-Fi, letting users schedule, monitor and remotely control home temperatures. These devices also learn homeowners' behaviours and automatically modify settings to provide them with maximum comfort and efficiency. Smart thermostats can also report energy use and remind users to change filters.

Smart door locks and garage door openers. Homeowners can use smart locks and garage-door openers to grant or deny access to visitors. Smart locks can also detect when residents are near and unlock the doors for them.

Smart security cameras and systems. With smart security cameras and doorbells, such as Ring, residents can monitor their homes when they're away. Smart motion sensors can identify the difference between residents, visitors, pets and burglars and can send notifications to authorities if suspicious behaviour is detected.

Smart pet and lawn care. Pet care can be automated with connected feeders. Houseplants and lawns can be watered using connected timers.

Smart kitchen appliances. Brands such as LG, GE and Samsung offer smart kitchen appliances of all sorts. These appliances include smart coffee makers that can brew a fresh cup automatically at a programmed time; smart refrigerators that keep track of expiration dates, make shopping lists or even create recipes based on ingredients currently on hand; slow cookers and toasters; and, in the laundry room, washing machines and dryers.

Smart household monitors. Household system monitors can, for example, sense a power surge and turn off appliances, sense water failures or freezing pipes and turn off the water so the home doesn't flood.

Smart plugs. These connect to wall sockets to transform simple home devices, such as lamps and ceiling fans, so they can be controlled remotely via mobile apps and voice assistants such as Alexa.

Smart Building: A smart building is an implementation of a smart (connected) world. A smart world, like a smart building is, for the most part, only different from the IoT (internet of things) in name; both the IoT and smart worlds share the same frameworks, benefits, and challenges. The subtle difference between the generic IoT and a type of smart world is that a smart world usually describes the usage of an IoT network in a specific implementation or industry, in this case, a smart building.

Smart buildings include private homes, offices and commercial buildings, workplaces, and factories and warehouses.

Smart buildings deliver actionable information about a building itself or a specific room inside it so that owners or tenants can better manage it. The term smart building usually refers to commercial buildings, while the term smart home usually refers to private residences, but much of the functionality is the same and so the terms overlap.

The goal of creating a smart building is to reduce operating expenses, improve occupant comfort, automate energy consumption management, track the status of core building assets, and meet global regulations and sustainability standards in the industry.

To be effective, smart buildings require complex monitoring of the IoT networks that control the building system.

Types of smart buildings

Smart buildings go beyond the concept of automation, a key feature of the IoT. A smart building system must be able to evaluate the data it gathers from sensors and automatically be able to act on the data, for example being able to activate a sprinkler system without human intervention if there is a fire.

1. Smart private homes

Smart homes are designed to improve residents' security and comfort, enable the remote control of many home appliances, automate home maintenance schedules, monitor energy usage, and control home security systems.Central to the development of smart homes is the concept of assistive technologies. Assistive technologies traditionally described aids, like wheelchairs, designed to help people with disabilities in their daily lives.

In the IoT era, the concept of assistive technologies is extended. Examples of assistive technologies are devices that enable the automated scheduling of when appliances like lights and washing machines are switched on or off. Smart medical and health devices are assistive technologies used in smart homes for the remote monitoring of elderly or sick residents, and children. Wearables sensors in smart homes automatically open doors, maintain an ambient temperature, and monitor and analyze energy usage in the home.Security sensors in smart homes can detect and report gas leaks, water leaks, and security vulnerabilities.

2. Smart offices and commercial buildings

A smart office building or commercial complex enables the automated, centralized control of the structure's water and electricity, lighting, heating, ventilation, security, parking spaces, waste management, elevators and emergency exits, access control to computer systems, and garden and equipment maintenance over an IoT network. In the retail industry, IoT sensors around stores can help businesses collect data such as at what time a customer entered a shop, what they showed interest in, and what they bought. Smart commerce helps marketing and product teams to optimize a store's layout, maintain optimal stock levels, monitor staff behaviour, improve product tracking like return rates, monitor wait times in queues and foot traffic, and automate checkouts.

Commercial IoT applications deployed at supermarkets, malls, hotels, healthcare facilities, museums and exhibitions, and leisure complexes aim to create an enjoyable consumer experience outside people's home environments. To create a comfortable environment, sensors monitor and automatically adjust air quality, lighting, and temperature in public buildings. Commercial IoT applications manage access control and security, monitor inventory in retail stores, gather data about people's behaviour in public places, and provide location services for visitors to hospitality venues. Commercial IoT is not to be confused with consumer IoT, which is concerned with personal wearables and smart home devices.

Edge computing is a growing trend in commercial IoT. Edge computing provides capabilities for devices to collect, process, and act on data gathered close to its source, for example foot traffic in a supermarket, without having to backhaul to a data center. Communication in commercial IoT solutions is effected by numerous connectivity types, including Bluetooth, Wi-Fi, LoRa, 4G LTE, and ZigBee, depending on the application.

3. Smart workplaces

Smart workplaces feature hardware and software for improved communication and collaboration like video conferencing. In smart workplaces, sensors can keep track of business assets like company laptops. Smart workplaces enable automated monitoring of IT security vulnerabilities and remote management of off-site employees and contractors. In smart workplaces, many mundane tasks like scheduling a suitable conference room or catering for a meeting can be done remotely or by digital business assistants. In smart workplaces, new employees may receive push notifications to guide them around their new offices, for example notifying them where they are in the building or what security clearance they need to enter a particular office. In a smart workplace, the coffee never runs out, toilets are always flushed, and visitors never have to circle the block for a parking space.

4. Smart factories and warehouses

In the industrial sphere, smart factories and warehouses are managed over industrial IoT (IIoT) networks. The IIoT is a combination of smart factories and warehouses, smart supply chains, smart logistics, and smart industrial machinery, creating a smart industrial ecosystem.

An example of how smart buildings are managed in the industrial sphere is the use of robots in factories and warehouses. The use of robots in the smart industry is called the Internet of Robotic Things (IoRT).

4.1.2 Smart Lighting

Smart lighting is a technology driven concept that links three main features of solid state lighting (SSL) technologies, universal communication interfaces and advanced control. However, this conceptualization is continuously progressing to comply with the guidelines of the next generation of devices that work in the Internet of Things (IoT) environment.

Modern smart lighting systems are based on Light Emitting Diode (LED) technology and involve advanced technology drivers. Now the lighting systems are evolving to support different wireless communications interfaces well suited with the IoT environment. Market propensity of SSL systems forecast the accelerated growth of connected IoT lighting control systems in different markets from smart homes to industrial lighting systems. These systems offer advanced features such as spectral control of the light source and also, the inclusion of several communication interfaces.

Smart lighting is a system of lights, which holds energy efficient LED drivers, advanced control algorithms, lighting sensors, and communication interfaces to collaborate and inter connect in a lighting network. At its core, a smart lighting system is being conceived as a flexible lighting system with the objective to improve visual comfort, as well energy efficiency.

Diverse implementations of smart lighting systems involve different communication interfaces and additional capabilities such as light spectral reproduction in real-time, advanced detection options with illuminance sensors and colour sensors. The latest lighting solutions include many features beyond conventional illumination purposes.

Lighting Sources

White light based on LED: Humans are adapted to working in healthy environments that mimic the sun daylight spectrum. For this reason, we generally seek to illuminate the space with white light that imitate the solar spectrum. The most common method to obtain white light for illumination purposes, or optical communications, employs a combination of red, green and blue (RGB) LEDs as shown in Image 2.

Energy efficient LED drivers: Electronic drivers for lighting purposes are devices. Which regulate the power for LEDs and provide varying output current for matching light source characteristics. Most lighting systems prepared for the IoT environment include a power conversion stage with a constant-current LED driver, several LEDs organized in arrays and the inclusion of sensors and a communication interface as shown in Image 3.

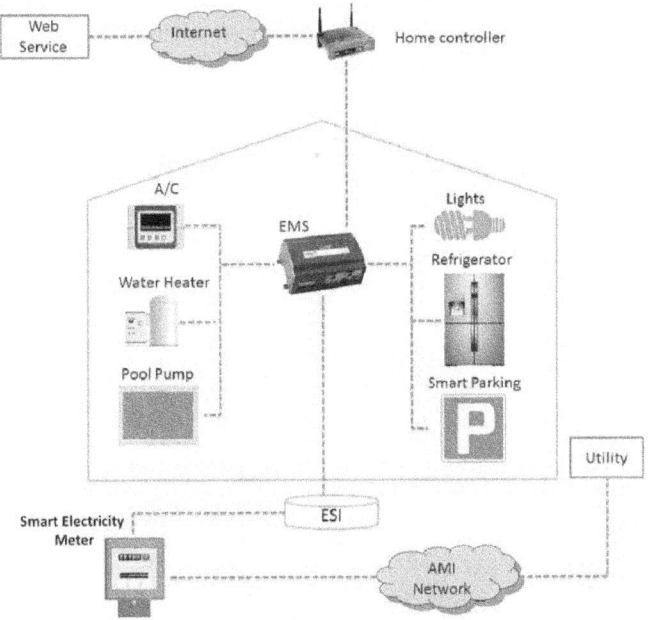

Architectural elements: Smart lighting solutions include various devices, systems and network types. Devices are mainly luminaires containing sensors, actuators, and advanced algorithms. A combination of advanced algorithms allows for the observation of daylight levels, light spectrum, and user occupation to decide a final action. The algorithms run inside devices, or to alleviate the workload of the device the algorithm can run directly in the cloud stored as a web service to send command messages to execute the different control actions. Several algorithms for smart lighting are related to advanced operations such as to tune the colour reproduction in real-time. In the next page, Image 4 showcases the Architecture of smart lighting system.

Sensors for smart lighting platforms

Smart lighting system works with different sensor technologies and communication interfaces. The modern day IoT lighting principles aim to control lighting depending on varying the environment with a wide range of digital sensors. Image 5 showcases various sensor types to implement in such systems. RGB colour sensors are intended to detect red-green-blue content of light and tune white light in LED luminaires. For optical communications including Visible Light Communication (VLC) connectivity several technologies of photodiodes can be used in wireless links mainly in indoor environments.

In addition, more advanced functionalities such as spectral detection of light are covered with micro-spectrometers to detect the light spectrum in the visible range that can be detected by our eyes. In addition, it is well known that LEDs decrease their maximum luminous flux over time mainly due to temperature or aging effects, and therefore, such sensors and advanced control systems are of use to ensure best performance of the system.

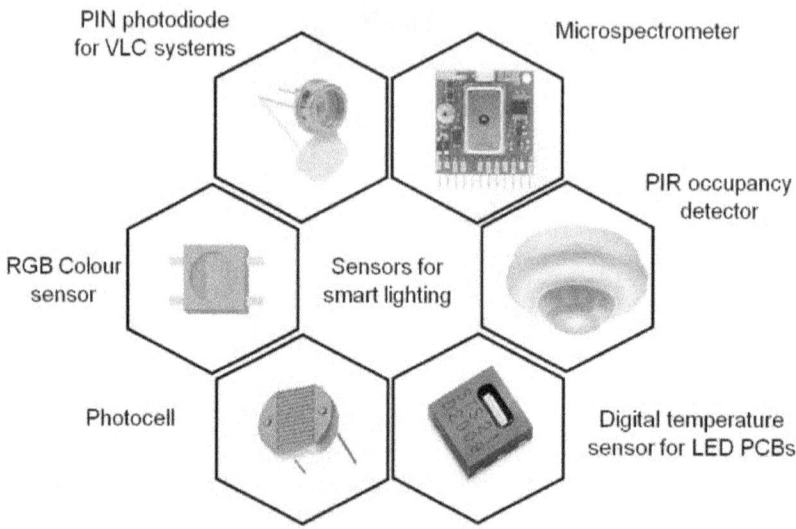

4.1.3 Security and surveillance system

IoT applications can significantly enhance security and surveillance systems by **enabling remote monitoring, real-time data collection, and intelligent analysis**. This allows for proactive threat detection, faster response times, and improved overall security.

Here's how IoT enhances security and surveillance:

> ➢ **Remote Monitoring and Control:** IoT devices like CCTV cameras, sensors, and access control systems can be monitored remotely, providing instant access to live video feeds and data.

> ➢ **Real-time Data Collection and Analysis:** IoT sensors can collect various data, such as temperature, humidity, motion, and audio,

which can be analyzed in real-time to identify anomalies and potential threats.

- **Intelligent Threat Detection:** AI-powered IoT systems can detect patterns and anomalies in data, triggering alerts and enabling faster responses to security breaches.

- **Automated Incident Response:** IoT-based systems can automate certain security tasks, such as locking doors, deploying alarms, or notifying authorities in case of a threat.

- **Improved Efficiency and Cost Savings:** By automating tasks and providing real-time data, IoT systems can improve the efficiency of security operations and reduce costs.

Examples of IoT applications in security and surveillance:

- **Smart Buildings:** IoT can be used to monitor and control various aspects of a building's security, including access control, intrusion detection, and video surveillance.

- **Smart Cities:** IoT can help manage urban infrastructure, improve public safety, and enhance security by monitoring traffic, parking, and lighting, as well as detecting and responding to emergencies.

- **Industrial IoT (IIoT):** IIoT can improve the security of industrial sites by monitoring equipment, detecting potential hazards, and ensuring compliance with safety regulations.

- **Drones and Robotics:** IoT-enabled drones and robots can be used for surveillance, patrols, and security operations in public and private spaces.

Key Considerations:

- **Data Security and Privacy:** Implementing strong data encryption, access controls, and oversight mechanisms is crucial to protect sensitive data and ensure privacy.

- **Cybersecurity Threats:** IoT devices can be vulnerable to cyberattacks, so it's essential to implement robust cybersecurity measures to protect against unauthorized access and data breaches.

- **Interoperability and Scalability:** Ensuring that different IoT devices and systems can communicate and work together seamlessly is essential for creating a comprehensive security solution.

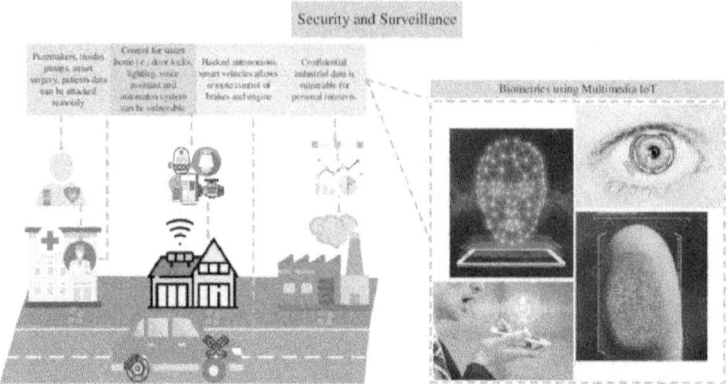

4.2 Industrial IoT (IIoT)

4.2.1 IoT in Manufacturing

Today, every industry is turning to the Internet of Things (IoT) to optimize and automate processes, take advantage of the power of edge processing, and gain actionable insights from across the network. Manufacturing is no exception. IoT in manufacturing is an increasing trend where companies can take advantage of faster networks, smarter devices and improvements in edge technology.

The Impact of IoT in the Manufacturing Industry

Industrial robots have become commonplace on the factory floor thanks to their accuracy, precision, endurance and speed. Now, manufacturers can extend the impact of industrial robots by connecting them to IoT devices. Connected manufacturing IoT sensors enable machines to communicate with each other, share data, and coordinate their activities autonomously. By sharing data between machines, IoT devices improve robotic efficiency and productivity while also improving safety and reducing unscheduled maintenance.

Benefits of IoT in Manufacturing

There are many measurable benefits of IoT for manufacturing. Automated manufacturing systems are engineered to orchestrate complex workflows with minimal human intervention. These systems leverage cutting-edge technologies such as robotics, artificial intelligence (AI), and smart edge devices to optimize every facet of the production cycle. By seamlessly integrating disparate components and processes, automated manufacturing systems dramatically improve efficiency and agility, empowering organizations to meet evolving market demands.

The following are some of the key benefits of IoT in manufacturing.

Improved Operational Efficiency: By implementing IoT solutions, manufacturers can automate more processes, detect anomalies and reduce errors, and therefore increase operational efficiency. IoT enables industrial robots to operate autonomously using sensors, cameras, wireless devices and edge computing, conducting tasks such as assembly, defect detection, sorting, stacking and routing. Intelligent automation gathers data on machine performance, inventory levels, and other metrics that then allow manufacturers to optimize processes and make data-driven decisions.

Improved Safety: Automation enhances workplace safety by reducing the risk of accidents and injuries associated with manual labor and hazardous tasks. Automated systems adhere to strict safety standards and regulations, mitigating the potential for human error and ensuring compliance with industry guidelines and protocols. And today manufacturing companies are increasingly investing in wearable technology wearable technology solutions, such as IoT-enabled smart glasses and vests, to support better posture for heavy lifting, and alerts to hazardous behaviors.

Reduced Costs: Automation reduces the need for human intervention in repetitive or labor-intensive tasks, which not only minimizes labor costs but also frees up human workers to focus on higher-value activities such as problem-solving, innovation, and process optimization.

Additionally, with the maintenance of industrial equipment contributing to nearly 70 percent of overall cost, operational efficiency and predictive maintenance are key. Industrial IoT technology offers significant benefits, such as improving remote troubleshooting and reducing the number of service calls when no maintenance is required. And finally, the use connected devices and sophisticated management platforms allows operators to remotely manage operations including remote out-of-band management.

Scalability: Automated systems are inherently scalable and adaptable to changing production requirements and market dynamics, vs. the traditional method of scaling up or scaling down staffing. Whether ramping up production volumes or diversifying product offerings, automation allows manufacturers to respond quickly and effectively to evolving business needs, maintaining competitiveness and agility.

IoT Use Cases in Manufacturing: The manufacturing industry often contends with supply chain shocks, talent shortages, the effects of inflation and geopolitical instability. The net result is that manufacturers must continually seek ways to reduce costs and leverage technology to optimize output to manage complexity and dynamic conditions.

- Factory floors and fields
- Supply chain management
- Remote operations

IoT Challenges in Manufacturing

Clearly, IoT provides tremendous value to manufacturing. The right IoT solution provider can help address these challenges to ensure your deployment is scalable, secure and integrated with existing infrastructure. Here are a few key challenges that manufacturers should consider when implementing IoT systems:

Security — Security remains one of the biggest risks to industrial IoT systems. Hackers who break into an industrial IoT environment might steal or modify critical process information, potentially compromising product quality. For highly regulated industries such as defense, healthcare and critical infrastructure, these issues are paramount. If IoT devices are not properly updated, attackers pose risks from business disruption to enormous impacts on revenue and reputation.

Interoperability — IoT platforms and protocols are subject to a range of standards, which means manufacturers, systems integrators and organizations must manage interoperability issues when incorporating IoT devices into existing IT systems.

Data privacy — By connecting IoT sensors to the Internet, manufacturers become immediately exposed to cyber threats that create potential data privacy risks.

4.2.2 Predictive Maintenance with IoT

The Internet of things (IoT) is transforming the way manufacturers operate. One of the greatest advantages of IoT technology is its use in predictive maintenance, which focuses on preemptive planning for equipment breakdowns, helping businesses make the most out of their resources. This reliable data gives manufacturers greater control over when service needs are required and what components may need replacing so that proper allocation of resources can be planned out in advance. This, in turn, can save manufacturers on expensive repair costs while forecasting future requirements more easily.

How does IoT help in predictive maintenance?

IoT-based predictive maintenance is crucial for ensuring machine reliability and safety. Machine data is collected, which can include operating temperature, supply voltage, current, and vibration, through sensors and wireless transmission. The collected data is sent in real time to a cloud-based centralized data storage platform. Maintenance teams gather data from the centralized storage system and analyze it using predictive analytics programs, powered by AI, and machine-learning (ML) algorithms to derive actionable insights to guide repair or preventative maintenance. Security is another important factor to consider when implementing an IoT solution for predictive maintenance. IoT technologies gather personal information from various sources that must be stored securely to prevent malicious activity like cyberattacks or data breaches. Data privacy regulations can differ depending on the country or region, and compliance is necessary. ML technology and IoT solutions together can transform preventative maintenance.

Implementing IoT-based predictive maintenance has multiple benefits to manufacturers. Reducing maintenance costs is a primary concern, with the ability to schedule optimal inspection and maintenance routines that can avoid unplanned downtime to remain cost-efficient. Enhanced asset reliability is another benefit that can result from accurate forecasting and avoidance of machine failures, leading to higher rates of machine utilization and increased profitability. Using sensors on machines gives continuous feedback regarding data such as temperature, vibration levels and operating conditions. The data gathered by sensors and connected analytics tools can be converted into actionable insights that reveal potential maintenance issues before they cause equipment failure or a costly repair job. With IoT-based predictive maintenance identifying potential errors before they occur, operational efficiency can be maximized as unexpected downtime and other associated risks are minimized.

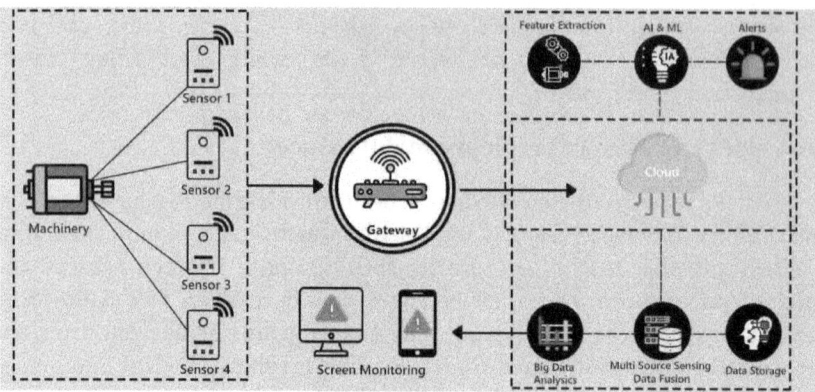

Components of IoT-based predictive maintenance

The components that comprise IoT-based predictive maintenance are sensors, data communication, central data storage, and predictive analytics.

Sensors: Sensors have become an integral part of modern technology, enabling the real-time collection of data from various devices, systems, assets, and locations. This data is critical for businesses to optimize their operations, improve efficiency, and make informed decisions. With sensors, the performance of machines, inventory levels, energy consumption, and much more can be monitored, tracked, or measured.

Data communication: Data communication is the process of transmitting or transferring data from one device to another. It plays a crucial role in sending data collected from various devices to a central data storage system in the cloud for the efficient management and storage of data, as well as easy access to data from anywhere at any time. The data communication process can involve various protocols and technologies such as TCP/IP, Wi-Fi, Bluetooth, and Ethernet.

Central data storage: Central data storage in the cloud is becoming increasingly popular. Data can be stored and accessed from anywhere at any time with an internet connection, meaning that businesses can centralize their data storage for easier management of and access to important information. Cloud storage is often more secure than traditional methods of data storage, with advanced encryption and backup systems in place to protect against data loss or theft. Central data storage in the cloud offers many benefits and is quickly becoming the preferred method of data storage for both businesses and individuals.

Predictive analytics: Predictive analytics is a powerful tool that enables maintenance teams and repair engineers to stay ahead of equipment failures and breakdowns. By using real-time data streams, predictive analytics can identify potential issues before they become major problems, saving not only time and money, but also helping to improve the overall efficiency of the maintenance process. In addition to real-time data, periodic reports are also available for further analysis and to provide valuable insights into equipment performance to fine-tune maintenance schedules and repair procedures. Predictive analytics is a critical component of modern maintenance and repair operations.

IoT predictive maintenance industry applications

Manufacturing: Manufacturing industries are among the largest adopters of IoT predictive maintenance. The manufacturing industry uses this technology to monitor equipment, detect anomalies, and identify potential failures to help manufacturers to schedule maintenance and repairs before machinery breaks down, reducing unplanned downtime and increasing production capacity.

Service: IoT-based predictive maintenance helps the service industry to monitor equipment performance, predict potential failures, and schedule maintenance and repairs, reducing time spent on reactive maintenance. It also helps service-related companies to provide better customer service by reducing downtime and improving equipment reliability.

Life sciences: Life sciences companies have also adopted IoT-based predictive maintenance to ensure equipment reliability, monitor laboratory equipment such as refrigerators, freezers, and incubators, and reduce downtime. IoT-based predictive maintenance in the life sciences industry helps to ensure that equipment is maintained at the correct temperature and humidity to reduce the risk of equipment failure and protect valuable samples.

Benefits of IoT-based predictive maintenance

Reduce maintenance cost: IoT-based predictive maintenance uses sensors, analytics, and ML algorithms to predict when a machine or piece of equipment will require maintenance, enabling companies to reduce not only maintenance costs, but also downtime. This also helps companies to identify potential problems and address them before they become major issues. IoT-based predictive maintenance is a powerful tool that can help companies keep costs down and improve overall efficiency.

Increase asset utilization: Businesses can increase asset utilization with IoT-based predictive maintenance by predicting and preventing equipment failures before they occur. Using sensors and other IoT devices for data collection about equipment performance can provide businesses with valuable insights into potential issues and proactive steps to address them.

This not only helps to avoid costly downtime and repairs, but it also allows businesses to maximize the lifespan of their equipment, as well as overall productivity. IoT-based predictive maintenance lets businesses stay ahead of the curve with the confidence that their assets are always working at peak efficiency.

Improve technician efficiency: IoT-based predictive maintenance can also improve technician efficiency by providing real-time information about equipment performance that can help technicians identify potential issues before they become major problems, enabling them to schedule maintenance at a time that is convenient and cost-effective. This approach can help businesses reduce the time and resources required for maintenance, freeing up technicians to focus on other tasks.

Reduce equipment downtime: Detecting issues early and scheduling maintenance at a time that's both convenient and cost-effective can reduce equipment downtime. IoT-based predictive maintenance is rapidly gaining popularity in the manufacturing, energy, and transportation industries to reduce equipment downtime and optimize operations. By utilizing sensors, data analytics, and ML algorithms, businesses can predict equipment failures before they occur and schedule maintenance proactively to not only reduce the cost of unscheduled downtime, but also improve the overall efficiency and lifespan of equipment.

Improve safety and compliance—IoT-based predictive maintenance can also be a powerful tool for the improvement of safety and compliance in a variety of industries by monitoring equipment in real time and ensuring that equipment is always in good working order. With potential safety hazards identified, steps can be taken to address them before they present a safety hazard or lead to regulatory noncompliance of equipment standards.

4.2.3 Industrial automation and robotics

Industrial Internet of Things (IIoT) is fundamentally intertwined with both industrial automation and robotics, enabling them to achieve greater efficiency, data-driven decision-making, and overall performance improvement. IIoT connects industrial devices like sensors, controllers, and robots, allowing them to communicate and share data, which in turn facilitates remote monitoring, control, and optimization of processes. This connectivity enhances the capabilities of both industrial automation and robotics, enabling them to perform more effectively and intelligently.

Elaboration:

- **Industrial Automation:** IIoT enhances industrial automation by providing real-time data and remote control capabilities. This allows for more precise control over processes, optimized resource allocation, and reduced downtime.

- **Industrial Robotics:** IIoT enables industrial robots to operate more autonomously, gather data from their environment, and adapt to changing conditions. This integration, often referred to as the "Internet of Robotic Things" (IoRT), allows for continuous monitoring of robot performance, component health, and remote support.

- **Data-Driven Decision Making:** The data collected through IIoT allows for the analysis of operational performance, identification of bottlenecks, and the optimization of processes. This data-driven approach enables more informed decision-making and continuous improvement in both automation and robotics.

- **Remote Monitoring and Control:** IIoT allows for remote monitoring of industrial processes and robots, enabling quick response to issues, and potentially extending the lifespan of equipment through predictive maintenance.

- **Improved Efficiency and Productivity:** By connecting devices and enabling real-time data analysis, IIoT helps improve operational efficiency, reduce waste, and increase overall productivity in industrial settings.

- **Enhanced Safety:** IIoT can be used to improve safety by providing remote monitoring of dangerous processes and enabling faster response to emergencies.

- **Industry 4.0:** IIoT is a key enabler of Industry 4.0, a concept that emphasizes the integration of advanced technologies like AI and robotics for enhanced manufacturing automation and process connectivity.

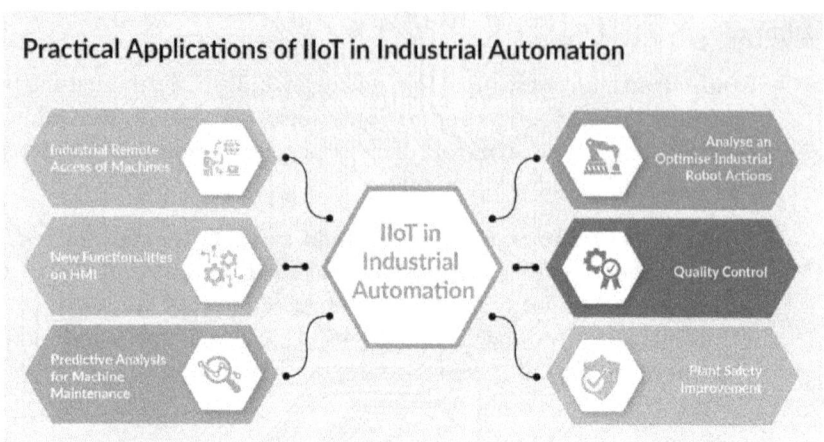

4.2.4 Supply Chain Management

Supply chain management (SCM) is the monitoring and optimization of the production and distribution of a company's products and services. It seeks to improve and make more efficient all processes involved in turning raw materials and components into final products and getting them to the ultimate customer. Effective SCM can help streamline a company's activities to eliminate waste, maximize customer value, and gain a competitive advantage in the marketplace.

How Supply Chain Management (SCM) Works

SCM represents an ongoing effort by companies to make their supply chains as efficient and economical as possible. Typically, SCM attempts to centrally control or link the production, shipment, and distribution of a product. By managing the supply chain, companies can cut excess costs and needless steps and deliver products to the consumer faster. This is done by keeping tighter control of internal inventories, internal production, distribution, sales, and the inventories of company vendors. SCM is based on the idea that nearly every product that comes to market does so as the result of efforts by multiple organizations that make up a supply chain. Although supply chains have existed for ages, a lot of companies didn't pay attention to them as a value-add to their operations until recently.

5 Phases of Supply Chain Management (SCM)

A supply chain manager's job is not only about traditional logistics and purchasing. They have to find ways to increase efficiency and keep costs down while also avoiding shortages and preparing for unexpected contingencies. Typically, the SCM process consists of these five phases:

1. Planning: To get the best results from SCM, the process usually begins with planning to match supply with customer and manufacturing demands. Companies must try to predict what their future needs will be and act accordingly. That means taking into account the raw materials or components needed during each stage of manufacturing, equipment capacity and limitations, and staffing needs. Large businesses often rely on enterprise resource planning (ERP) software to help coordinate the process.

2. Sourcing: Effective SCM processes rely very heavily on strong relationships with suppliers. Sourcing entails working with vendors to supply the materials needed throughout the manufacturing process. Different industries will have different sourcing requirements. In general, SCM sourcing involves ensuring that. The raw materials or components meet the manufacturing specifications needed for the production of the goods. The prices paid to the vendor are in line with market expectations. The vendor has the flexibility to deliver emergency materials due to unforeseen events. The vendor has a proven record of delivering goods on time and of good quality.

3. Manufacturing: Using machinery and labor to transform the raw materials or components the company has received from its suppliers into something new is the heart of the supply chain management process. This final product is the ultimate goal of the manufacturing process, though it is not the final stage of SCM. The manufacturing process may be further divided into sub-tasks such as assembly, testing, inspection, and packaging. During the manufacturing process, companies must be mindful of waste or other factors that may cause deviations from their original plans. For example, if a company is using more raw materials than planned and sourced for due to inadequate employee training, it must rectify the issue or revisit the earlier stages in SCM.

4. Delivery: Once products are made and sales are finalized, a company must get those products into the hands of its customers. A company with effective SCM will have robust logistic capabilities and delivery channels to ensure timely, safe, and inexpensive delivery of its products. This includes having a backup or diversified distribution methods should one method of transportation temporarily be unusable. For example, how might a company's delivery process be impacted by record snowfall in distribution center areas?

5. Returns: The SCM process concludes with support for the product and customer returns. The return process is often called reverse logistics, and the company must ensure it has the capabilities to receive returned products and correctly assign refunds for them. Whether a company is conducting a product recall or a customer is simply not satisfied with the product, the transaction with the customer must be remedied. Returns can also be a valuable form of feedback, helping the company to identify defective or poorly designed products and to make whatever changes are necessary. Without addressing the underlying cause of a customer return, the SCM process will have failed, and returns will likely persist into the future.

Types of Supply Chain Models

Supply chain management does not look the same for all companies. Each business has its own goals, constraints, and strengths that will shape its SCM process. These are some of the models a company can adopt to guide its SCM efforts:

- ➤ **Continuous Flow Model:** The continuous flow model relies on a manufacturer producing the same good over and over and expecting customer demand will show little variation. One of the more traditional supply chain methods, this model is often best for mature industries.

- ➤ **Agile Model:** The agile model prioritizes flexibility, as a company may have a specific need at any given moment and must be prepared to pivot accordingly. This method works best for companies with unpredictable demand or custom-order products.

- ➤ **Fast Model:** This model emphasizes the quick turnover of a product with a short life cycle. Using a fast chain model, a company strives to capitalize on a trend, quickly produce goods, and ensure the product is fully sold before the trend ends.

- ➤ **Flexible Model:** The flexible model works best for companies affected by **seasonality**. Some companies may have much higher demand requirements during peak season and low volume requirements in others. A flexible model of supply chain management ensures that production can easily be ramped up or wound down.

- ➤ **Efficient Model:** Companies competing in industries with very tight profit margins may strive to get an advantage by making their supply chain management process the most efficient. That could involve coming up with ways to do a better job of utilizing equipment and machinery, managing inventory, and processing orders.

> **Custom Model:** If any model above doesn't suit a company's needs, it can always apply a custom model. This is often necessary for highly specialized industries with high technical requirements, such as an automobile manufacturer.

4.3 Healthcare and Wearables

4.3.1 IoT in Healthcare Systems

The IoT is transforming healthcare in many tangible ways by introducing innovative ways to approach traditional tasks such as monitoring, diagnosing and treating patients. The patients' experiences are significantly improved through these innovations. Not only is their care improved, but they profit by the benefit of severely reduced costs. IoT achieves that in many ways. Here's an in-depth look at key IoT applications in healthcare.

1. Remote patient monitoring (RPM)

Wearable devices such as smartwatches, phones, or wearable sensors automatically collect health metrics. These remote patient monitoring devices collect healthcare data such as body temperature, blood pressure, body-fat percentage, etc, while recommending medical treatment or generating alerts based on that information. Many conditions require continuous health monitoring, and collecting data would require a stay at the healthcare facility. This is an issue that RPM largely fixes by providing a stream of constant information to information to healthcare workers who can provide quality remote patient care to even the most isolated of communities

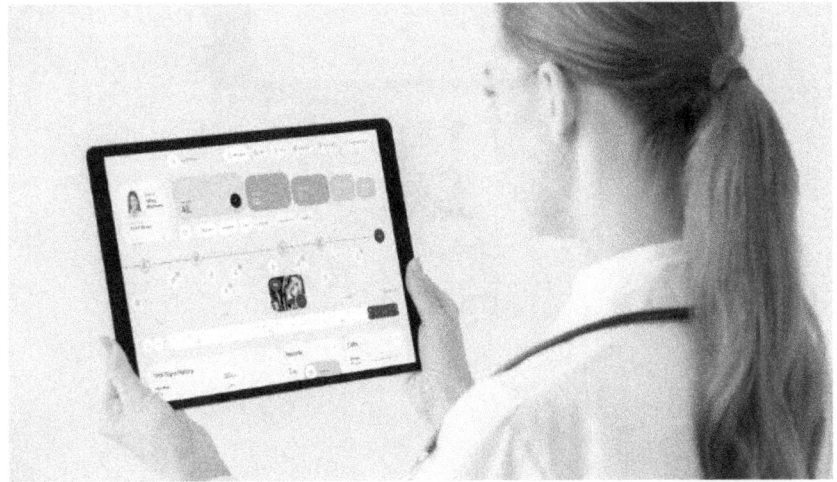

2. Glucose monitoring

Glucose monitoring devices include embedded or wearable sensors that automatically monitor a patient's glucose level, keep a record of the data, and similarly alert medical professionals. Some devices which can be embedded even have the functionality of **automatically supplying insulin** when needed. More importantly, these medical devices assist patients in monitoring their sugar levels themselves more. Some devices can even automatically regulate insulin levels, which leads to an increased quality of life. All of which lead to **more precise monitoring and patient care.**

3. Heart-rate monitoring

Unlike glucose monitoring devices, IoT devices monitoring the heart-rate of a patient are already portable. Many devices like smartwatches or **IoT sensors** already provide effortless constant monitoring of a person's heart rate or other **vital signs**. Thus, **data can be collected even while the patient is sleeping.** That data can then be stored in the patient's **electronic health records.** Monitoring the fluctuation of the heart rate is more challenging when compared to glucose monitoring since it is affected by various activities during the day. Continuous cardiac monitoring allows patients to avoid stays at **healthcare facilities** and still have their condition be monitored. These devices can also serve as emergency response systems that can alert health workers should the heart rate be out of norm.

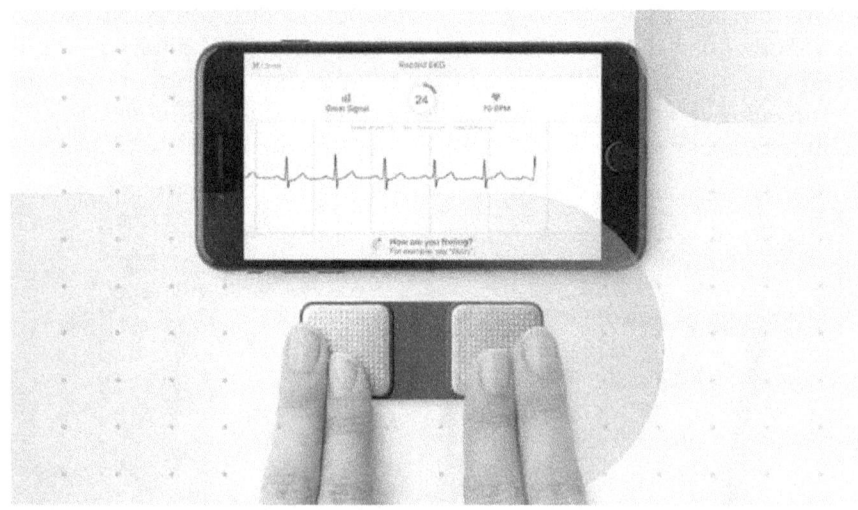

4. Hand hygiene monitoring

Lately, many hospitals and other healthcare facilities are using **hygiene monitoring IoT devices** to ensure proper standards of cleanliness. People use these healthcare devices to remind them to sanitize their hands at regular intervals or whenever they enter a specific room. Many hospital rooms often house critically ill patients. Introducing any pathogens may further complicate the conditions of these patients. Even if **working with relatively healthy patients**, proper decontamination procedures are necessary for the work of any hospital. Hand hygiene IoT health devices can remind people to wash their hands, but they can also give instructions on how to clean their hands or sanitize objects. Where people use these devices, there is an estimated 60 per cent reduction in infection rates.

5. Depression or mood monitoring

By monitoring the heart rate, blood pressure, and other biometric data, **Internet of Things healthcare devices** can infer information about the patient's current mood and **mental health**. More advanced IoT devices can even track the movement of a person's eyes. Traditionally, the continuous patient monitoring of **mental health** is quite challenging. Medical professionals must periodically **ask about the patient's feelings** to determine their diagnosis. The experts, however, cannot predict the mood swings of patients or the latter may decide to omit some information from their **medical records** or refuse to share their medical history with the professional. The main advantage of IoT devices is that they rely on objective biometrics rather than the testimony of a person. These **health indicators** are not controlled by the patient and serve as a good indication of a person's **mental health**. Further, patient monitoring may continue while they are sleeping as well.

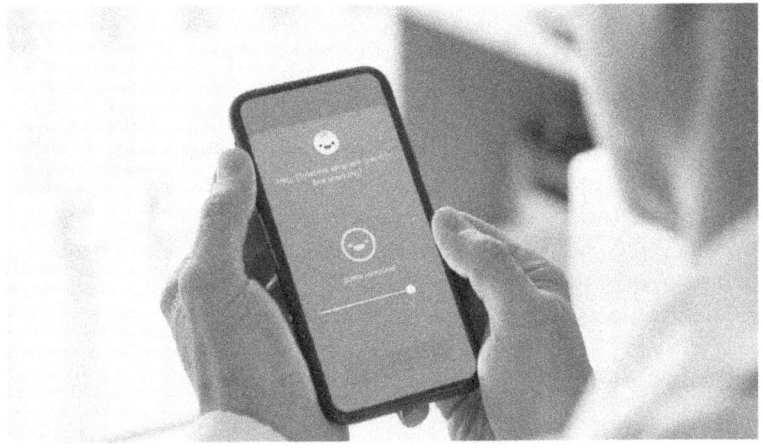

6. Ingestible sensors

Much as the name suggests, these medical devices are small sensors that are ingested and designed to either pass through or dissolve in the digestive tract. A lot of these devices resemble the shape of a pill that a person must swallow. Their purpose is to collect various biometric data, such as **determining the PH level of the stomach** or identifying the presence of internal bleeding.

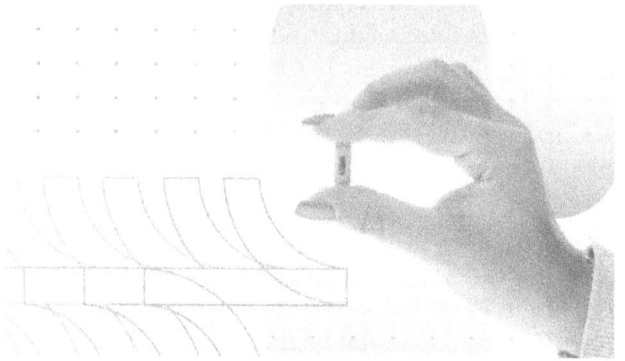

Using digestible sensors enables patients to choose a much less intrusive procedure. Unlike traditional methods, using ingestible sensors is much less messy and disruptive since the sensor can either independently pass or dissolve in a patient's digestive tract. The process is smoother since a **medical professional** does not need to manually insert the sensor into the digestive system. Recent **advancements in healthcare technology** have even suggested the possibility of easily ingestible yet small pills being developed.

7. Robotic surgery

A new way of conducting surgeries is through IoT medical devices. Surgeons can inject small devices like **Internet-connected robots** into the human body to perform surgeries. Professionals use these to reduce human error when the operation requires precision. The main issue is that the incisions required to conduct surgeries by hand are bigger when compared to their robotic counterparts. Human hands need more space when they **perform complex procedures.** When using these IoT robotic devices, **surgeons can do more precise and effective operations**. The incisions are smaller due to easier insertion of the IoT devices. All of which leads to a less invasive procedure for the patient and shorter recovery times. The main requirement for such devices is that they must be small and reliable enough to **perform complex procedures.** They must also be able to accurately analyze the conditions inside a person's body and formulate an appropriate decision for the surgery

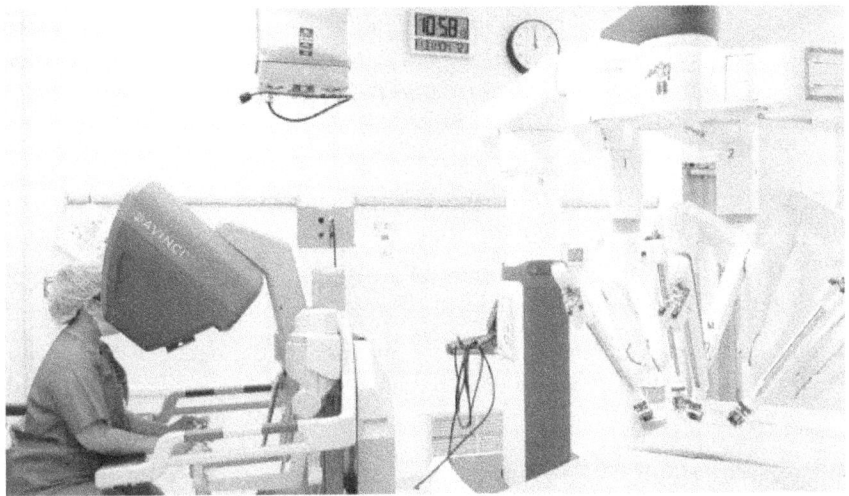

Benefits

> - **Constant monitoring** has the unique benefit of being **immune to human error**. Without having the data collected, a patient would be susceptible to missing their dose, forgetting to report something to their medical professional and even deciding to ignore certain **health issues**. IoT devices do that work for them in a data-driven way.

> - Some patients are susceptible to hypochondriac use of medicine that could damage their health. IoTs make sure that **any dose is just the right amount**. IoT devices prevent this other extreme from coming to fruition;

> - Medical professionals benefit from **reduced paperwork and bureaucracy**, because IoT devices digitize all reliable data.

> - They also can be used to perform **easier and more effective interventions**. Examples would include the ingestible sensors and the robot surgeries.

4.3.2 Remote Patient Monitoring and Telemedicine

Definition of telemedicine: Telemedicine refers to the use of telecommunication and information technologies to provide clinical health care services remotely. This means that patients can receive medical consultations from the comfort of their homes, without needing to visit a doctor's office or hospital.

Types: Telemedicine services can include virtual consultations, remote monitoring, and patient education. Some telemedicine services also offer specialized services, such as remote surgery and mental health counselling.

Advantages

Improved access to healthcare: Telemedicine has improved access to healthcare, especially for people living in rural areas or those with mobility issues. With telemedicine, patients can receive medical consultations without travelling long distances.

Cost-effectiveness: Telemedicine has the potential to reduce healthcare costs by eliminating the need for patients to travel to see a doctor and reducing the need for in-person appointments.

Improved patient satisfaction: Patients are generally more satisfied with telemedicine than traditional in-person appointments because it is more convenient and less time-consuming.

Increased efficiency: Telemedicine can help healthcare providers see more patients in a day, as virtual consultations take less time than in-person appointments.

Challenges of telemedicine

Reimbursement: Reimbursement for telemedicine services is still an issue, as some insurance companies do not cover virtual consultations.

Technical difficulties: Technical difficulties, such as poor internet connection or the need for specialized equipment, can make telemedicine difficult to implement.

Data security and privacy: The security and privacy of patient data is a concern with telemedicine, as sensitive information is transmitted over the internet.

Definition of remote patient monitoring

Remote patient monitoring refers to the use of technology, such as wearable devices, sensors, and mobile applications, to collect and transmit health data from a patient to healthcare providers, allowing for continuous monitoring and assessment of the patient's health status outside of a traditional clinical setting. The goal of remote patient monitoring is to improve patient outcomes and reduce healthcare costs by reducing the need for in-person visits and hospitalizations, while still ensuring timely and effective care.

Importance of telemedicine and remote patient monitoring

Telemedicine and remote patient monitoring are two key applications of the Internet of Things in healthcare that are transforming the way patients receive care. Telemedicine enables patients to receive medical consultations from their homes, while remote patient monitoring allows healthcare providers to monitor patient's health remotely, in real-time.

The potential impact of Telemedicine and Remote patient monitoring

Telemedicine and remote patient monitoring have the potential to significantly improve access to healthcare, especially for patients living in remote or underserved areas, and those with mobility issues. By enabling virtual consultations and continuous health monitoring, these technologies can help to:

- ➢ Reduce the burden on hospitals and clinics, leading to faster and more efficient care for patients

- ➢ Increase patient satisfaction by reducing the need for in-person visits and providing more convenient access to care

- ➢ Improve patient outcomes by enabling healthcare providers to detect and respond to health problems early, reducing the risk of complications and hospitalization

- ➢ Lower healthcare costs by reducing the need for in-person visits and reducing the length of hospital stays

- ➢ Increase the efficiency and effectiveness of healthcare delivery by enabling healthcare providers to access and review patient data in real-time, improving decision-making and collaboration between care teams.

4.3.3 Health and wearables IoT:

fitness and health tracking wearables

Wearables equipped with Internet of Things (IoT) technology are **revolutionizing fitness and health tracking, enabling continuous** monitoring of vital signs and personalized insights. These devices, like smartwatches and fitness bands, collect data on activity, heart rate, sleep patterns, and more, empowering users to make informed decisions about their health and fitness routines.

Key Features and Benefits:

- **Continuous Monitoring:** Wearables track health metrics like heart rate, steps, calories burned, and sleep patterns, providing real-time data and feedback.

- **Personalized Insights:** Analysis of collected data offers tailored recommendations for fitness routines, sleep improvement, and other aspects of well-being.

- **Early Disease Detection:** Real-time data can alert users to potential health issues, enabling proactive management and early intervention.

- **Motivation and Engagement:** Immediate feedback on activity and health metrics can motivate users to stay active and achieve their goals, often with gamification features like challenges and rewards.

- **Improved Communication:** Wearables facilitate communication between users and healthcare providers, allowing for more efficient monitoring and care.

Examples of Wearable IoT Devices:

- **Fitness Trackers:** These devices track physical activity, sleep patterns, and other metrics, often with features like step counting, calorie tracking, and heart rate monitoring.

- **Smartwatches:** Beyond timekeeping, smartwatches offer health and fitness tracking capabilities, along with communication and entertainment features.

- **Smart Clothing:** Wearable technology can be integrated into clothing, providing continuous health monitoring and data collection.

- **Medical Wearables:** These devices are designed for specific medical needs, such as monitoring blood glucose levels or delivering medication.

How Wearable IoT Devices Work:

- ➢ **Data Collection:** Wearables use sensors to collect data on various health and fitness metrics.
- ➢ **Connectivity:** Data is transmitted to the cloud or local devices for processing and analysis.
- ➢ **Data Analysis:** Algorithms analyze the data to provide insights and personalized recommendations.
- ➢ **User Interface:** Data is presented to users through wearable displays, apps, or other platforms.

In conclusion, wearable IoT devices are transforming health and fitness tracking by providing continuous monitoring, personalized insights, and early detection capabilities, ultimately empowering individuals to take a proactive approach to their well-being.

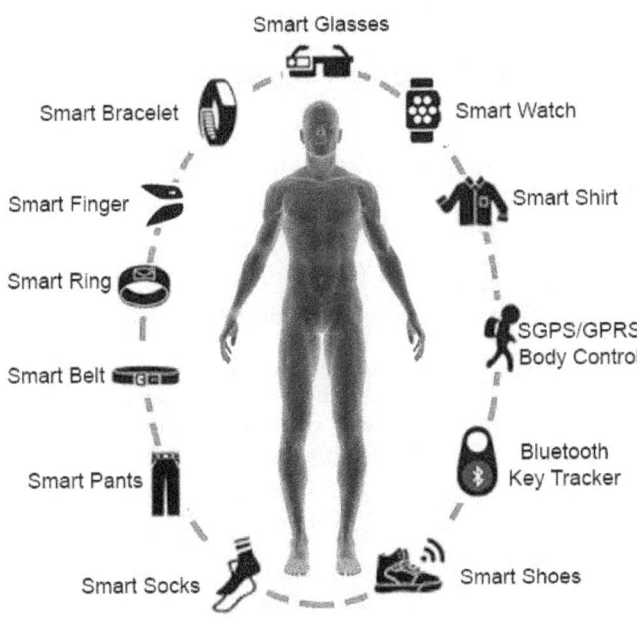

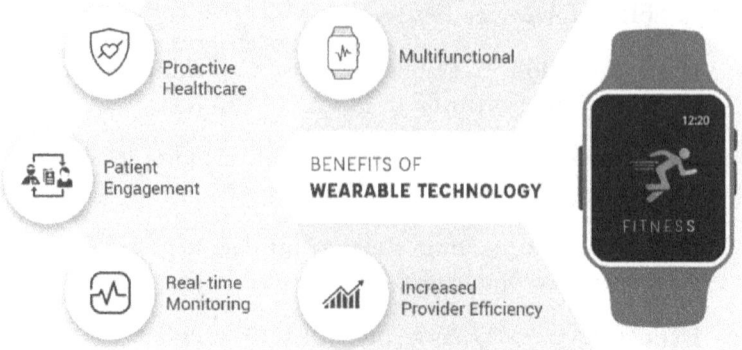

4.3.4 Challenges in IoT healthcare Applications

What are the challenges of IoT in healthcare?

1) Data Security and Privacy:

One of the most significant challenges faced by IoT is Data Security and Privacy. IoT-enabled mobile devices capture data in real-time, but most of them lack adherence to data protocols and standards.

There is significant ambiguity regarding data ownership and regulation. Hence, the data stored within IoT-enabled devices are prone to data thefts and it makes the data more susceptible to cybercriminals that can hack into the system to compromise personal health information.

Some examples of misuse of IoT device data are fraudulent health claims and the creation of fake IDs for buying and selling drugs

2) Integration: Multiple Devices & Protocols:

The integration of multiple types of devices causes hindrance in the implementation of IoT in the healthcare sector. The reason behind this hindrance is that device manufacturers haven't reached a consensus regarding communication protocol and standards.

This results in a scenario where every manufacturer creates its own separate ecosystem of IoT devices that do not work with the devices and applications of competing manufacturers. In such a situation, there is no synchronous protocol that could be followed for data aggregation. This non-uniformity slows down the process and reduces the scope of scalability of IoT in healthcare.

3) Data Overload and Accuracy:

Due to the non-uniformity of data and communication protocols, it is difficult to aggregate data for vital insights and analysis. IoT collects data in bulk and for proper data analysis, the data need to be segregated in chunks without overloading with precise accuracy for better results. Moreover, the overloading of data might affect the decision-making process in the hospitality sector in the longer run.

4) Cost:

You might not be surprised to see this point here. Costs are one of the greater challenges when planning to consider IoT app development for healthcare mobility solutions. However, the costs are completely worth it if the IoT implementation is one that solves a genuine problem.

While you will spend a significant amount of money and resources in developing an IoT application, the returns will be equally huge when your business saves time and manpower, all while improving the business processes, generating more revenue streams, and creating more business opportunities through IoT.

What Are The Applications of IoT in Healthcare?

- IoT applications in healthcare are meant not just for the healthcare institutions, but for the patients too! In a nutshell, IoT in healthcare does the following:
- Reducing emergency room wait time
- Tracking patients, staff, and inventory
- Enhancing drug management
- Ensuring the availability of critical hardware
- Now, these benefits cannot be realized without the various types of IoT devices leveraged in the healthcare sector, some of the popular
- aspects of the city, such as traffic flow, air quality, and energy consumption.
- **Data Analytics:** The collected data is analyzed to identify trends, optimize resource allocation, and make data-driven decisions.
- **Smart Transportation:** Systems like smart traffic lights, public transportation optimization, and connected vehicles contribute to smoother and more efficient mobility.

- **Smart Grids:** These systems manage energy distribution more efficiently, reducing waste and promoting renewable energy sources.
- **Smart Water Management:** Technologies like smart meters and leak detection systems help conserve water resources and reduce waste.
- **Smart Waste Management:** Systems that optimize collection routes, monitor waste levels, and promote recycling contribute to a cleaner and more sustainable environment.

Benefits of Smart Infrastructure:

- **Improved Efficiency:** Optimized resource management and data-driven decision-making lead to increased efficiency across various urban systems.
- **Reduced Costs:** Smart technologies can help reduce energy consumption, water waste, and transportation costs, leading to savings for both governments and citizens.
- **Enhanced Sustainability:** Smart cities can promote sustainable practices through energy conservation, waste reduction, and renewable energy adoption.
- **Improved Quality of Life:** Better transportation, cleaner air, and more efficient public services contribute to a higher quality of life for residents.
- **Resilience to Climate Change:** Smart infrastructure can help cities adapt to climate change by improving resource management, reducing emissions, and enhancing resilience to extreme weather events.

Challenges and Considerations:

- **Data Privacy and Security:** Ensuring the privacy and security of data collected by smart infrastructure is crucial.
- **Digital Divide:** Addressing the digital divide and ensuring equitable access to smart city technologies is important.
- **Public Acceptance:** Engaging with the public and ensuring their acceptance of smart city initiatives is essential for success.
- **Integration with Existing Infrastructure:** Integrating new smart technologies with existing infrastructure can be challenging, requiring careful planning and coordination.

> Smart cities and their smart infrastructure are transforming urban environments, offering numerous benefits for residents and the environment. By embracing innovative technologies and data-driven solutions, cities can create more sustainable, resilient, and livable communities for the future.

4.4 Smart Cities and Infrastructure:

4.4.1 Smart Transportation System

Smart transportation and smart city traffic management are revolutionizing how cities approach mobility and emergency response, while reducing congestion on city streets. How? With sensors, advanced communication technologies, automation and high-speed networks.

The art and science of moving from one place to another is an inherent part of our lives — not just today but throughout history. From chariots and horses to carriages, automobiles, steam trains and spacecraft — being on the move is a part of being human.

Civilization has come a long way from riding horses and camels to get from place to place. With the emergence of intelligent transportation systems and the Internet of Things (IoT), the world is entering the next stage of movement — smart transportation. If the term sounds vague or triggers mental images of autonomous flying cars and hamster-like, high speed tubes, don't worry.

This article will lay out what exactly smart transportation is, how it works, and many of the benefits it brings along with some real world examples in use today. And we'll also cover the different types of intelligent transportation systems being deployed today.

What Is Smart Transportation?

According to the goverment "Intelligent Transportation Systems (ITS) apply a variety of technologies to monitor, evaluate, and manage transportation systems to enhance efficiency and safety." Putting visions of science fiction style transportation aside for the moment, this definition can be simplified into the following concepts for what makes up smart transportation: management, efficiency, and safety. In other words, smart transportation uses new and emerging technologies to make moving around a city more convenient, more cost effective (for both the city and the individual), and safer.

What emerging technologies are facilitating these new opportunities? Primarily the proliferation of IoT devices and 5G communication technology. The former provides for inexpensive sensors and controllers that can be imbedded into nearly any physical machine to be controlled and managed remotely. The latter provides the high speed communications needed for managing and controlling transportation systems in real time with minimal latency.

Smart transportation is not just a theory for the future; it is being implemented today in several cities with their successes and failures being used to improve systems in new locations. Some of the cities that are implementing new transportation technologies may surprise you at first. Of course, global hubs like **New York City** have embraced smart transportation for their ever increasingly intelligent city. However, the rural **state of Wyoming** is also a leading testbed for connected vehicles. This is because the cowboy state is a major freight corridor — autonomous transportation of goods across the country can drastically improve supply chain efficiency and reduce the need for long-haul drivers forced to balance tight timelines with their human need for rest.

The Main Benefits of Transportation Technology

The benefits of smart technology and the advantages they bring to transportation within a smart city are numerous.

- **Smart Transportation is safer:** By combining machine learning with IoT and 5G, autonomous transportation systems (both in vehicles and in stationary infrastructure such as intersections) have proven to reduce the "human factor" in accidents. Computers don't get distracted or fatigued or emotional.

- **Smart Transportation is better managed:** Data collection is an important key to responsible public management of infrastructure. Smart transportation not only provides detailed data points for every aspect of the transportation system, but allows administrators to better monitor operations, track maintenance needs, and identify key sources of problems that need to be fixed.

- **Smart Transportation is more efficient:** With better management comes more efficient use. Quality data can help to pinpoint areas where efficiency can be improved. Maybe a slight adjustment in train schedules would provide for better fill rates, Or, perhaps bus routes would better serve the community if stops were allocated differently.

- **Smart Transportation is cost effective:** Because smart transportation makes better use of the resources available, it can cut down costs thanks to preventative maintenance, lower energy consumption, and fewer resources used towards accidents. Cost savings can also be gained by riders when inexpensive public transit is efficient enough to compete with private vehicle ownership.

- **Smart Transportation provides rapid insights**: City traffic management centers (TMCs) can get rapid visibility and notifications for trouble spots or city-wide issues affecting congestion on city streets, public safety and emergency response systems, in order to take action or communicate more effectively with other agencies and emergency responders.

Beyond the better management, safety, and efficiency already discussed, there are several additional benefits that the general public, local governments, and the world at large can enjoy. These are:

- Security
- Environmental Considerations

- Supply Chain Resiliency

Security

One major fear among smart city skeptics is its vulnerability to cyber attacks. After all, as the world grows more connected, cyber attacks have become nearly commonplace among criminals and even nation states as they target critical infrastructure such as <u>Internet connected power grids</u> and banking systems.

However, the attacks themselves are nothing new—only the tools are novel. Banks, power grids, and other critical infrastructure to include transportation have been vulnerable to physical attacks long before computers have been around. Physical threats such as criminals stealing cars, terrorists using vehicles as weapons (as in the <u>2016 Lorry attack in France</u>), and bad actors holding <u>public transportation hostage</u> can all be mitigated when vehicles and infrastructure are integrated, networked, and autonomous.

As for the risk of cyber attacks, they are much easier to defend against than the physical threats listed above. Proper software updates, encrypted communications through virtual private network (VPN) tunnels and <u>other multilayered security practices</u> can mitigate the risk of cyber attacks. This means that smart transportation for intelligent cities can make modern public transport safer overall by reducing the opportunities for both physical and cyber attacks.

Environmental Considerations

The history of transportation is inexorably tied to the environment. From steam vehicles that burned coal and wood to today's gasoline hungry combustion engines, transportation takes a toll on the planet's resources and atmosphere.

While scientific advances are made every day to find alternative sources of energy to power transportation, another benefit of smart transportation technology is that it allows cities to use their current resources more responsibly.

Mass transit is better for the environment than private vehicles but is not widely used across the US and other countries because it is often impractical in some regions. With the efficiency boosts that come from smart transport solutions, however, modern public transport can be made lucrative for more portions of the population. As urban transportation technology improves in large cities, the proven methods can be replicated and spread to regions that want the benefits of a smart city.

Supply Chain Resiliency

Global crises such as the Coronavirus pandemic have proven that the world's supply chains are vulnerable to disruption. When workers and drivers are ill and traveling from one region to another becomes a public health hazard, autonomous transportation of goods can become a literal lifesaver.

Projects such as Wyoming's connected vehicle project might be the key to forming an autonomous supply chain powered by smart, city-to-city transport and logistics systems to move critical goods such as food and emergency supplies without the need to risk human drivers. Minimally, the human supply chain workforce can be augmented wherever safety and efficiency can be improved using automation, artificial intelligence and robotics. The good news is that experts believe these innovations will support creation of more jobs — and safer ones — as developers, technicians, analysts and administrators help to bring the advancements to market and maintain them.

Are There Disadvantages of Smart Cities?

For all their benefits, some disadvantages may come to the surface as smart city transportation systems are implemented. These problems center mainly around power consumption and responsible data management.

Smart cities require sensors — *a lot of sensors* — and those sensors all require power. For sensors attached to moving objects, this will require batteries. Stationary sensors may be able to use solar power, but more often than not will need to be wired into the city's electrical grid. The sheer number of sensors required for the world to transition to smart cities (estimated in the trillions) makes powering so many devices a daunting problem. Even for sensors wired into the power grid, the amount of raw material necessary (such as copper) is significantly high compared to what the world population is accustomed to producing.

Beyond power, there is significant debate in the world today regarding personal data online. Data is the lifeblood that smart cities need in order to operate. While much of the information needed is anonymous compared to online data, this will require a mental and behavioral shift among populations. Cars will need to collect positional information and sensors around a city will need to passively collect the signals that a smart phone emits throughout the day. Responsible laws and policies for managing data, no matter how anonymous, will need to be enacted in order for smart cities to thrive into the future.

4.4.2 IoT in Urban Planning

The Internet of Things is a network of interconnected devices and sensors that collect and exchange data. IoT is driving urban development by transforming how cities manage resources, infrastructure, and public services.

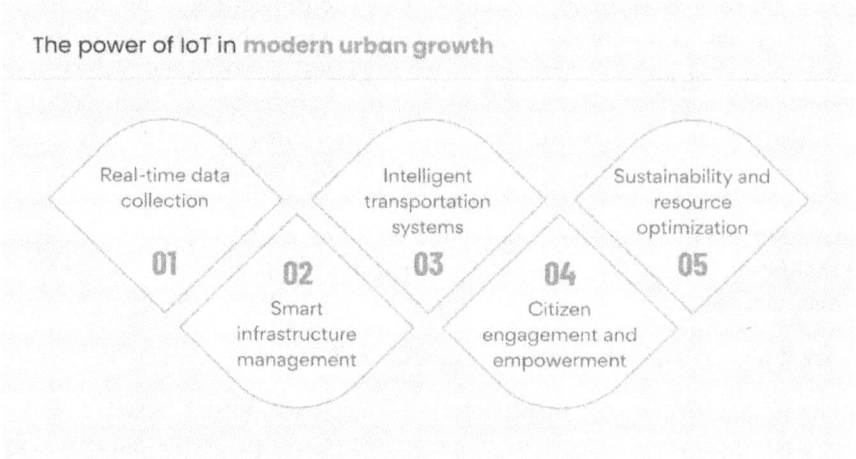

1. Real-time data collection

IoT applications in smart cities include sensors and cameras deployed across urban areas to gather real-time data on traffic patterns, energy usage, air quality, and waste management.

This information provides city planners and administrators with actionable insights to optimize operations and improve urban planning.

2. Smart infrastructure management

IoT Smart city infrastructure relies on sensors embedded in critical assets like buildings, utilities, and transportation networks. These sensors help monitor and manage systems in real-time.

For instance, IoT-enabled smart grids optimize energy distribution, minimizing wastage and promoting renewable energy integration.

3. Intelligent transportation systems

IoT Traffic Monitoring is transforming urban mobility. Connected sensors, cameras, and GPS devices provide live data on traffic conditions, parking availability, and public transportation.

This data supports IoT Traffic Management strategies that reduce congestion and improve public transit services.

4. Citizen engagement and empowerment

IoT for smart urban solutions encourages public participation. Through mobile applications, residents can access real-time information, report issues, and interact with city services.

This improves transparency and inclusivity in urban decision-making.

5. Sustainability and resource optimization

Urban IoT solutions play an important role in managing energy consumption, water usage, and waste disposal.

Cities can optimize resources, minimize environmental impact, and promote sustainable practices by analysing real-time data.

Efficient infrastructure management is a key component of IoT for urban development, ensuring smarter resource utilization, sustainability, and improved quality of life for residents.

4.4.3 Waste and water management

Smart cities leverage technology to optimize waste and water management for efficiency, sustainability, and resource conservation. This includes smart waste collection systems, advanced water distribution networks, and wastewater treatment technologies, all monitored and managed through data analytics and real-time feedback.

Waste Management:

IoT sensors embedded in waste bins and collection trucks provide real-time information on waste levels.

This data supports IoT for smart urban solutions by enabling efficient waste collection routes, minimizing unnecessary trips, and improving waste disposal processes.

- ➤ **Optimized Collection:** Smart bins with sensors monitor fill levels, triggering automated alerts for waste pickup trucks, optimizing routes and reducing waste generation.
- ➤ **Real-time Monitoring:** IoT devices and data analytics provide real-time data on waste volumes, composition, and collection efficiency, enabling proactive waste management strategies.
- ➤ **Waste Reduction and Recycling:** Smart cities encourage participation in waste reduction and recycling programs through educational campaigns and incentives, as well as promoting composting and other sustainable waste management practices.
- ➤ **Smart Bin Infrastructure:** Waste bins can be equipped with solar panels and compactors to further enhance efficiency and reduce the need for frequent collection.
- ➤ **Water Management:** IoT sensors in water supply networks track usage, detect leaks, and monitor water quality. Cities can identify high-consumption areas, reduce wastage, and take steps to conserve water resources by collecting real-time data.
- ➤ **Smart Water Infrastructure:** Smart water meters and sensors monitor water usage, detect leaks, and manage water pressure, optimizing water distribution and minimizing water loss.
- ➤ **Wastewater Management:** Smart wastewater systems detect leaks, prevent overflows, and monitor water quality, ensuring efficient treatment and minimizing water wastage.
- ➤ **Predictive Maintenance:** Data analytics can predict infrastructure failures and optimize maintenance schedules, reducing downtime and water loss.
- ➤ **Water Reuse:** Smart cities explore water reuse opportunities, such as using treated wastewater for irrigation or industrial processes, reducing reliance on freshwater sources.

- **Smart Metering:** Advanced metering infrastructure (AMI) enables real-time monitoring of water consumption, allowing for targeted interventions and water conservation initiatives.

4.4.4 Environmental monitoring

Environmental monitoring is a crucial aspect of smart cities, leveraging technology to track various parameters and support data-driven decisions for sustainable urban development. This involves deploying sensors and networks to monitor air quality, weather, noise levels, and other environmental factors, enabling authorities to identify pollution sources and implement corrective measures. By analyzing this data, smart cities can optimize infrastructure, manage waste, and reduce pollution, ultimately improving the quality of life for residents.

1. Air Quality Monitoring:

- **Purpose:** To track pollutants like particulate matter, ozone, and greenhouse gases, helping identify pollution hotspots and sources.
- **Techniques:** Using sensors embedded in streetlights or other infrastructure to collect real-time data on air quality parameters.
- **Benefits:** Enables authorities to implement targeted measures to reduce pollution, such as optimizing traffic flow, promoting public transportation, or enforcing stricter emissions standards.

2. Water Quality Monitoring:

- **Purpose:** To monitor water levels, quality (e.g., pH, dissolved oxygen), and detect leaks or pollution events.
- **Techniques:** Deploying sensors in water networks, including those for smart irrigation systems, to monitor water flow and detect anomalies.
- **Benefits:** Supports water conservation efforts, prevents waterborne diseases, and helps manage flood events by identifying potential issues in real-time.

3. Waste Management Monitoring:

- **Purpose:** To track waste collection efficiency, identify overflowing bins, and optimize waste transportation routes.

- **Techniques:** Using sensors in waste bins to monitor fill levels, detect leaks, and track their movement.
- **Benefits:** Reduces waste collection costs, minimizes littering, and supports recycling efforts by providing real-time data on waste volumes and composition.

4. Noise Pollution Monitoring:

- **Purpose:** To track noise levels in different areas of the city and identify noise sources, particularly during construction or transportation.
- **Techniques:** Using noise sensors strategically placed in urban areas to monitor noise levels and identify potential violations.
- **Benefits:** Helps authorities implement noise control measures, improve public health by reducing noise-related stress, and support urban planning by considering noise levels in zoning and transportation design.

5. Meteorological Monitoring:

- **Purpose:** To track weather patterns, predict extreme weather events (e.g., floods, heatwaves), and prepare for potential emergencies.
- **Techniques:** Using weather sensors to monitor temperature, humidity, rainfall, and wind speed.
- **Benefits:** Enables early warning systems for extreme weather events, supports urban planning by considering weather patterns in infrastructure design, and helps optimize resource allocation during emergencies.

Benefits of Environmental Monitoring in Smart Cities:

- **Improved public health:** By monitoring air and water quality, smart cities can reduce the risk of respiratory and waterborne diseases.
- **Reduced environmental impact:** Monitoring waste and pollution sources helps cities reduce their carbon footprint and other environmental damages.
- **Enhanced resource management:** By monitoring water and energy consumption, smart cities can optimize resource allocation and reduce costs.

> **Improved urban planning:** Environmental data helps city planners make informed decisions about infrastructure development, transportation, and zoning.

> **Increased citizen engagement:** By providing access to environmental data, smart cities can empower citizens to participate in environmental initiatives and monitor their local environment.

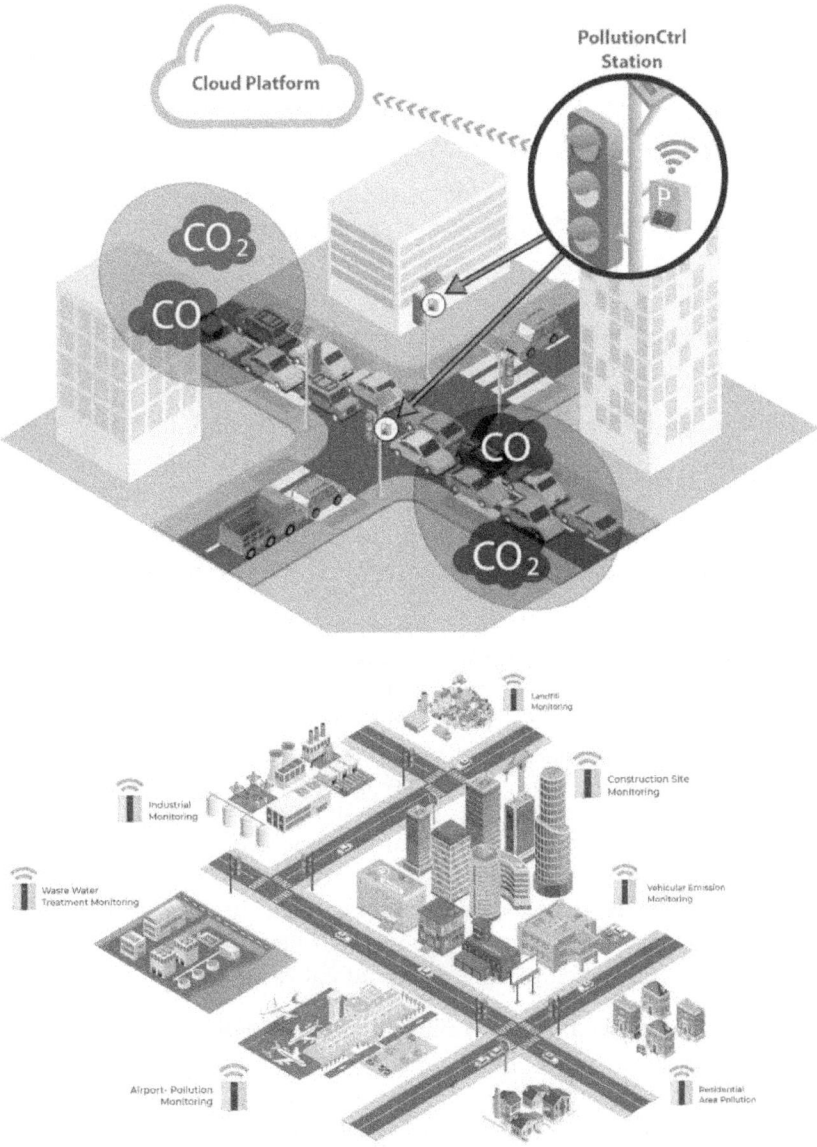

4.5 IoT in Agriculture and Environment

4.5.1 Precision Agriculture with IoT

IoT-based precision farming uses various technologies like GPS, GIS, sensors, aerial devices, or field mapping to streamline crop management processes, increase production levels, and improve profitability. It also optimizes the use of such traditional resources as electricity, fuel, and water, contributing to sustainable agriculture growth.

Precision farming technologies help obtain the following goals:

- Collecting real-time farming data, including crop status, environmental changes, and weather conditions
- Choosing the crops with better yields
- Managing fields by dividing them into separate zones for improved irrigation, fertilization, pest control, and fuel use
- Enhancing the sustainability and profitability of farms
- Forecasting natural hazards and timely response to them

Thus, precision agriculture facilitates decision-making by leveraging farming data for optimized sowing, reduced crop waste, and lowered harmful impact on the environment.

Key Benefits: Today, farmers are increasingly turning to precision agriculture technology. It's not surprising since this tech brings numerous benefits to agricultural processes, including more effective decision-making, increased ROI, and producing more with fewer resources.

Improved Farming Monitoring: With numerous tools and techniques, precision agriculture enables farmers to monitor fields more effectively by tracking various metrics. In particular, growers can check the rainfall levels, study soil samples, estimate fertilizer use, or evaluate the number of nutrients needed for the crops. All this contributes to a better understanding of the conditions that promote the highest agricultural yields.

Better Decision-Making: Following the previous point, all real-time data on the environment, soil condition, and crops enable farmers to make better decisions regarding agricultural management. As a result, thanks to IoT-based smart farming, field owners can timely respond to local changes and eliminate risks that may affect yield.

Unified Farming Data: Precision agriculture technologies make it possible to store agricultural data in one place, especially with the involvement of cloud-based tech. This way, crop management becomes much easier, as farmers can effortlessly access data from any device.

Enhanced Crop Protection: Farmers tend to use excessive amounts of chemicals to control pests in the fields. It not only harms the condition of the soil and crops but also significantly affects the budget. However, with IoT systems for precision farming, everything changes. This tech allows using chemicals only when necessary while effectively protecting crops.

Improved Irrigation: Effective irrigation management is critical in farming, as this industry is among those that consume the most significant amount of water. Precision farming enables measuring soil moisture and rainfall levels to determine the best time to irrigate a field.

Reduced Waste: Precision farming using IoT allows farmers to determine the exact amount of fertilizers, herbicides, and chemicals needed for a specific field. It also helps optimize the use of fuel, water, and electricity. All this benefits the environment and reduces the amount of harmful waste.

Advantages

Advanced Insights: Thanks to IoT solutions in precision agriculture, farmers can better analyze the processes on their sites. IoT sensors and devices installed on the farm will instantly send data on crop status, soil quality, weather conditions, or worker performance, giving a better understanding of all agricultural processes.

Optimized Resources: Precision farming using IoT makes it possible to optimize the use of resources. This tech allows for accurate harvest volume estimation and the assessment of the required amount of water, fertilizers, etc., reducing operating costs and boosting production

Advanced Aerial Data: The IoT in agriculture allows farmers to leverage drones with hyperspectral and multispectral sensors. These devices help to get deeper insights into the state of crops and soil moisture. On top of that, IoT-enabled drones can assist in natural disaster management.

Improved Internal Process Management: IoT technology used in precision farming can facilitate internal management procedures. With this tech, field managers can effectively supervise their workers and increase their productivity by sending them real-time data on field conditions.

4.5.2 Smart Irrigation Systems

Smart irrigation system using IoT have revolutionized agriculture offering unprecedented control and efficiency. These systems utilize Internet of Things (IoT) technology to enhance traditional irrigation methods providing real time data and automation for optimized water usage. In an era where water scarcity is a growing concern, smart irrigation system using IoT play a pivotal role in water conservation. By leveraging IoT in agriculture these systems enable farmers to monitor soil moisture levels and weather conditions ensuring water is used efficiently. Smart irrigation is the integration of IoT devices in traditional irrigation systems, offering farmers precise control over watering processes. This article explores the multiple benefits, components, challenges and future trends associated with smart irrigation system.

How does a Smart Irrigation System using IoT work?

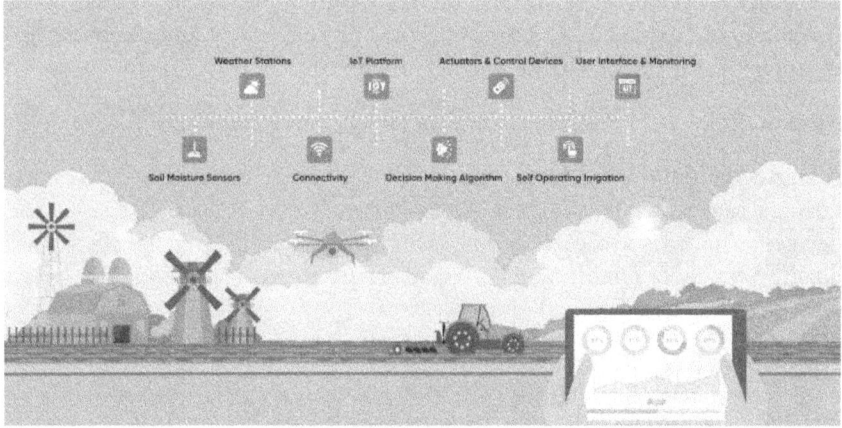

A Smart Irrigation System using IoT (Internet of Things) incorporates sensors, connectivity and data analytics to optimize the irrigation process. Here is a summary of how it functions.

Soil Moisture Sensors: The system utilizes soil moisture sensors placed in the soil at different locations within the irrigation area. These sensors measure the moisture content in the soil, providing real-time data about the soil's water saturation levels.

Weather Stations: Weather stations collect data about environmental conditions such as temperature, humidity, wind speed and precipitation. This information is crucial for understanding the atmospheric conditions that may affect plant water requirements.

Connectivity: The sensors and weather stations are connected to a central control unit or a gateway device using wireless communication protocols (e.g., Wi-Fi, Bluetooth, or Zigbee). The central control unit acts as a bridge between the sensors, weather stations and the IoT platform.

IoT Platform: The data collected from soil moisture sensors and weather stations are transmitted to an IoT platform or cloud-based system. The IoT platform processes and analyzes the data, considering factors such as soil type, plant type and weather conditions.

Decision Making Algorithm: The IoT platform uses intelligent algorithms to make decisions about when and how much to irrigate based on the analyzed data. Factors like current soil moisture levels, weather forecasts and plant water requirements are taken into account.

Actuators and Control Devices: Based on the decisions made by the IoT platform, control signals are sent to actuators that manage the irrigation system. Actuators control valves, pumps and other devices to adjust the flow of water to specific zones or plants.

Self Operating Irrigation: The irrigation system is self-operating and water is supplied precisely when and where it is needed. This self-operating system reduces water wastage, promotes efficient water use and ensures that plants receive the optimal amount of water for their growth.

User Interface and Monitoring: Users can monitor and control the smart irrigation system through a user interface, which can be a web application, mobile app or a dedicated control panel. The interface provides real-time information on soil moisture levels, weather conditions and irrigation activities.

Advantages of Smart Irrigation System Using IoT

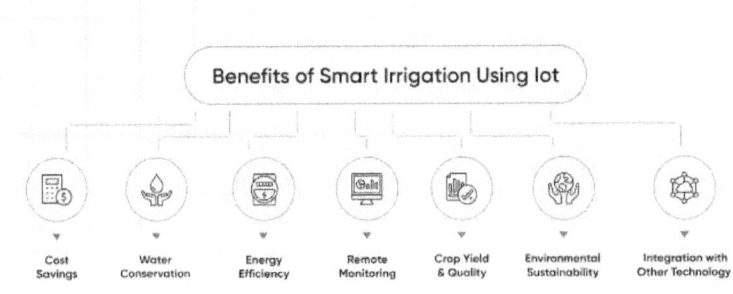

Cost Savings: By using data from sensors and weather forecasts, farmers can optimize irrigation schedules and resource usage. This results in cost savings by reducing water and energy consumption, as well as minimizing the need for fertilizers and other inputs.

Water Conservation: IoT enabled sensors and actuators allow farmers to precisely control the amount of water delivered to crops based on real time data, such as soil moisture levels and weather conditions.

Energy Efficiency: Smart irrigation systems can be automated to respond to environmental conditions. This reduces the need for manual intervention and ensures that irrigation activities are synchronized with the specific requirements of the crops.

Remote Monitoring: IoT devices enable farmers to monitor the irrigation system remotely in real-time. This allows for quick detection and response to issues such as leaks or equipment malfunctions, minimizing downtime and preventing potential crop damage.

Improved Crop Yield and Quality: Smart irrigation system ensure that crops receive the right amount of water at the right time. This optimized irrigation leads to improved crop yield, quality and uniformity, ultimately enhancing the overall productivity of the farm.

Environmental Sustainability: By minimizing water wastage and using resources more efficiently, smart irrigation contributes to environmental sustainability. This is particularly important in regions facing water scarcity and where agriculture is a major consumer of water resources.

Integration with Other Technologies: Smart irrigation systems can be integrated with other agricultural technologies, such as precision farming tools and automation systems. This integration enhances overall farm management and creates a more connected and efficient agricultural ecosystem.

Challenges and Limitations of Smart Irrigation System Using IoT

Dependency on Connectivity: Smart irrigation systems rely heavily on stable and continuous internet connectivity. In areas with poor network coverage or frequent outages. The effectiveness of these systems can be compromised. Leading to delayed or inaccurate data transmission.

Training Requirement for Farmers: Farmers and agricultural workers may lack the technical expertise required to set up, configure and troubleshoot IoT based irrigation systems. Training programs and ongoing technical support are essential for successful implementation.

Scalability Challenges: Adapting smart irrigation systems to various agricultural contexts and scales can be challenging. The diversity of crops, soil types and climate conditions requires customizable solutions and scalability may pose logistical and technological challenges.

Maintenance and Upkeep: Regular maintenance is essential for the proper functioning of IoT devices. Sensors may degrade over time and software updates. So they required to address emerging issues or improve system efficiency.

4.5.3 IoT for Livestock Monitoring

IoT solutions and smart devices are making considerable transformations in sectors like farming and livestock. When everything is connected around us via the Internet, it is nearly impossible for us to imagine life without the Internet of things.

The internet of things has changed the way the livestock industry works. The use of battery-powered sensors and smart devices has helped farmers in keeping track of their livestock without running around with them wherever they go. Livestock **monitoring using IoT** helps ranchers to keep track of their livestock in real-time. It helps in combating many problems faced in the livestock industry.

A list of problems faced by the livestock industry is as follows:

- Animals eat noxious things like plastic and fall sick.
- High animal mortality rate.
- No track of livestock if the number is significant.
- If a farm animal is lost, there is no track.

How IOT Solutions are Helpful in Livestock Monitoring Systems?

The livestock industry is huge, and therefore it is essential to keep track of livestock and other farm animals. A Livestock monitoring system is a revolutionary solution architected and developed using sensors, GPS, etc. and integrating all these with a network protocol for communication. This monitoring system helps the farmers to keep a check on their farm animals remotely. The tracker device is attached to collars and **keeps track of animal health, chewing patterns, location details, pasture management, etc.**

The Livestock monitoring system not only helps in managing farm animals but also other farm equipment. The use of sensors on livestock, where the data is sent to a central unit for monitoring, is an implementation known as Wireless Sensor Network.

How Can IOT Reduce the Spread of Lumpy Disease?

Lumpy Skin disease is a contagious viral disease that spreads among cattle through vectors like mosquitoes, flies, lice and wasps by direct contact, as also through contaminated food and water

Studies have also shown that it can spread through animal semen during artificial insemination.

The symptoms include high fever, reduced milk production, skin nodules, loss of appetite, increased nasal discharge and watery eyes.

As the early symptoms of Lumpy Disease are fever and Loss of appetite, temperature rise and rumination, which can be tracked by IoT cattle tracking devices. This can help in quarantining the cattle before spreading it to others.

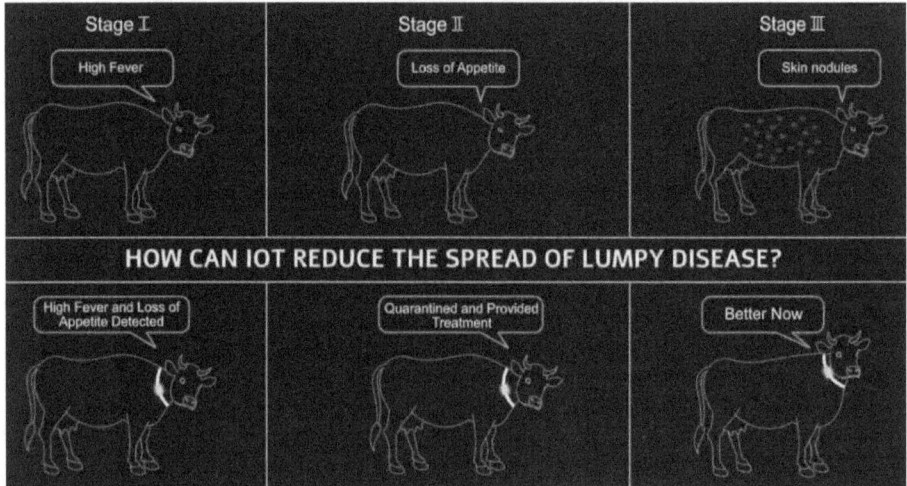

Working on an IOT-Enabled Livestock Monitoring System

The IoT-enabled livestock monitoring platform can turn out to be a boon for livestock farming. IoT-enabled livestock management solutions provide data on various aspects of cattle health. Using a wearable collar or tag, equipped with sensors, monitoring of the location, temperature, blood pressure, and heart rate of animals can be done. These Wearable IoT devices wirelessly send the data of every cattle on the farm to a central unit, called IoT Gateway.

The tracker device is made small in size and light weighted so that animals don't find it bulky over their body. The GPS tracker and sensors are integrated into the device so that the animals' movements and health can be monitored 24*7. The behavioral tracking feature of the system can help the farmers to know what their livestock are eating.

There are mobile applications and web apps or IoT Dashboards associated with the hardware. With the help of the application associated with the device, farmers can create virtual boundaries with geofencing to secure the locations where the livestock can move freely. The tracker sends alerts to the mobile application if the livestock moves beyond defined boundaries. It also sends alerts if the livestock is eating or drinking something toxic or inappropriate. This way, the farmers can save their livestock from health issues.

The system can work on LPWAN, which works everywhere, hence ensuring the proper connections. There are LPWAN protocols that are opted for according to the application.

Benefits of an IOT-Enabled Livestock Monitoring System

Farms now have huge numbers of animals making the direct interaction of staff with all the animals impossible. IoT-enabled monitoring for Livestock helps in checking on all the animals remotely and also provides information on every animal on the farm to rely on.

Key benefits of IoT Cattle tracking and monitoring system are: -

- ➢ Monitor the health and vitality of livestock in real-time, enabling farmers to quickly treat animals and prevent the spread of disease.
- ➢ To monitor grazing patterns and nutritional changes.
- ➢ Track grazing animals.
- ➢ Gather and analyze historical data to identify trends in cattle health.
- ➢ Accurate heat detection in cattle's for optimized breeding practices.
- ➢ Cloud-based integration and dashboard solutions to provide real-time information as well as historic data to vets, nutritionists etc.

4.5.4 Environment and Climate Monitoring

IoT in agriculture enables environment and climate monitoring through various sensors that gather data on soil conditions, temperature, humidity, and other factors. This data is then used to optimize irrigation, fertilizer application, and pest control, leading to improved crop yields and resource efficiency.

What can IoT do for Smart Agriculture & Smart Environment?

IoT in Agriculture:

The use of IoT in agriculture is referred to as "smart agriculture," which involves the integration of IoT technologies to improve crop yields and quality, reduce costs, and optimize resource usage. IoT sensors, drones, and autonomous vehicles are used to collect real-time data on soil moisture, temperature, and nutrient levels, as well as plant growth and animal behaviour. This data is then analysed using machine learning algorithms to provide insights into crop health and yield, enabling farmers to make informed decisions about irrigation, fertilization, and pest management.

One of the most significant benefits of IoT in agriculture is precision farming. This involves the use of real-time data to optimize crop management practices. Farmers can tailor inputs such as water, fertilizer, and pesticides to the specific needs of each crop, reducing waste and improving efficiency. For example, farmers can use soil moisture sensors to monitor moisture levels in a field and adjust irrigation accordingly. This can lead to significant water savings, as well as improved crop yield and quality.

IoT technologies are also being used to monitor animal health and welfare, providing farmers with real-time data on factors such as feed consumption, activity levels, and body temperature. This data can be used to identify health issues early and intervene before they become serious, leading to improved animal welfare and reduced veterinary costs.

In addition to improving productivity and efficiency, IoT technologies in agriculture can also help to reduce the environmental impact of farming. By optimizing inputs such as water and fertilizer, farmers can reduce the amount of waste and pollution generated by their operations. Precision farming can reduce water use by up to 30% and fertilizer use by up to 25%, while improving crop yields, according to a report by the Food and Agriculture Organization of the United Nations.

Examples of IoT in Agriculture:

One of the most notable examples of IoT in agriculture is John Deere's precision farming technology. John Deere's precision farming system uses GPS technology, sensors, and other IoT devices to provide farmers with real-time data on soil moisture, temperature, and other environmental factors.

This data is then used to optimize inputs such as water, fertilizer, and pesticides, leading to higher crop yields and quality.

Another example of IoT in agriculture is the use of drones for crop monitoring. Drones equipped with cameras and sensors can fly over fields, providing farmers with real-time data on crop health, water levels, and other factors. This data can then be used to make informed decisions about irrigation and fertilization, reducing waste and improving crop yields.

IoT in Environmental Monitoring:

IoT technologies are also being used to monitor the environment, including air quality, water quality, and weather conditions. This data can be used to inform decision-making in areas such as urban planning, disaster response, and environmental protection.

In urban areas, IoT sensors can be used to monitor air quality and noise levels, providing insights into the impact of traffic and industry on the environment and human health. In the event of a natural disaster such as a flood or earthquake, IoT sensors can be used to monitor water levels, temperature, and seismic activity, enabling authorities to respond quickly and effectively.

IoT technologies are also being used to monitor the health of ecosystems such as forests and oceans. In forests, IoT sensors can be used to monitor factors such as temperature, humidity, and soil moisture, providing insights into the health and growth of trees and other vegetation. This data can be used to inform forest management practices, such as controlling wildfires, managing pests and diseases, and reducing deforestation.

In oceans, IoT sensors can be used to monitor water quality, temperature, and acidity, providing insights into the health of marine ecosystems. This data can be used to inform policy decisions aimed at reducing pollution and protecting marine biodiversity.

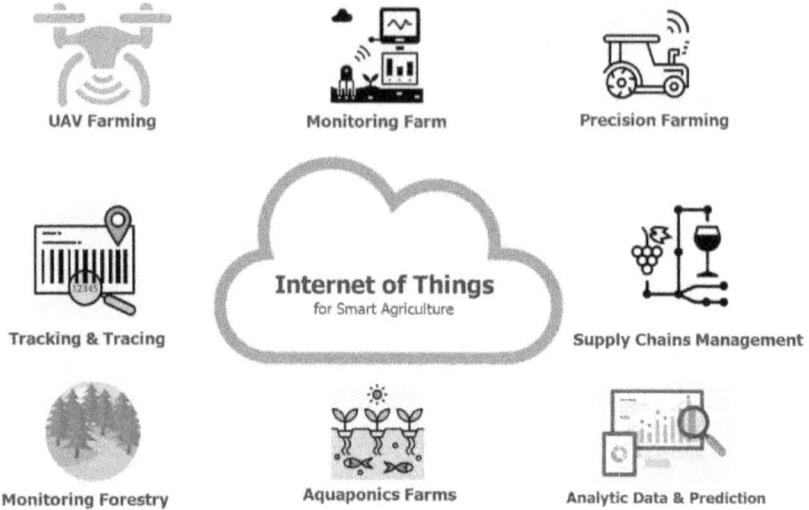

Examples of IoT in Environmental Monitoring:

One example of IoT in environmental monitoring is the CityAir app, developed by Imperial College London. The app uses IoT sensors to monitor air quality in London, providing residents with real-time information on pollution levels in their area. The app also provides recommendations on how to reduce exposure to pollutants and improve air quality.

Another example of IoT in environmental monitoring is the use of underwater drones to monitor coral reefs. The drones are equipped with sensors that can monitor factors such as water temperature, acidity, and clarity, providing insights into the health of coral reefs. This data can be used to inform conservation efforts aimed at protecting these fragile ecosystems.

4.6 IoT in Retail

4.6.1 Inventory Management with IoT

Inventory management is a critical function for businesses in manufacturing, retail, logistics, and warehousing. Traditional inventory tracking methods are prone to human errors, inefficiencies, and delays. The integration of **IoT (Internet of Things)** in inventory management revolutionizes how businesses monitor, track, and control their stock in real-time, leading to improved efficiency, cost reduction, and better decision-making.

The Role of IoT in Inventory Management

Now, let's talk inventory management. Inventory management is the process of overseeing stock levels to ensure product availability and minimize storage costs. Traditionally, it's performed manually and involves physical counts and barcode scanning, which are prone to errors and inefficiencies. For anyone who's ever tried to keep track of products in a warehouse or a store in a traditional way, you know it can be a logistical nightmare.

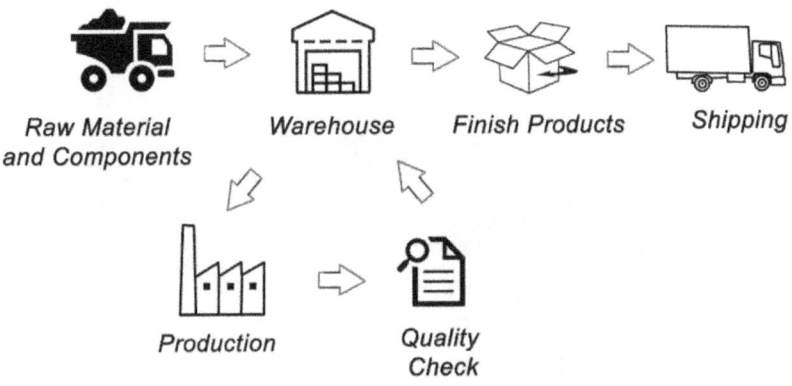

So, how is IoT used in inventory management, and what perks does it offer? By embedding sensors in products, smart shelves, and placing cameras throughout a warehouse, IoT easily integrates with inventory management systems. These inventory sensors continuously collect data on:

Location: Monitor the inventory movements across the entire supply chain.

Quantity: Maintain accurate stock levels to prevent stockouts and overstocking.

Condition: Monitor temperature, humidity, or other environmental factors for items that are perishable or require delicate handling.

The information collected on goods is then sent to a central system, where it's processed and used to make decisions.

Key IoT Technologies in Inventory Management

As you could guess, an IoT management system consists of several components that make the whole thing run. Here's an overview of IoT technology in inventory management and its major elements:

RFID Tags

RFID (Radio Frequency Identification) tags are tiny stickers with radio waves that act like unique digital codes for your inventory. They contain a microchip and antenna to be able to communicate with RFID readers, which are usually placed throughout a warehouse or store. When the tagged item passes by a reader, the reader picks up the unique code from the tag and updates the smart inventory system with the item's location and status. You have an up-to-the-minute overview of your entire inventory at the click of a button.

Smart Sensors

Sensors can be described as the eyes and ears of the IoT inventory management system due to the function they perform. They monitor and report on the warehouse's environmental conditions (temperature, humidity levels, light exposure, pressure, vibration, etc.) to help keep inventory safe and in good condition. Let's suggest you're running a warehouse storing perishable goods. A sudden spike in temperature could spoil an entire batch before anyone notices. But with smart sensors in place, you'll receive instant alerts if conditions deviate from the acceptable range so you can take immediate action. While considering implementing these technologies, it's crucial to understand the cost of IoT sensors, as this investment can significantly impact your overall budget.

GPS and Beacon Technology

GPS technology, familiar to anyone who's used a smartphone to find directions, can also be applied within large-scale smart inventory management. You may argue that the GPS signal is weak indoors and, therefore, not reliable for tracking inventory within a warehouse. Yet, when combined with a beacon technology, it creates a powerful hybrid solution. Beacons are compact transmitters that use low-energy Bluetooth signals to talk to nearby devices. As items equipped with GPS and beacon receivers move through the warehouse, their exact locations can be easily tracked. Just imagine how much time and cost savings you can achieve when you know exactly where each item is positioned.

Challenges and Considerations of IoT Implementation

IoT inventory management facilitates a number of operations simply by delivering sufficient information on inventory levels. Outdated systems replaced with IoT devices improve your tracking capabilities, item traceability, and quality control. Yet, the way to these benefits is filled with certain challenges that companies should be aware of to overcome them with confidence.

CHALLENGES AND CONSIDERATIONS OF IOT IMPLEMENTATION

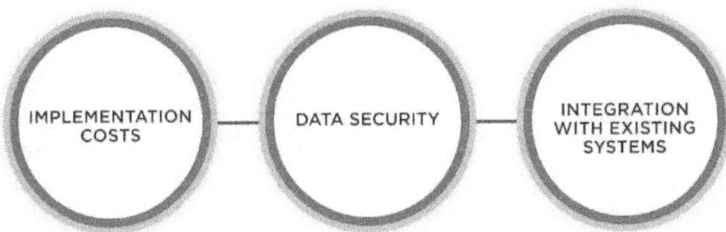

Implementation Costs

Internet of Things adoption is a substantial investment that requires careful budgeting. The initial costs can be hefty, as you need to purchase sensors and devices and perhaps upgrade your infrastructure to support the increased data flow. Software platforms, staff training, and potential new hires with the necessary expertise can also add to the expenses. The upfront investment is indeed high, but the ROI from improved supply chain efficiency and better decision-making will pay off the initial expenditure.

Data Security

IoT devices generate vast amounts of data, much of which is sensitive and, therefore, requires even stronger protection. Each implemented sensor, and the device is a point of data transmission that hackers may exploit. Securing the IoT system may sound like a very difficult task, yet it is not insurmountable. What you need is to follow some best security practices:

Data encryption. Ensure all data transmission and storage are encrypted to safeguard sensitive information from unauthorized access.

Device security. Implement robust security protocols on your IoT devices to prevent hacking and malware attacks.

Access control. Establish clear access control measures to restrict who can access and modify data within the system.

If you are not sure about the level of your system protection, turn to relevant cybersecurity specialists to help you boost security.

4.6.2 Strategies to Enhance Customer Experience Through IoT

Enable Proactive Monitoring and Instant Alerts

IoT enables enterprise-wide monitoring of operations, products, and services so that companies can stay informed and address any customer-impacting issues proactively.

For instance, sensors embedded in manufacturing equipment can continuously transmit performance data over the IoT network. Analytics dashboards analyze this data to detect early warning signs of potential malfunctions. Technicians are instantly alerted to conduct preventive maintenance before an actual breakdown happens. This minimizes disruptions to production and enables meeting customer delivery timelines consistently.

In supply chain logistics, IoT tracking devices attached to shipped goods relay location, condition, speed, and other metrics in real-time to logistics control centers. Shipments falling behind scheduled routes are instantly flagged. Transporters can accordingly optimize routes on the fly to avoid delays that affect client supply chains negatively. Customers also get automated status alerts on the expected delivery time for their packages rather than anxiously tracking them manually. Such IoT-enabled supply chain visibility offers peace of mind.

As another real-time example, wearable medical devices with sensors allow healthcare providers to monitor at-risk patients remotely 24/7. Vital health parameters like heart rate, blood pressure, respiratory rate, etc., can be continuously tracked to enable timely medical interventions instead of the patient visiting hospitals frequently for routine checks. This improves clinical outcomes, recovery, and overall well-being for the patient while saving avoidable hospitalization costs.

Facilitate Self-Service Options

IoT-enabled smart devices automate tasks that previously required human assistance. For example, ATMs connected to the IoT network can self-diagnose technical glitches like being out of cash, jammed card input slots, etc., and directly send alerts to the bank's service team to dispatch personnel to fix the issues. The ATM can even order cash replenishment autonomously when the currency chest is nearly empty.

Airport self-service kiosks allow passengers to print boarding passes and baggage tags without waiting in long check-in queues. Retail chains are implementing IoT-powered self-checkout stations for faster billing. Smart vending machines can handle the entire purchase journey, from order placement to digital payments and contactless product delivery.

Such self-service functionality provides consumers with more flexibility and control over their experience. Moreover, the user data collected via IoT-connected self-service channels provides companies with valuable insights to improve operations. IoT integration's automation and personalization potential empowers customers and redefines service delivery across industries.

Leverage Predictive Maintenance Capabilities

IoT-driven digital transformation facilitates gathering product usage data from sensors installed at customer locations or embedded inside offerings. For example, automobile companies get real-time driving pattern data and diagnostic trouble codes from connected cars that help them forecast demand for spare parts. Production and inventory at regional warehouses can accordingly be optimized to avoid stockouts.

Industrial equipment manufacturers leverage IoT sensor data about operating temperatures, pressures, vibrations, etc., to schedule predictive maintenance on customer assets before issues arise. This proactive service approach increases uptime and lifespan for customers, avoiding disruptions to their operations and ensuing revenue losses. It also makes servicing more cost-effective for manufacturers than traditional reactive break-fix maintenance.

Home appliance companies get performance data from IoT-enabled refrigerators, washers, etc., to detect emerging problems while still under warranty and arrange timely repairs. This prevents avoidable malfunctions later and improves customer longevity, safety, and efficiency rather than just reacting post-failure. The preventive insights facilitated by IoT integration enable a greater ownership experience.

Develop Immersive Smart Environments

IoT digital transformation allows businesses to create 'smart' environments tailored to users' habits and needs. For example, an office workspace can have IoT-enabled HVAC, lighting, and other systems that automatically adjust ambient conditions based on the employee's comfort preferences logged over time. Smart street lighting can optimize intensity based on real-time traffic and pedestrian volumes to balance visibility, ambiance, and energy efficiency.

Hotels can store a guest's room settings, like temperature, lighting, TV channels, etc., from previous stays to automatically orchestrate their preferred ambiance once they check in again. Shopping malls have cameras, Bluetooth beacons, and other sensors continuously tracking customer movements across stores anonymously. Digital signage then provides personalized promotions to shoppers based on real-time heatmaps.

Smart headphones may monitor biometrics like the listener's heartbeat rhythms to curate suitable music selections for a more immersive audio experience. Driverless cars collect inputs from an array of LiDAR, radar, and other sensors to dynamically assess driving hazards and take over control when needed to prevent accidents. The hyper-personalized, intelligent, and predictive environments enabled by IoT integration take customer experiences to the next level.

Reimagine Interactive Engagement

Digital transformation with IoT allows brands to reinvent customer engagement across the lifecycle more experientially. For example, fashion retail stores can implement smart changing rooms with interactive mirrors, letting shoppers request alternate apparel sizes or colors from in-store assistants without repeatedly stepping out.

Quick-service restaurants may have tables embedded with tablets enabling customers to self-order food, play games, stream video content, and even have the tabletop projector display visual menus. Sports stadiums have thousands of IoT motion and noise sensors networked to monitor crowd density across seating zones in real-time. Ushers are empowered with mobile apps to guide fans to vacant seats efficiently.

Cosmetics brands can develop virtual try-on apps powered by augmented reality to overlay products on shoppers' faces after scanning their skin tone. The app suggests the best-matched foundation shades to try. Connected packaging tracks consumer usage patterns enabling replenishment deliveries right before emptying products. The immersive and personalized engagement possible via creative IoT applications serves to build customer relationships for life.

Additional IoT Transformation Strategies to Further Enhance Customer Experience

Apply Advanced Analytics for Deeper Insights

IoT generates enormous amounts of temporally and spatially rich data about equipment performance, operational processes, customer usage patterns, and environmental conditions. Big data analytics techniques like machine learning can help derive deeper insights from the data.

Predictive analytics on machine sensor data can forecast asset degradation ahead of failure. Prescriptive analytics can even recommend optimal maintenance policies. This enhances asset utilization and uptime.

Adopt Robotic Process Automation

Robotic Process Automation (RPA) tools can be integrated with IoT networks to automate repetitive administrative tasks across operations like processing transactions, updating records, generating invoices, etc.

RPA bots continuously pull and analyze data from IoT-enabled assets and systems. Based on programmed rules, they can autonomously trigger appropriate actions like placing service requests, adjusting inventory orders, updating customer records, etc.

By automating high-volume routine tasks, RPA allows human staff to focus on higher-value creative work like product innovation and customer service enhancement.

Prioritize Cybersecurity and Privacy

With the exponential increase in attack vectors due to billions of connected devices, cybersecurity is a key concern in IoT transformation implementations. Neglecting security can endanger customer safety and trust. A prudent security-by-design approach is essential right from the product design phase. Regular firmware updates and patches will enhance device-level security throughout the product lifecycle.

Encrypting IoT data communications through protocols like SSL/TLS safeguards privacy. Strict access controls must govern data usage. Customers should have options to delete their data or opt out of tracking. Transparent privacy policies and compliance audits build confidence.Blockchain-based distributed ledgers can provide immutable audit trails of all IoT data exchanges to enable forensic analyses in case of breaches. IoT security should be an enterprise imperative rather than an afterthought.

Cultivate a Data-Driven Culture

Deriving customer and business value from IoT transformation requires building organizational capabilities like data engineering, analytics, automation, and security. Upskilling workforces via training in digital and analytical competencies is key.Creating cross-functional teams, including engineering, IT, design, and business roles, facilitates creative IoT solutions to enhance customer experiences across touchpoints.

Instilling an agile, experimental, and data-driven culture enables continuous innovation. Collaboration with external partners like startups and academia also catalyzes IoT innovation.Executive leadership should actively evangelize and incentivize the adoption of IoT capabilities for managing human capital. Nurturing appropriate organizational culture and talent is vital to harness the full potential of IoT.

4.7 IoT in Energy Management

4.7.1 Smart Grids and Energy Distribution

A smart grid is a digitally enabled electrical grid that collects, distributes and works on the information about the behaviour of all suppliers and consumers in order to improve the efficiency, reliability and sustainability of electricity service.

Smart Grid = Information Technology + Electrical Grid

The smart grid uses a two-way digital communication of technologies and computer processing which enables electricity industry to better manage energy delivery and transmission. It is capable of providing real time information and enable the nearby quick balancing of supply and demand.

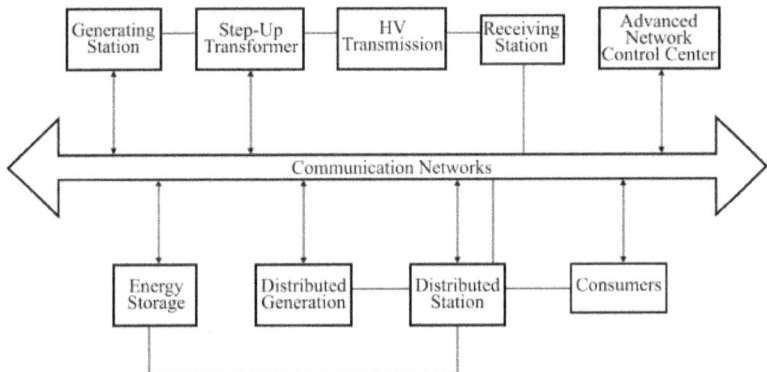

How does a Smart Grid Work?

In addition to the traditional grid's generating facilities and transmission network the smart grid consists of three new components

- ➤ Smart control and measuring devices
- ➤ Digital communication systems
- ➤ Computer software programs

The smart devices include computer controlled generators and other power sources as well as meters, monitors and intelligent electronic devices that gather information about the demand for power, its availability from various sources, the delivery capacity of each part of the grid and the flow of power throughout the system. The computer software programs for the grid help to determine electricity efficiency and monitor the electrical functions of generators and consumers.

The digital communication and control is what makes the grid smart. Sensors that monitor and report conditions on the grid enable switches and other controls to respond instantly. Real time information permits system operators to predict, diagnose and reduce issues that have caused interruptions or serious power disturbances. With smart grid technologies end users have more control over their energy consumption and cost.

IoT applications in smart energy

1. Grid monitoring and management: **IoT facilitates real-time monitoring of the entire grid infrastructure.** Sensors deployed across substations and transmission lines capture data on voltage, current, and other vital

parameters. This data is transmitted in real-time, enabling utilities to monitor grid health, detect abnormalities, and proactively address potential issues.

2. Demand response optimization: IoT-enabled smart grids empower utilities to implement demand response programs efficiently. By integrating smart meters and IoT devices in homes and businesses, utilities can remotely manage and optimize energy consumption during peak hours, reducing strain on the grid and minimizing the need for costly infrastructure upgrades; see IoT in energy management.

3. Distributed energy resources integration: Smart grids leverage IoT to seamlessly integrate renewable energy sources, energy storage systems, and electric vehicles. This integration allows for efficient management of distributed energy resources, optimizing their contribution to the grid and ensuring a smoother transition to a cleaner, more sustainable energy ecosystem.

4.Predictivemaintenance: **IoT sensors** play a crucial role in predictive maintenance, offering real-time insights into the condition of grid components. By continuously monitoring equipment health, utilities can identify potential failures before they occur, reducing downtime, lowering maintenance costs, and improving overall grid reliability.

Smart Grid Characteristics

A Smart Grid would have the following fundamental characteristics −

Optimised Operation of the System − A smart grid allows consumers to play a part in optimising the operation of the system and provides consumers with greater information and choice of supply.

Enables Demand Response and Demand-Side Management − The smart grid enables demand response and demand-side management through the integration of smart meters, smart appliances and consumer loads, micro-generation and electricity storage and by providing consumers with information related energy use and price.

Reduces the Environmental Impacts − The smart grid facilitates the connection and operation of generators of all sizes and technologies and accommodates intermittent generation and storage options. It accommodates and facilitates all renewable energy sources, distributed generation, residential micro-generation and storage options, thus significantly reducing the environmental impact of the whole electricity supply system. It also provide simplified interconnection just like *'plug-and-play'*.

Optimised and Efficient use of Assets – The smart grid optimises and efficiently operates assets by intelligent operation of the delivery system and pursuing efficient asset management. This includes utilising assets depending on what is needed and when it is needed.

Improves Reliability and Security of Supply – The smart grid operates resiliently in disasters, physical or cyber-attacks and delivers enhanced levels of reliability and security of supplying energy. It assures and improves reliability and security of supply by anticipating and responding in a self-healing manner and strengthening the security of supply through enhanced transfer capabilities.

4.7.2 Renewable Energy Integration

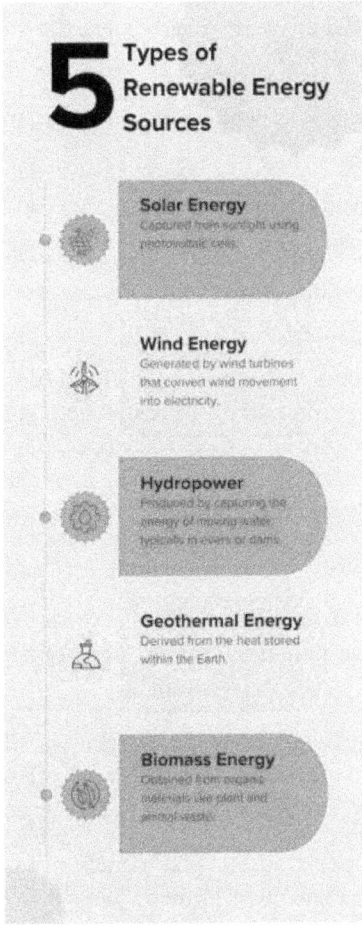

Definition of Renewable Energy Sources

Renewable energy comes from natural processes that are continuously replenished. Unlike fossil fuels, which are finite and contribute to environmental pollution, renewable energy sources are sustainable and have minimal environmental impact.

Common examples of renewable energy sources include:

- **Solar Energy:** Captured from sunlight using photovoltaic cells.
- **Wind Energy:** Generated by wind turbines that convert wind movement into electricity.
- **Hydropower:** Produced by capturing the energy of moving water, typically in rivers or dams.
- **Geothermal Energy:** Derived from the heat stored within the Earth.
- **Biomass Energy:** Obtained from organic materials like plant and animal waste.

Solar Energy in day today life:

Solar energy is one of the most accessible and widely adopted forms of renewable energy for residential use. Here's a closer look at how solar panels work and their benefits:

How Solar Panels Work: Solar panels, also known as photovoltaic (PV) panels, consist of numerous solar cells made from semiconductor materials like silicon. When sunlight hits these cells, it excites electrons, creating an electric current. This direct current (DC) is then converted to alternating current (AC) by an inverter, making it usable for home appliances.

Benefits of Solar Energy:

- **Environmental Impact:** Solar energy is clean and produces no greenhouse gas emissions during operation, significantly reducing the household's carbon footprint.
- **Cost Savings:** By generating their own electricity, homeowners can reduce or even eliminate their utility bills. Excess energy can often be sold back to the grid in a process known as net metering.
- **Energy Independence:** Solar panels provide a level of energy independence, protecting homeowners from rising electricity costs and power outages.

- **Incentives and Rebates:** Many governments offer incentives, tax credits, and rebates to encourage the installation of solar panels, making them more affordable.

INTERNET OF THINGS

CHAPTER 5

INDEX

IOT DATA ANALYTICS AND AI

5.1 IoT Data Analytics 293
    5.1.1 Data Processing in IoT Systems 293
    5.1.2 Real time vs Batch analytics 295
    5.1.3 IoT Visualization Tools 296
    5.1.4 Use of AI in IoT Analytics 300
5.2 Machine Learning in IoT 305
    5.2.1 Predictive Models in IoT 305
    5.2.2 Anomaly Detection 307
    5.2.3 Machine learning algorithm for iot applications 311
    5.2.4 Deploying ML models on IoT devices 317
5.3 Bigdata and IoT: 319
    5.3.1 Big data characteristics in IoT 319
    5.3.2 Storage and processing of IoT bigdata 322
    5.3.3 Hadoop, Spark and IoT 327
    5.3.4 Challenges in Big Data Management for IoT: 333
5.4 Digital Twins 337
    5.4.1 Concept of Digital Twins 337
    5.4.2 Implementing digital twins in iot systems: 342
    5.4.3 Applications of Digital Twins 348
    5.4.4 Future Trends in Digital Twin Technology 351

5.5 Federated Learning in IoT 354
    5.5.1 Privacy-Preserving AI Models 354
    5.5.2 Distributed System and IoT Devices... 356
5.6 Natural Language Processing (NLP) in IoT 360
    5.6.1 Natural Language Processing's Role in Advancing IoT
    Applications 360
    5.6.2 Natural Language Processing apply to IoT................................... 363

CHAPTER 5:

IOT DATA ANALYTICS AND AI

5.1 IoT Data Analytics

5.1.1 Data Processing in IoT Systems

The Internet of Things (IoT) refers to a network of physical devices interconnected through the internet, enabling them to collect, exchange, and process data. These devices range from sensors, wearables, smart home appliances, and industrial machines. With the rapid growth of IoT, the amount of data being generated is enormous, creating a need for efficient data processing methods. Data processing in IoT systems refers to the techniques and technologies used to analyze, store, and interpret data collected by IoT devices to extract meaningful insights. The complexity of IoT systems comes from the sheer volume, variety, and velocity of data produced. Real-time data processing, edge computing, and cloud computing are common strategies employed to manage and process the data effectively.

Types of Data Processing in IoT

Real-Time Data Processing

Real-time data processing involves the immediate analysis of data as it is generated. This type of processing is essential for IoT systems that require instant actions based on the data collected, such as in autonomous vehicles, smart cities, or industrial automation.

Example: A smart thermostat adjusting the temperature based on real-time environmental data.

Batch Data Processing

In batch processing, data is collected and stored temporarily before being processed in chunks. It is not time-sensitive and can be processed in intervals. This is often used for data that does not require immediate attention, such as historical analysis or periodic reporting.

Example: A weather monitoring system processing data collected over the past week to predict trends.

Edge Computing

Edge computing involves processing data at or near the data source (i.e., at the "edge" of the network) rather than sending all the data to a central server. This reduces latency, saves bandwidth, and allows for faster decision-making.

Example: A smart security camera processing video feeds locally to detect motion or unusual activities before sending relevant data to the cloud.

Cloud Computing

Cloud computing processes and stores IoT data on remote servers, providing virtually unlimited storage and computational resources. Data can be analyzed in the cloud for complex analytics, long-term storage, and large-scale integration.

Example: A smart health-monitoring system sending patient data to the cloud for analysis by doctors or medical AI algorithms.

Examples of Data Processing Applications in IoT Systems

Smart Homes: IoT devices in smart homes collect data on energy usage, room temperatures, lighting conditions, and occupancy. Data processing allows these systems to optimize energy usage, improve comfort, and enhance security.

Wearables: Smartwatches and fitness trackers continuously collect health-related data, such as heart rate, step count, and sleep patterns. Data processing in these devices allows users to track their health and make lifestyle improvements.

Industrial IoT (IIoT): Sensors in manufacturing plants and factories collect data on machine performance, temperature, humidity, and other parameters. Real-time processing can help detect faults, predict maintenance needs, and optimize production efficiency.

Smart Cities: IoT systems in cities monitor traffic, pollution levels, weather conditions, and public services. Data processing enables city management systems to optimize traffic flow, waste collection, energy usage, and public safety.

5.1.2 Real time vs Batch analytics

In the realm of IoT data analytics, both real-time and batch analytics play distinct roles. Real-time analytics focuses on immediate data analysis, enabling rapid decision-making and action, while batch analytics processes data in larger, delayed batches, often for in-depth analysis and historical trends. The choice between the two depends on the specific needs of the application, including data freshness requirements, cost considerations, and the type of insights needed.

Real-time analytics is crucial for applications demanding swift responses, such as:

- **IoT device monitoring:** Detecting anomalies and failures in real-time to prevent downtime.
- **Predictive maintenance:** Forecasting equipment failures based on real-time sensor data.
- **Supply chain optimization:** Tracking shipments and optimizing logistics in real-time.
- **Smart city management:** Monitoring traffic flow, resource consumption, and public safety.

Batch analytics, on the other hand, excels in:

- **Historical trend analysis:** Uncovering long-term patterns and insights from accumulated data.
- **Data warehousing and reporting:** Storing and querying large datasets for business intelligence.
- **Deep dive analysis:** Performing complex statistical analysis on large datasets.
- **Cost optimization:** Processing large datasets efficiently, saving on infrastructure costs.

Key Differences:

Feature	Real-Time Analytics	Batch Analytics
Data Freshness	Highly fresh, near instantaneous	Delayed, processed in batches
Processing Speed	Fast, immediate	Slower, batch-oriented
Resource Requirements	May require more resources for real-time processing	Can be more resource-efficient for large datasets
Use Cases	Time-sensitive decisions, real-time monitoring	Historical analysis, deep dive analysis

Real-time analytics provides immediate insights for proactive decision-making, while batch analytics offers in-depth analysis of historical data for strategic insights. The optimal approach depends on the specific application and the desired balance between speed, accuracy, and cost-effectiveness.

5.1.3 IoT Visualization Tools

The process of converting vast volumes of IoT data into graphical displays such as dashboards, graphs, charts, and maps is known as IoT visualization. Through IoT visualization, stakeholders can monitor system performance, identify abnormalities, gain insightful information, and make data-driven decisions. This article aims to explore the need for IoT visualization, the tools and techniques used, as well as its applications

Need for IoT Visualization

Data visualization plays a crucial role in the field of IoT (Internet of Things) for several reasons:

Understanding Complex Data: IoT systems generate large volumes of data from various sources such as sensors, devices, and networks. Visualization helps in understanding this complex data by providing insights and patterns that might not be apparent from raw data.

Real-Time Monitoring: IoT applications often require real-time monitoring of data streams. Visualization dashboards allow users to monitor multiple parameters simultaneously and quickly identify any anomalies or trends.

Decision Making: Visual representation of IoT data enables stakeholders to make informed decisions quickly. Whether it's optimizing operations, predicting maintenance needs, or improving efficiency, visualization aids in interpreting data for better decision-making.

Identifying Patterns and Trends: Visualization tools allow users to identify patterns, trends, and correlations within IoT data. This can be valuable for predictive analytics, anomaly detection, and forecasting.

Communication: Visualization provides a common language for communicating insights and findings across different teams within an organization. It helps bridge the gap between technical and non-technical stakeholders by presenting information in an intuitive and accessible format.

User Engagement: Interactive visualizations engage users more effectively than static reports or spreadsheets. They empower users to explore data, drill down into details, and gain deeper insights, leading to better engagement and understanding.

Resource Optimization: By visualizing IoT data related to resource usage, such as energy consumption, water usage, or equipment utilization, organizations can identify inefficiencies and opportunities for optimization, leading to cost savings and sustainability benefits.

Data Sources for IoT Visualization

IoT data comes from many different sources, and for successful visualization, it is important to understand these sources:

Sensors and Devices: Internet of Things (IoT) sensors and devices record a variety of data, such as temperature, humidity, pressure, speed, and location. These sensors are incorporated into many different products, including wearable technology, industrial gear, and smart home appliances.

Network Data: Data on connectivity, signal strength, data transfer speeds, and network performance are produced by the Internet of Things networks. By making this data visually appealing, network performance may be improved and any bottlenecks or poor coverage regions can be found.

Cloud Platforms: To store and analyze data, cloud platforms are used in many Internet of Things implementations. Users may analyze and visualize data in real time using visualization tools coupled with cloud platforms, giving them a thorough understanding of device performance and data patterns.

Data Streams: Real-time streams of IoT data are often delivered, and seeing this data as it happens may provide quick insights. Live dashboards, for instance, may show current numbers, notify users of abnormalities, and facilitate quick decision-making.

IoT Visualization Techniques

Various visualization methods are commonly used to analyze and understand Internet of Things (IoT) data. Here are some examples:

Time Series Visualization: This involves using heatmaps, line charts, and area charts to analyze data patterns over time. For example, a line chart can be used to track temperature changes over time to identify trends or anomalies.

Geospatial Visualization: Geospatial visualization involves plotting IoT data on maps to gain location-based insights. Tools such as GIS mapping, choropleth maps, and heatmaps can be used to visualize network coverage, device density, and data distribution across different locations.

Dashboard Creation: Dashboards provide a consolidated view for monitoring important metrics and key performance indicators (KPIs). They combine multiple visualizations into a single screen, making it easier to monitor IoT data and make informed decisions.

Interactive Visualization: Adding interactivity to IoT data visualization allows users to explore the data in more detail. Features like drill-down capabilities, filtering options, and hover-over insights enable users to uncover hidden patterns or correlations.

Effective IoT visualization requires a thorough understanding of the data sources, the environment in which they are generated, and the specific insights that need to be derived. By selecting the right visualization approaches and tools, organizations can maximize the potential of their IoT data and achieve increased operational efficiency, creative problem-solving, and enhanced decision-making capabilities.

Popular Tools for IoT Data Visualization

Tableau: A widely used data visualization tool that provides extensive features for IoT data visualization, including interactive dashboards and maps.

Power BI: Comprehensive analytics and data visualization capabilities are offered by Microsoft Power BI, which integrates seamlessly with other Microsoft products and services.

ThingSpeak: ThingSpeak is an IoT analytics platform that lets users gather, view, and evaluate data in real time from sensors and devices.

InfluxDB: An open-source time series database called InfluxDB has data visualization capabilities integrated right in, made especially for real-time and Internet of Things data.

Grafana: A robust analytics and visualization platform with configurable dashboards that works with a variety of data sources, including Internet of Things devices.

Applications of IoT Visualization

Applications for IoT visualization are many and span several industries:

Smart Cities: By analyzing data from linked sensors and devices across the city infrastructure, visualization can assist city administrators and planners in bettering waste management, understanding traffic flow, and enhancing municipal services.

Industrial Internet of Things (IoT): IoT visualization helps manufacturers monitor their production processes, spot bottlenecks, and maximize productivity. Predictive maintenance may be made possible by visualizing sensor data on machines, which will cut down on downtime.

Healthcare: By tracking patient health, identifying abnormalities, and offering remote monitoring options, wearable technologies and medical equipment provide data that may be viewed to enhance patient care and facilitate early action.

Agriculture: Data on crop health, weather, and soil moisture is provided via Internet of Things sensors installed in farms and greenhouses. Farmers can maximize crop yields, use less water, and make data-driven choices by visualizing this data.

Retail: By analyzing consumer behavior, optimizing product placement, and improving inventory management, physical retailers may use IoT data visualization to enhance the whole shopping experience.

Smart Homes: Data visualization from smart devices may help homeowners monitor energy use, identify security breaches, and set up customized automation schedules.

Challenges and Considerations in IoT Data Visualization

Among the difficulties and factors to take into account while visualizing IoT data are:

- **Data Volume and Velocity:** Managing the pace at which IoT data is created and handling massive amounts of data may be difficult tasks that call for scalable and effective data processing solutions.

- **Security and Privacy:** It's essential to protect the security and privacy of Internet of Things data, particularly when handling sensitive data. Adequate safeguards for data must be put in place.

- **Data Quality:** Data from IoT devices might be erratic and noisy. Techniques for data cleansing and validation are required to provide accurate and trustworthy visualizations.

- **Real-Time changes:** Effective streaming and data processing skills are necessary for visualizations to manage real-time data changes.

- **Contextual Understanding:** In order to aid users in accurately interpreting the data and prevent biases or misinterpretations, visualizations should provide the data context.

5.1.4 Use of AI in IoT Analytics

IoT analytics refers to collect, process and analyze data that are generated by IoT devices. As more devices are connected in the internet, it generate a large amount of data that provides a valuable insights and provide valuable information from that particular data. IoT can be the subset of Bigdata and it consist of heterogenous streams that combined and transformed to correct information.

The Significance of Data Analytics in IoT

Data analytics is a process of analyzing unstructured data to give meaningful conclusions. Numerous of the methods and processes of data analytics are automated and algorithms designed to process raw data for humans to understand.IoT devices give large volumes of precious data that are used for multiple applications. The main goal is to use this data in a comprehensive and precise way so that it's organized, and structured into a further usable format.

A Data analytics uses methods to process large data sets of varying sizes and characteristics, it provides meaningful patterns, and extracts useful outputs from raw data.Manuallyanalyzing these large data sets is veritably time consuming, resource intensive, and expensive. Data analytics is used for saving time, energy, resources and gives precious information in the form of statistics, patterns, and trends.Organizations use this information to improve their decision-making processes, apply further effective strategies, and achieve desired outcomes.

The 7 Roles of Data Analysts in IoT

The roles of data analysts within organizations are contingent on their knowledge, skills, and expertise. Here are seven prominent roles that data analysts fulfil:

Determining Organizational Goals: A data analyst's most crucial part is helping a business define its primary organizational objectives. This original step is vital for setting a business apart, outperforming challengers, and attracting the right audience. Data analysts collaborate with staff and team members to monitor, track, gather, and analyze data, necessitating access to all available data used within the organization.

Data Mining: Data analysts gather and mine data from internet sources and company databases, conducting analysis and research. This research helps businesses understand market dynamics, current trends, competitor activities, and consumer preferences.

Data Cleaning: Data analysts play an essential part in data cleansing, a critical aspect of data preparation. Data cleansing involves correcting, identifying, and analyzing raw data, significantly improving decision making by providing accurate and precise data.

Data Analysis: Data analysts offer data entry services that include data analysis. They employ ways to efficiently explore data, excerpt relevant information, and give accurate answers to business-specific questions. Data analysts bring statistical and logical tools to the table, enhancing a business's competitive advantage.

Recognizing Patterns and Identifying Trends: Data analysts excel in recognizing trends within industries and making sense of vast datasets. Their expertise in identifying industry trends enables businesses to enhance performance, estimate strategy effectiveness, and more.

Reporting: Data analysts convert essential insights from raw data into reports that drive advancements in business operations. Reporting is vital for monitoring online business performance and safeguarding against data misuse. It serves as the primary means to measure overall business performance.

Data and System Maintenance: Data analysts also contribute to maintaining data systems and databases, ensuring data coherence, availability, and storage align with organizational requirements. Data analysts employ ways to enhance data gathering, structuring, and evaluation across various datasets.

Why is IoT data analytics important?

IoT (Internet of Things) data analytics is pivotal for several reasons:

Practicable Insights: IoT devices generate massive amounts of data from various sources. Analyzing this data allows organizations to extract precious insights and make informed decisions. By understanding patterns and trends, businesses can optimize processes, upgrade effectiveness, and enhance overall performance.

Real- Time Decision: Making IoT data analytics enables real- time processing and analysis of data aqueducts. This is particularly important in applications where quick decisions are essential, such as in industrial settings, healthcare monitoring, and smart megacity infrastructure. Real- time insights empower organizations to respond instantly to changing conditions.

Predictive Maintenance: IoT data analytics can be used to predict when equipment or devices are likely to fail. By covering and analyzing performance data, organizations can apply predictive maintenance strategies, reducing time-out and minimizing the costs associated with unanticipated failures.

Cost effectiveness Analyzing: IoT data helps identify areas for optimization and cost reduction. Whether it's streamlining operations, enhancing resource utilization, or minimizing energy consumption, data analytics plays a crucial part in achieving cost effectiveness.

Enhanced Customer Experience: In sectors like retail and healthcare, IoT data analytics can be leveraged to understand customer behavior and preferences. This information can be used to personalize services, enhance customer satisfaction, and tailor offerings to meet specific requirements.

Security and Anomaly Detection: With the increasing number of connected devices, security becomes a paramount concern. IoT data analytics can be applied to detect anomalies and possible security pitfalls. By continuously monitoring data streams, organizations can identify unusual patterns that may indicate a security breach.

Scalability and Flexibility: As IoT ecosystems grow, traditional techniques of data analysis may become inadequate. IoT data analytics platforms are designed to handle the scalability and diversity of data generated by a multitude of devices. This ensures that analytics capabilities can evolve alongside expanding IoT infrastructures.

Regulatory Compliance: In certain industries, there are regulatory demands regarding data collection, storage, and privacy. IoT data analytics platforms can help organizations adhere to these regulations by delivering tools for secure data management and compliance reporting.

Innovation and Product Development: Understanding how customers interact with IoT devices can inform the development of new products and services. Analytics on usage patterns and user feedback can guide innovation and lead to the creation of further effective and user-friendly solutions.

What can IoT analytics do?

IoT analytics can do the following:

Data Processing and Integration: Handle large volumes of data generated by IoT devices, integrating and processing different data types for meaningful insights.

- ➤ **Real-Time Decision-Making:** Give nonstop monitoring of IoT data streams, enabling immediate responses to changing conditions or events.
- ➤ **Predictive Analytics:** Forecast trends and potential issues based on historical data, facilitating visionary decision-making and preventative measures.
- ➤ **Functional Effectiveness:** Optimize processes, resource allocation, and energy usage by identifying patterns and inefficiencies in IoT-generated data.
- ➤ **Predictive conservation:** Anticipate equipment failures or maintenance requirements, reducing time-out and minimizing functional dislocations.
- ➤ **Cost Optimization:** Identify areas for cost reduction and efficiency enhancement by analyzing IoT data for resource utilization and process optimization.
- ➤ **Security and Anomaly:** Detection Monitor IoT data for irregularities and potential security pitfalls, enabling timely detection and response to cybersecurity issues.
- ➤ **Customer Perceptivity:** Analyze user behavior and preferences from IoT data to enhance customer experiences, personalize services, and tailor offerings.

- **Supply Chain Optimization:** Improve supply chain visibility and effectiveness by analyzing data from connected devices throughout the supply chain process.
- **Regulatory Compliance:** Helps organizations in adhering to data privacy and regulatory essentials by providing tools for secure data management and compliance reporting.

IoT Analytics Tools

There are several IoT analytics tools available that cater to different aspects of data processing, analysis, and visualization in the context of the **Internet of Things (IoT)**. Here are some notable ones:

- **Microsoft Azure IoT Analytics:** Description Part of the Azure IoT Suite, it offers capabilities for processing and analyzing large quantities of IoT data. It includes tools for data storage, transformation, and querying.
- **AWS IoT Analytics:** Description A service provided by Amazon Web Services (AWS), it allows users to clean, process, store, and analyze IoT data. It integrates with other AWS services for comprehensive IoT solutions.
- **IBM Watson IoT Platform:** Description Offers analytics and AI capabilities for IoT data, allowing organizations to conclude actionable insights. It includes features for real-time data analysis and predictive maintenance.
- **Google Cloud IoT Core and Cloud IoT Analytics:** Description Google Cloud offers IoT Core for device management and Cloud IoT Analytics for processing and analyzing IoT data. It integrates with other Google Cloud services for comprehensive data solutions.
- **Thing Speak:** Description An IoT analytics platform by Math Works, it allows users to collect, analyze, and visualize IoT data in real-time. It's well-suited for applications involving sensor data and monitoring. **DescriptionC3.ai** provides an IoT analytics platform that enables organizations to build and deploy AI-driven applications for various use cases, including predictive maintenance and energy management.
- **Predix(by GE Digital):** Description Predix is a platform specifically designed for industrial IoT applications. It provides tools for data analytics, machine learning, and application development in the artificial sector.
- **Ubidots:** Description Ubidots is a cloud-based IoT platform that offers analytics and visualization tools. It's designed to simplify the process of building IoT applications and dashboards.

> **Particle:** Description Particle provides an IoT platform that includes tools for device management, connectivity, and data visualization. It's suitable for IoT systems ranging from prototypes to product.
> **Kaa IoT Platform:** Description Kaa is an open-source IoT platform that offers features for data analytics, device management, and application development. It provides flexibility for customization based on specific IoT project requirements.

5.2 Machine Learning in IoT

5.2.1 Predictive Models in IoT

Predictive modelling is a process used in data science to create a mathematical model that predicts an outcome based on input data. It involves using statistical algorithms and machine learning techniques to analyze historical data and make predictions about future or unknown events. In predictive modelling, the goal is to build a model that can accurately predict the target variable (the outcome we want to predict) based on one or more input variables (features). The model is trained on a dataset that includes both the input variables and the known outcome, allowing it to learn the relationships between the input variables and the target variable. Once the model is trained, it can be used to make predictions on new data where the target variable is unknown. The accuracy of the predictions can be evaluated using various metrics, such as accuracy, precision, recall, and F1 score, depending on the nature of the problem. Predictive modelling is used in a wide range of applications, including sales forecasting, risk assessment, fraud detection, and healthcare. It can help businesses make informed decisions, optimize processes, and improve outcomes based on data-driven insights.

Applications of Predictive Modeling

The practical impact of predictive modeling across various domains are:

1. Finance

Risk Assessment: Predictive modeling helps banks and financial institutions assess the creditworthiness of individuals and businesses, making lending decisions more informed and reducing the risk of defaults.

Fraud Detection: By analyzing patterns in transactions and account activity, predictive modeling can detect fraudulent activities and prevent financial losses.

2. Healthcare

Disease Prediction: Predictive modeling can help healthcare professionals predict the likelihood of diseases such as diabetes, heart disease, and cancer in patients, allowing for early intervention and personalized treatment plans.

Resource Allocation: Hospitals and healthcare facilities can use predictive modeling to forecast patient admissions, optimize staffing levels, and ensure the availability of resources such as beds and medications.

3. Marketing and Customer Relationship Management (CRM)

Customer Segmentation: Predictive modeling enables businesses to segment customers based on their behavior, preferences, and likelihood to purchase, allowing for targeted marketing campaigns.

Churn Prediction: By analyzing customer data, predictive modeling can predict which customers are likely to churn (stop using a service or product), enabling companies to take proactive steps to retain them.

4. Supply Chain Management

Demand Forecasting: Predictive modeling helps companies forecast demand for their products, ensuring that they maintain optimal inventory levels and reduce stockouts or overstock situations.

Logistics Optimization: By analyzing historical data and external factors, predictive modeling can optimize logistics operations, such as routing, transportation modes, and warehouse locations, to improve efficiency and reduce costs.

5. Human Resources

Talent Acquisition: Predictive modeling can help HR departments identify the best candidates for job openings by analyzing resumes, past performance, and other relevant data.

Employee Retention: By analyzing factors that contribute to employee turnover, predictive modeling can help companies implement strategies to retain top talent and reduce turnover rates.

Types of Predictive Models

There are several types of predictive models, each suitable for different types of data and problems. Here are some common types of predictive models:

Linear Regression: Linear regression is used when the relationship between the dependent variable and the independent variables is linear. It is often used for predicting continuous outcomes.

Logistic Regression: Logistic regression is used when the dependent variable is binary (i.e., has two possible outcomes). It is commonly used for classification problems.

Decision Trees: Decision trees are used to create a model that predicts the value of a target variable based on several input variables. They are easy to interpret and can handle both numerical and categorical data.

Random Forests: Random forests are an ensemble learning method that uses multiple decision trees to improve the accuracy of the predictions. They are robust against overfitting and can handle large datasets with high dimensionality.

Support Vector Machines (SVM): SVMs are used for both regression and classification tasks. They work well for complex, high-dimensional datasets and can handle non-linear relationships between variables.

Neural Networks: Neural networks are a class of deep learning models inspired by the structure of the human brain. They are used for complex problems such as image recognition, natural language processing, and speech recognition.

Gradient Boosting Machines: Gradient boosting machines are another ensemble learning method that builds models sequentially, each new model correcting errors made by the previous ones. They are often used for regression and classification tasks.

Time Series Models: Time series models are used for predicting future values based on past observations. They are commonly used in finance, economics, and weather forecasting.

5.2.2 Anomaly Detection

Anomaly Detection, additionally known as outlier detection, is a technique in records analysis and machine studying that detects statistics points, activities, or observations that vary drastically from the dataset's ordinary behavior. These abnormalities may sign extreme conditions which include mistakes, flaws, or fraud. Anomaly Detection is critical in lots of fields, which includes finance for detecting fraudulent transactions, manufacturing for identifying flaws, healthcare for odd clinical conditions, and cybersecurity for detecting protection breaches or threats. The essential idea is to locate patterns or statistical factors that do not observe predicted behavior.

What is Anomaly Detection?

Recognizing odd data patterns is called anomaly detection. It discovers unexpected stuff that doesn't fit normal trends. These irregular findings often signal major troubles. Think mistakes, wrongdoing, or unauthorized access. Many fields rely on spotting anomalies. Take finance detecting fraud. Also, manufacturing finds defects. And cybersecurity uncovering breaches or harmful actions. Identifying oddities are crucial across industries. To summarize, anomaly detection is a critical aspect of hazard control, operational overall performance, patron happiness, and protection across a wide range of industries. Its significance is heightened by using the increasing volume of facts and sophistication of threats within the virtual age, making it a critical tool in the arsenal of companies in search of to keep a competitive gain and secure their operations.

What is an Anomaly?

Anomaly is the deflection from usual behaviors or patterns. In data analysis and monitoring systems, these deviations signify potential issues. Anomalies may indicate errors, irregular conditions, or security breaches. Detecting anomalies accurately allows organizations to maintain proper operations by quickly identifying potential problems.

How Does Advanced Load Balancer Help with Anomaly Detection?

Advanced load balancers can enhance anomaly detection by incorporating several features:

Traffic Checking: They constantly screen traffic examples and framework execution, empowering continuous recognition of uncommon spikes or drops in rush hour gridlock that might show expected issues or assaults.

Versatile Burden Adjusting: They use AI calculations to adjust to changing traffic designs and recognize abnormalities in view of deviations from anticipated conduct.

Rate Restricting and Choking: They can naturally choke demands from dubious sources, decreasing the effect of odd traffic and forestalling over-burdens.

Incorporation with Security Frameworks: High level burden balancers frequently coordinate with security data and occasion the board (SIEM) frameworks to correspond irregularity information with other security occasions, improving by and large danger discovery.

Traffic Examination: They break down examples and patterns continuously, assisting with recognizing designs characteristic of irregularities, for example, DDoS assaults or strange client conduct.

Computerized Reactions: They can naturally change steering strategies or scale assets because of recognized peculiarities, relieving possible effects before they heighten.

Anomaly Detection Techniques

Here are some common techniques:

Factual Techniques: Utilize measurable measures like mean, difference, and z-scores to recognize exceptions. For instance, pieces of information past a specific number of standard deviations from the mean are viewed as peculiarities.

Thickness Based Techniques: Survey information thickness to recognize inconsistencies. Strategies like DBSCAN (Thickness Based Spatial Bunching of Utilizations with Commotion) characterize focuses in low-thickness areas as anomalies.

Distance-Based Techniques: Measure the distance between information focuses to distinguish irregularities. For example, the k-closest neighbors (k-NN) calculation recognizes focuses that are a long way from their neighbors as peculiarities.

Troupe Strategies: Consolidate various inconsistency recognition methods to further develop precision. Models incorporate consolidating factual techniques with AI models.

Time-Series Examination: Utilized for consecutive information, techniques like Occasional Pattern disintegration utilizing LOESS (STL) or autoregressive models recognize peculiarities in worldly examples.

Anomaly Detection Machine Learning Techniques

Certainly, anomaly detection strategies include statistical methods, device learning (ML), and deep mastering (DL), each of which provides unique approaches to finding outliers. These techniques may be divided into three classes primarily based on the nature of the learning process: supervised, unsupervised, and semi-supervised ML anomaly detection. Let's get into the complexities of each.

Supervised Anomaly Detection

To train a version for supervised anomaly detection, a dataset classified "normal" and "anomalous" ought to be provided. This approach considers anomaly detection as a type of trouble, with the version studying to differentiate between ordinary and odd cases based on facts attributes.

Techniques and Models: Common fashions consist of decision trees, support vector machines (SVMs), and neural networks. The desired version is decided by using the dataset's complexity and the relationship between regular and anomalous information factors.

Advantages: When classified information is available, supervised approaches can be extremely effective, generating precise fashions that could distinguish between normal and atypical behavior.

Limitations: The most big problem is the requirement for a well-categorized dataset, which can be pricey or impractical to get. Furthermore, those fashions may not generalize nicely to new varieties of abnormalities that have been now not present in the schooling information.

Unsupervised Anomaly Detection

Unsupervised anomaly detection would not need categorized statistics. Instead, it believes that anomalies are unusual and distinguishable from the bulk of statistics points. These techniques try to expect the distribution of normal facts and become aware of deviations from them as anomalies.

Techniques and Models: Common techniques and fashions consist of clustering (e.g., K-means), density-based strategies (e.g., Local Outlier Factor), and dimensionality reduction (e.g., PCA). Autoencoders, a form of neural community, have additionally been used efficaciously in unsupervised environments.

Advantages: The important benefit is that it does now not require categorized information, making it more flexible and less difficult to use in many situations in which labeling isn't always achievable.

Limitations: Its performance is completely reliant on the assumption that regular and anomalous facts are sufficiently multiple to be separated without labels. It may war with datasets including anomalies that are not well-defined or too just like normal instances.

Semi-supervised Anomaly Detection

Semi-supervised anomaly detection assumes that the collection best contains classified normal statistics. The idea is to use these statistics to build a model of normality and discover deviations from that version as anomalies.

Techniques and Models: One common approach is to use a model to learn a representation of normality (e.g., a neural network trained to reconstruct normal data points accurately) and then measure deviation from this model for anomaly detection (e.g., using reconstruction error).

Advantages: This method is useful whilst anomalies are unknown or too uncommon to be correctly categorized, allowing the version to concentrate on studying normal behavior.

Limitations: If the model's normality illustration is simply too vast or too slender, it can forget anomalies or become aware of too many regular examples as anomalies. The great of the everyday samples is crucial to the achievement of this technique.

5.2.3 Machine learning algorithm for iot applications

Understanding machine learning and IoT

When the Internet of Things (IoT) and Machine Learning (ML) work together, your devices not only connect to the internet but also learn and adapt to your needs.

The Internet of Things (IoT) refers to the vast network of connected devices that gather and share data about their environment over the Internet. It's a digital universe where physical objects can "talk" to each other.

Machine Learning (ML), a type of artificial intelligence (AI), empowers computers (and IoT devices) to learn from data, identify patterns, and make predictions without explicit programming. It's a powerful data processor that effectively learns from experience and reprograms itself.

So, what makes ML and IoT a perfect pair?

IoT devices are smart sensors that capture a lot of data. For example, your fitness watch or smart ring is a complex IoT device that collects data about your daily activity. But it's the associated machine learning capabilities that make it a smart device. AI/ML algorithms process all that data to tell you how many calories you burned during your last run or how frequently you woke up last night.

When you consider that manufacturers shipped nearly a billion wearable devices in 2023, it's easy to see that this category creates vast amounts of data. All that data needs to get processed somehow, and traditional data processors aren't up to the task of analyzing and making sense of all this data. Machine learning takes care of this challenge because it scales better than any other data processing technique.

This table shows at a glance how well IoT and ML technologies work together:

Feature	Internet of Things (IoT)	Machine Learning (ML)
What it does	Connects devices and collects data	Analyzes data to uncover patterns
Data	Generates mass amounts of data for analysis	Works best when provided with large volumes of data
Intelligence	No inherent intelligence	Learns and improves over time
Applications	Smartwatches, fitness trackers, smart hearing aids, smart glasses, smart homes, connected medical devices, connected machinery	Personalization, voice detection, activity classification, natural language processing, anomaly detection

As we can see, the common thread between machine learning and IoT is data. IoT devices generate massive amounts of data, and ML algorithms thrive on this data. Machine learning for IoT uncovers insights and patterns that would be virtually impossible for humans to see.

> **ML technology is like a scientist** that gathers data (experiments), analyzes it (hypothesis testing), and draws conclusions (new

theories). The AI can learn from these conclusions to make predictions about future experiments.

> **A smart device is like a well-trained technician** recording data in an organized and defined manner and following instructions (programming) to perform a specific task (for example, changing the temperature). An IoT device can't independently deviate from its instructions or learn new tasks.

Some smart devices incorporate basic ML for limited purposes. For example, some smart hearing aids include a chip with AI/ML trained to detect certain sounds, and some security systems have built-in anomaly detection intelligence. The size and power of onboard intelligence models scale with the power capacity of the IoT device.

Generally speaking, though, an IoT device's core functionality relies on pre-programmed rules. A connection to a remote machine learning system opens doors for a much wider range of intelligent applications and adaptability for different conditions.

Since IoT devices generate massive amounts of data, machine learning is a perfectly matched technology for optimizing data handling—whether it happens at the edge or on the cloud. This synergy between IoT and ML provides numerous benefits for businesses, which we'll explore next.

The algorithms at the heart of machine learning in IoT

At their core, machine learning algorithms are super-powered pattern recognizers. ML can sift through massive amounts of data collected by IoT devices, uncovering hidden trends and relationships that would be impossible to see with the naked eye. But these algorithms come in different flavors. Each type is suited for a specific kind of task:

Supervised learning

Imagine a teacher showing a student labeled examples. This is how supervised learning works: we train the algorithm on data that's already been categorized. In the context of the Industrial Internet of Things (IIoT), categories could include "faulty machine" or "healthy machine." By analyzing these examples, the algorithm learns to identify patterns and predict what labels are appropriate for new data it's never seen before.

This type of algorithm is perfect for tasks like predictive maintenance, where IIoT sensor data can be used to predict equipment failures before they happen by recognizing patterns described by the systems.

Unsupervised learning

This is where things get interesting. Unlike supervised learning, where we feed the algorithm with both input data and the corresponding output labels, unsupervised learning takes a different approach. We do not provide pre-labeled data, so the algorithm isn't explicitly told what patterns or features to look for. Instead, it uses its own internal logic to explore the data to uncover hidden structures, relationships, or anomalies.

This capability is particularly valuable in areas like anomaly detection in IoT. For instance, an unsupervised algorithm analyzing traffic patterns in a smart city might detect unusual congestion or traffic slowdowns, which could signal an accident, road blockage, or abnormal events. Since it doesn't rely on pre-defined labels or patterns, the algorithm has the flexibility to detect novel or rare behaviors that might not be part of typical training data.

Reinforcement learning

This approach is like training a dog with treats. The algorithm interacts with its environment, receives rewards for desired actions, and learns to optimize its behavior over time. It's a powerful tool for applications like smart thermostats. By analyzing energy usage patterns and receiving positive reinforcement for reducing consumption, the thermostat can autonomously adjust temperature settings for optimal comfort and efficiency.

These are just a few examples, and you have a whole toolbox of algorithms to choose from. But what makes machine learning so powerful in IoT is its ability to handle the sheer volume and variety of data generated by connected devices. Imagine a wind farm with hundreds of sensors collecting data on wind speed, turbine performance, and weather conditions. Machine learning can analyze this data to optimize energy production, predict maintenance needs, and even forecast weather patterns.

The applications are endless. From optimizing traffic flow in smart cities to enhancing security in smart homes, machine learning is making the Internet of Things connected and intelligent.

Supervised, unsupervised, and reinforcement learning examples

Scenario	Best Algorithm	Explanation
Predictive maintenance for industrial machines	Supervised Learning (for example, Decision Trees)	Labeled data (for example, "faulty" or "healthy") allows the algorithm to predict when a machine will fail.
Energy consumption prediction in smart homes	Supervised Learning (for example, Neural Networks)	Neural networks learn from historical data (energy usage patterns) to forecast future consumption and optimize energy distribution.
Grouping similar pedestrian behaviors in a smart city system	Unsupervised Learning (for example, k-means Clustering)	Clustering helps identify groups of individuals with similar behaviors from unlabeled data (for example, travel patterns).
Anomaly detection in IoT network traffic	Unsupervised Learning (for example, Principal Component Analysis)	Detects unusual patterns in network data, identifying potential security breaches or abnormal usage without predefined categories.
Autonomous vehicle route optimization	Reinforcement Learning (for example, Q-Learning)	The algorithm learns the best routes by receiving rewards for more efficient paths, adjusting its behavior over time.
Smart thermostat energy optimization	Reinforcement Learning (for	Learns and adjusts temperature settings by receiving feedback on

Scenario	Best Algorithm	Explanation
	example, Deep Q-Networks)	energy savings and user comfort, continuously optimizing based on its environment.

Challenges (and solutions) of machine learning for IoT

As the Internet of Things continues its relentless march, integrating machine learning into IoT ecosystems offers immense potential and significant challenges. The ability of ML models to extract insights from IoT sensors could revolutionize everything from predictive maintenance to smart homes. However, a few hurdles must be overcome first.

- ➢ **Massive datasets**: IoT devices are notoriously data-hungry beasts. Given their massive data needs, cramming ML models onto small edge devices with limited computing power is effectively impossible. This restricts much of the heavy ML lifting to the cloud, which can create latency issues. Techniques like pruning, quantization, and federated learning can reduce model size and processing needs.

- ➢ **Security nightmares**: The diffuse nature of IoT networks substantially increases the attack surface for cyberattacks. ML models running on IoT devices could be reverse-engineered or poisoned with bad data. Federated learning techniques that keep training data local help mitigate exposure. IT security professionals are also exploring containerization, secure enclaves, and blockchain distribution of ML model updates.

- ➢ **Integration headaches**: IoT environments are a heterogeneous mess of devices, operating systems, network protocols, and data formats. Getting ML platforms to work robustly across this tangle is an ongoing struggle. To help wrestle IoT's diversity under control, we're seeing the rise of solutions like machine learning operations (MLOps) platforms and purpose-built ML tooling for IoT.

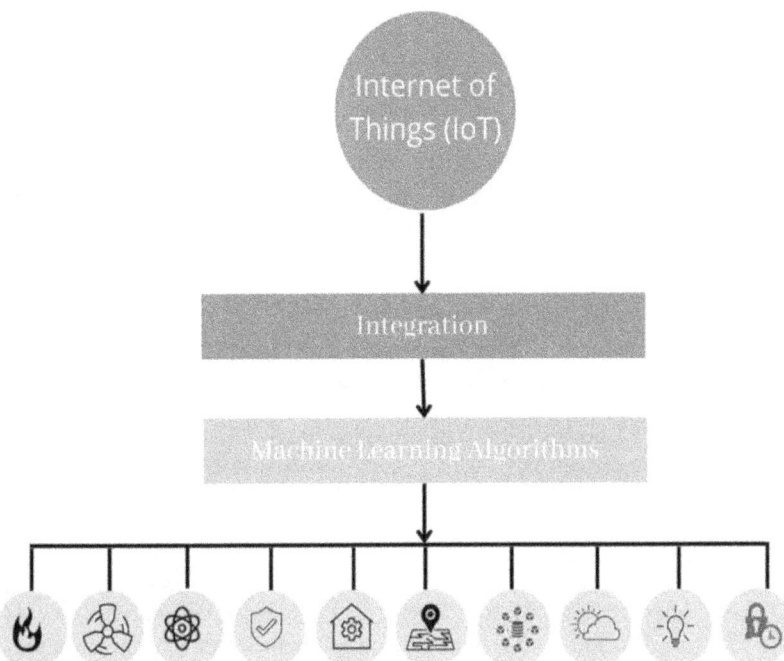

Intellias as your ML for IoT partner

The world is only going to get more connected and data-driven. As this trend continues, machine learning and the Internet of Things will continue to shape how we live, work, and interact with technology.

Intellias offers expertise in implementing machine learning IoT solutions. We tailor solutions to address specific business needs across multiple industries, including retail, financial services, healthcare, and mobility. Whether your current priority is enhanced data analysis, predictive maintenance, or improved security, we can help you explore what's possible.

5.2.4 Deploying ML models on IoT devices

Deploying ML models on IoT devices, often referred to as "Edge AI," involves running machine learning models directly on the device itself instead of relying on a central server. This approach offers benefits like reduced latency, enhanced privacy, and offline accessibility, making it ideal for real-time applications and sensitive data handling.

Here's a breakdown of key considerations for deploying ML models on IoT devices:

1. Model Optimization and Lightweight Frameworks:

- **Model Size and Complexity:** Edge devices typically have limited resources, so models need to be optimized for size and complexity. Techniques like model compression, pruning, and quantization can help reduce model size and processing requirements.

- **Lightweight Frameworks:** Frameworks like TensorFlow Lite (TFLite) and ONNX are specifically designed for edge deployments and offer efficient runtime environments.

- **Tiny Machine Learning (TinyML):** This emerging field focuses on deploying ML models on extremely resource-constrained devices, further optimizing model size and energy consumption.

2. Hardware and Software Considerations:

- **Device Selection:** Choose IoT devices that are suitable for the application and have sufficient processing power, memory, and storage capacity.

- **Operating System:** Select an appropriate operating system for the target device, considering factors like energy efficiency and compatibility with chosen frameworks.

- **Power Management:** Optimize power consumption to extend battery life, especially for battery-powered devices.

- **Communication:** Choose a communication protocol that minimizes data transmission and power consumption.

3. Deployment Strategies:

- **Cloud-based MLOps:** Platforms like AWS IoT Greengrass, Azure IoT Edge, and Google Cloud IoT Core provide tools for deploying and managing ML models on edge devices.

- **Over-the-Air (OTA) Updates:** Enable continuous model updates and improvements through OTA deployments, ensuring that models remain accurate and relevant.

4. Security and Privacy:

- **Data Encryption:** Securely transmit data between the edge device and any cloud infrastructure.

> **Access Control:** Implement appropriate access controls to protect sensitive data and models.

> **Threat Detection:** Utilize ML algorithms to identify and mitigate potential security threats.

5. Real-time Applications:

> **Edge AI for IoT:** Enables real-time analysis and decision-making on the device, reducing latency and dependence on cloud processing.

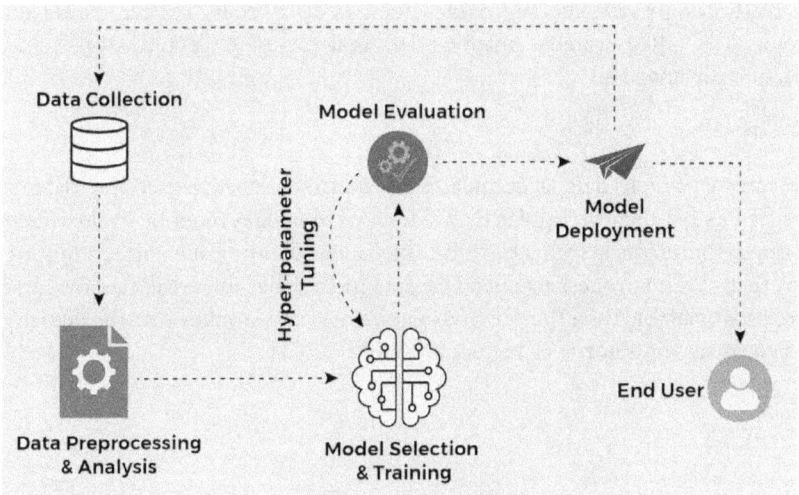

5.3 Bigdata and IoT:

5.3.1 Big data characteristics in IoT

Big data in the context of IoT is characterized by volume, velocity, variety, veracity, and value, often referred to as the 5 Vs. These characteristics describe the massive amounts of data generated by connected devices, the speed at which it's generated and processed, the diversity of data types, the accuracy and trustworthiness of the data, and the insights derived from its analysis

Volume

The prominent feature of any dataset is its size. Volume refers to the size of data generated and stored in a Big Data system. We're talking about the size of data in the petabytes and exabytes range. These massive amounts of data necessitate the use of advanced processing technology—far more powerful than a typical laptop or desktop CPU. As an example of a massive volume dataset, think about Instagram or Twitter. People spend a lot of time posting pictures, commenting, liking posts, playing games, etc. With these ever-exploding data, there is a huge potential for analysis, finding patterns, and so much more.

Variety

Variety entails the types of data that vary in format and how it is organized and ready for processing. Big names such as Facebook, Twitter, Pinterest, Google Ads, CRM systems produce data that can be collected, stored, and subsequently analyzed.

Velocity

The rate at which data accumulates also influences whether the data is classified as big data or regular data. Much of this data must be evaluated in real-time; therefore, systems must be able to handle the pace and amount of data created. The processing speed of data means that there will be more and more data available than the previous data, but it also implies that the velocity of data processing needs to be just as high.

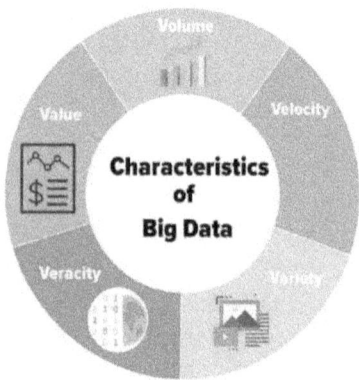

Value

Value is another major issue that is worth considering. It is not only the amount of data that we keep or process that is important. It is also data that is valuable and reliable and data that must be saved, processed, and evaluated to get insights.

Veracity

Veracity refers to the trustworthiness and quality of the data. If the data is not trustworthy and/or reliable, then the value of Big Data remains unquestionable. This is especially true when working with data that is updated in real-time. Therefore, data authenticity requires checks and balances at every level of the Big Data collecting and processing process.

What is Big Data?

Big Data, a popular term recently, has come to be defined as a large amount of data that can't be stored or processed by conventional data storage or processing equipment. Due to the massive amounts of data produced by human and machine activities, the data are so complex and expansive that they cannot be interpreted by humans nor fit into a relational database for analysis. However, when suitably evaluated using modern tools, these massive volumes of data provide organizations with useful insights that help them improve their business by making informed decisions.

Types of Big Data

As the Internet age continues to grow, we generate an incomprehensible amount of data every second. So much so that the number of data floating around the internet is estimated to reach 163 zettabytes by 2025. That's a lot of tweets, selfies, purchases, emails, blog posts, and any other piece of digital information that we can think of. These data can be classified according to the following types:

Structured data

Structured data has certain predefined organizational properties and is present in structured or tabular schema, making it easier to analyze and sort. In addition, thanks to its predefined nature, each field is discrete and can be accessed separately or jointly along with data from other fields. This makes structured data extremely valuable, making it possible to collect data from various locations in the database quickly.

Unstructured data

Unstructured data entails information with no predefined conceptual definitions and is not easily interpreted or analyzed by standard databases or data models. Unstructured data accounts for the majority of big data and comprises information such as dates, numbers, and facts. Big data examples of this type include video and audio files, mobile activity, satellite imagery, and No-SQL databases, to name a few. Photos we upload on Facebook or

Instagram and videos that we watch on YouTube or any other platform contribute to the growing pile of unstructured data.

Semi-structured data

Semi-structured data is a hybrid of structured and unstructured data. This means that it inherits a few characteristics of structured data but nonetheless contains information that fails to have a definite structure and does not conform with relational databases or formal structures of data models. For instance, JSON and XML are typical examples of semi-structured data.

5.3.2 Storage and processing of IoT bigdata

What is big data storage?

Big data storage is a scalable architecture that allows businesses to collect, manage, and analyze immense sets of data in real-time. The design of big data storage solutions is specifically tailored to address the speed, volume, and complexity of the data sets. Some examples of big data storage options are:

- **Data lakes** are centralized storage solutions that process and secure data in its native format without size limitations. They can enable different forms of smart analytics, such as machine learning and visualizations.

- **Data warehouses** aggregate data sets from different sources into a single storage unit for robust analysis, supporting data mining, artificial intelligence (AI), and more. Unlike a data lake, data warehouses have a three-tier structure for storing data.

- **Data pipelines** gather raw data and transport it into repositories, such as lakes or warehouses.

Data lakes, warehouses, and pipelines exist within several different storage options, including:

- **Cloud-based storage** system is where a business outsources the storage of its data to a vendor that operates a cloud storage system.

- **Colocation storage** is the process of a business renting space to store its servers rather than having it on-site.

- **On-premise storage** is where a business manages its network and servers on-site. This can include hardware, such as servers, that houses the data at an organization's premises.

What is big data storage used for?

The primary purpose of big data storage is to successfully store immense amounts of data for future analysis and use. Big data is crucial for businesses and organizations, from health care research to retailers and security, to make more efficient, informed, and effective decisions. Without big data storage, businesses wouldn't have the time, money, or technology to store and manage big data sets successfully.

Because big data is valuable for processing and understanding patterns and trends, it needs correct storage. Big data storage makes applying big data to business decisions possible.

How does big data storage work?

Big data storage employs a system of commodity servers and high-capacity disks capable of analyzing the data sets. For example, in a cloud storage scenario, the big data sets exist in a server hosted in an off-site location that can be accessed through the internet. Virtual machines provide the space for the data to live safely, and it's possible to quickly create more virtual machines when the amount of data grows past the servers' current capacity.

Pros and cons of using big data storage

The pros and cons of big data storage typically relate to the volume of data being handled. **Here are some advantages of using big data storage:**

- ➢ **Data-driven.** The large-scale data analysis allows businesses to become data-driven using concrete data to help make decisions and better inform strategic planning.

- ➢ **Make safe and informed decisions.** Big data storage keeps data safe and lets professionals apply analytical tools to the data sets, resulting in more informed decision-making, better customer service, more flexibility in strategic planning, and increased efficiency in operations.

- ➢ **Flexible.** Cloud-based storage is flexible and allows businesses to scale their needed servers up or down without up-front investment.

On the other hand, here are some factors to consider when using big data storage:

- ➢ **Costly.** It's expensive for a business to purchase the necessary space to store big data sets, and the cost will only increase as more data becomes available. For example, if a business opts to manage its servers on-site, it may face the risk of needing to purchase more systems and the staff to run them.

Big Data Processing:

Big data processing covers collecting, storing, and managing massive amounts of data (mostly in a semi- or unstructured form) that arrives from multiple sources. Big data processing stages include data ingestion into a data lake or a stream processing engine, data cleansing and transformation, and data loading into an analytics storage optimized for querying and reporting. Processed big data is used to derive insights (including real-time) and trigger immediate automated actions.

Key approaches: Batch processing and stream processing (also known as real-time processing, event streaming and complex event processing).

Batch processing deals with huge volumes of historical data by running parallel computations according to the defined schedule (entails latency from minutes to hours).

Stream processing deals with real-time data, which should be processed as soon as it arrives (entails latency from milliseconds to seconds).

The demand for stream processing has grown significantly in recent years due to its ability to simplify data architectures, provide real-time insights, and support use cases involving time-sensitive data like asset monitoring, personalization, clickstream, and multi-player video games.

Typical architecture modules: Data sources, a data bus, a stream processing component, a big data storage, batch processing, a data warehouse, and a big data governance component.

Popular architecture options: Lambda, Kappa.

1. **Lambda architecture**

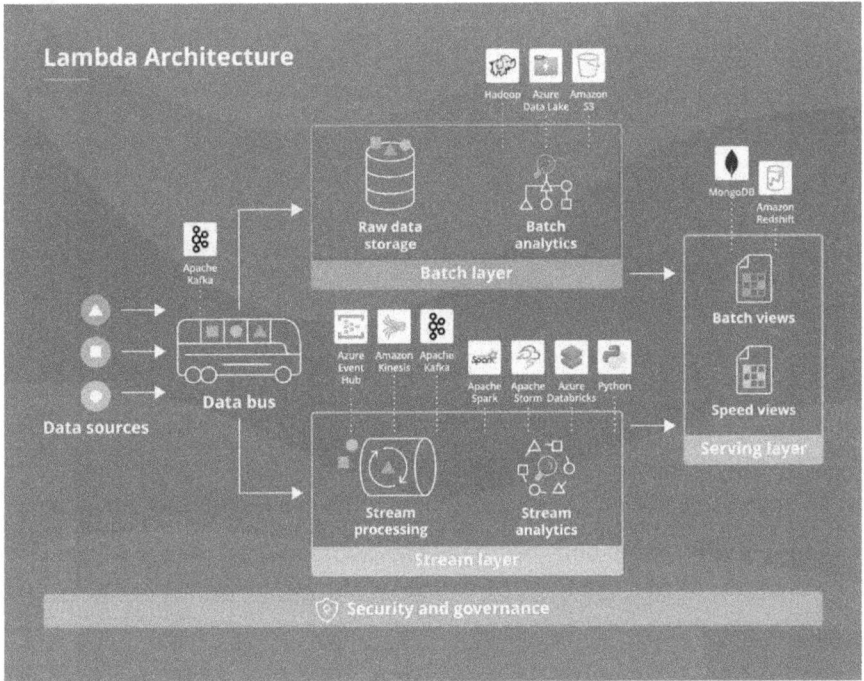

The Lambda architecture implies two separate data flows (= two technology stacks) – one for batch and the other for real-time processing. The complexity is to piece the output of these two flows together.

Pros:

> ➤ Existing ETL processes can be used as the batch layer.

> ➤ High performance.

> ➤ A low possibility of errors even if the system crashes, as a separate distributed storage will keep historical data intact.

> ➤ Fewer data streams with indefinite time-to-live, thus, cheaper PaaS and IaaS services.

> ➤ Lower development cost since there's no need to rewrite algorithms (not all algorithms can be made streaming).

2. Kappa architecture

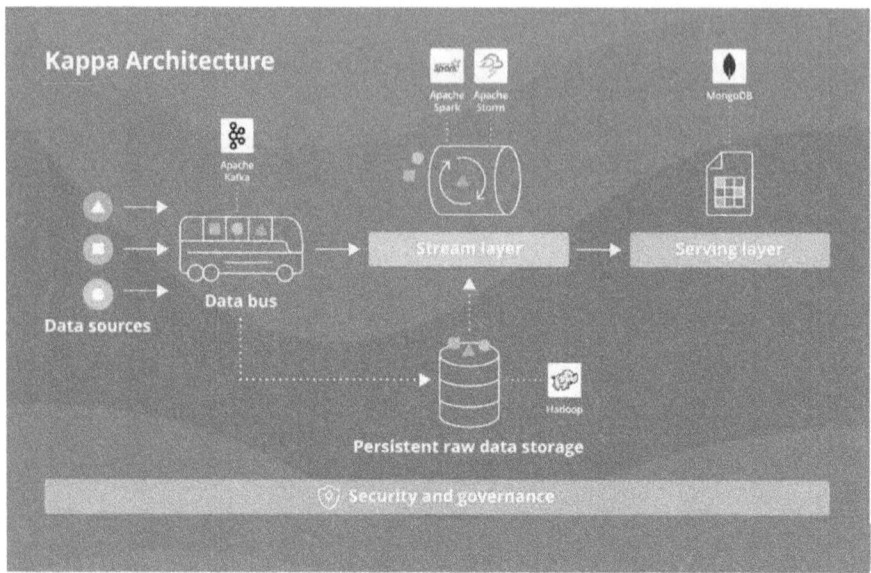

In Kappa Architecture, both real-time and batch processing of big data is performed within one data flow (= a single technology stack is used).

Pros:

- Easy to test and maintain. Only one set of infrastructure and technology is used.
- Data is easy to migrate and reorganize.
- Easy to add new functionalities and make hotfixes (since only one code base should be updated).
- High data quality with guaranteed data sequence and no mismatches.
- Lower infrastructure cost (storage, network, compute, monitoring, logs) since only one tech stack is used and data needs to be processed only once.

Popular Techs and Tools Used in Big Data Projects for processing:

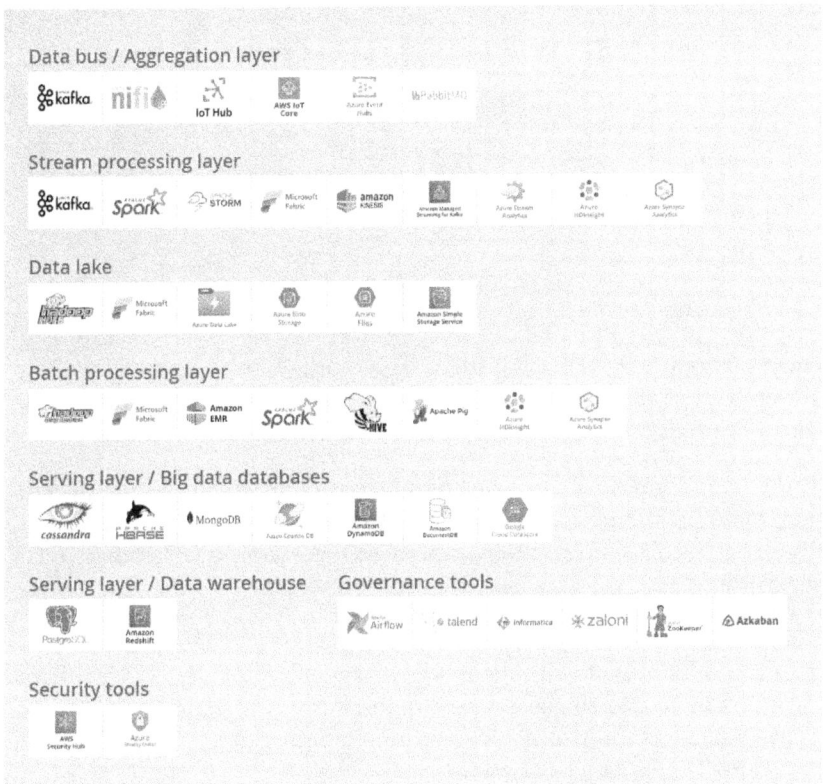

5.3.3 Hadoop, Spark and IoT

Apache Hadoop was born to enhance the usage and solve major issues of big data. The web media was generating loads of information on a daily basis, and it was becoming very difficult to manage the data of around one billion pages of content. In order of revolutionary, Google invented a new methodology of processing data popularly known as MapReduce.

Later after a year Google published a white paper of Map Reducing framework where Doug Cutting and Mike Cafarella, inspired by the white paper and thus created Hadoop to apply these concepts to an open-source software framework which supported the Nutch search engine project. Considering the original case study, Hadoop was designed with a much simpler storage infrastructure facilities.

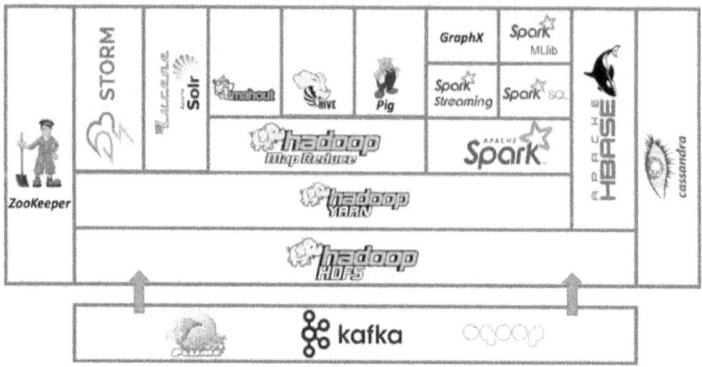

Apache Hadoop is the most important framework for working with Big Data. Hadoop biggest strength is scalability. It upgrades from working on a single node to thousands of nodes without any issue in a seamless manner.

The different domains of Big Data means we are able to manage the data'sare from videos, text medium, transactional data, sensor information, statistical data, social media conversations, search engine queries, ecommerce data, financial information, weather data, news updates, forum discussions, executive reports, and so on.

Hadoop is a framework which is based on java programming. It is intended to work upon from a single server to thousands of machines each offering local computation and storage. It supports the large collection of data set in a distributed computing environment.

Hadoop Distributed File System (HDFS):

HDFS is based on Google File System (GFS) that provides a distributed system particularly designed to run on commodity hardware. The file system has several similarities with the existing distributed file systems. However, HDFS does stand out among all of them. This is because it is fault-tolerant and is specifically designed for deploying on low-cost hardware.

HDFS is mainly responsible for taking care of the storage parts of Hadoop applications. So, if you have a 100 MB file that needs to be stored in the file system, then in HDFS, this file will be split into chunks, called blocks. The default size of each block in Hadoop 1 is 64 MB, on the other hand in Hadoop 2 it is 128 MB.

For example, in Hadoop version 1, if we have a 100 MB file, it will be divided into 64 MB stored in one block and 36 MB in another block. Also, each block is given a unique name, i.e., blk_n (n = any number). Each block is uploaded to one DataNode in the cluster. On each of the machines or clusters, there is something called as a daemon or a piece of software that runs in the background.

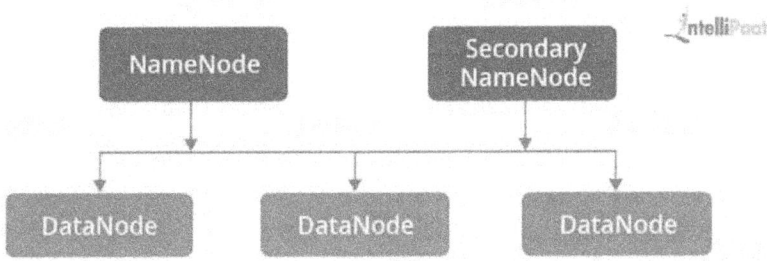

MapReduce Layer:

MapReduce is a patented software framework introduced by Google to support distributed computing on large datasets on clusters of computers. It is basically an operative programming model that runs in the Hadoop background providing simplicity, scalability, recovery, and speed, including easy solutions for data processing. This MapReduce framework is proficient in processing a tremendous amount of data parallelly on large clusters of computational nodes.

MapReduce is a programming model that allows you to process your data across an entire cluster. It basically consists of Mappers and Reducers that are different scripts you write or different functions you might use when writing a MapReduce program.

Mappers have the ability to transform your data in parallel across your computing cluster in a very efficient manner; whereas, Reducers are responsible for aggregating your data together. Mappers and Reducers put together can be used to solve complex problems.

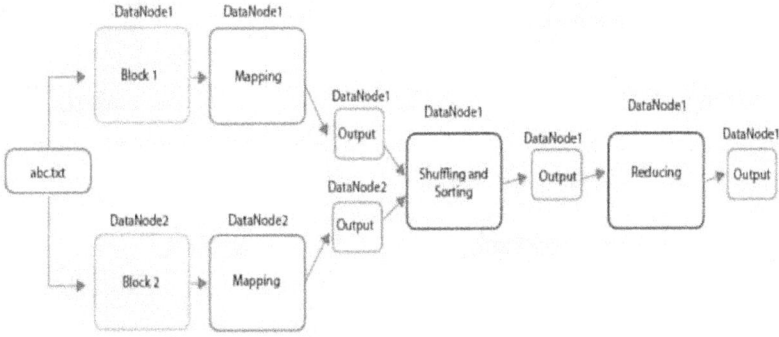

Apache Spark in IoT:

Apache Spark is an open-source distributed cluster-computing framework. Spark is a data processing engine developed to provide faster and easy-to-use analytics than Hadoop MapReduce. Before Apache Software Foundation took possession of Spark, it was under the control of University of California, Berkeley's AMP Lab.

Although it is known that Hadoop is the most powerful tool of Big Data, there are various drawbacks for Hadoop. Some of them are:

> **Low Processing Speed:** In Hadoop, the MapReduce algorithm, which is a parallel and distributed algorithm, processes really large datasets. These are the tasks need to be performed here:

> **Map:** Map takes some amount of data as input and converts it into another set of data, which again is divided into key/value pairs.

> **Reduce:** The output of the Map task is fed into Reduce as input. In the Reduce task, as the name suggests, those key/value pairs are combined into a smaller set of tuples. The Reduce task is always done after Mapping.

> **Batch Processing:** Hadoop deploys batch processing, which is collecting data and then processing it in bulk later. Although batch processing is efficient for processing high volumes of data, it does not process streamed data. Because of this, the performance is lower.

> **No Data Pipelining:** Hadoop does not support data pipelining (i.e., a sequence of stages where the previous stage's output ID is the next stage's input).

> **Not Easy to Use:** MapReduce developers need to write their own code for each and every operation, which makes it really difficult to work with. And also, MapReduce has no interactive mode.

> **Latency:** In Hadoop, the MapReduce framework is slower, since it supports different formats, structures, and huge volumes of data.

> **Lengthy Line of Code:** Since Hadoop is written in Java, the code is lengthy. And, this takes more time to execute the program.

Having outlined all these drawbacks of Hadoop, it is clear that there was a scope for improvement, which is why Spark was introduced. Spark provides:

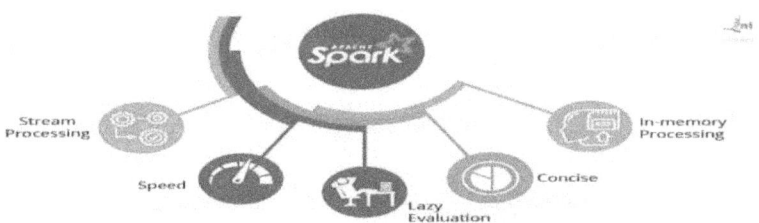

- **In-memory Processing:** In-memory processing is faster when compared to Hadoop, as there is no time spent in moving data/processes in and out of the disk. Spark is 100 times faster than MapReduce as everything is done here in memory.

- **Stream Processing:** Apache Spark supports stream processing, which involves continuous input and output of data. Stream processing is also called real-time processing.

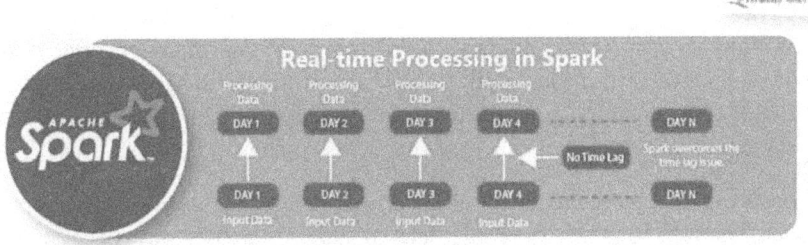

- **Less Latency:** Apache Spark is relatively faster than Hadoop, since it caches most of the input data in memory by the Resilient Distributed Dataset (RDD). RDD manages distributed processing of data and the transformation of that data. This is where Spark does most of the operations such as transformation and managing the data. Each dataset in an RDD is partitioned into logical portions, which can then be computed on different nodes of a cluster.

- **Lazy Evaluation:** Apache Spark starts evaluating only when it is absolutely needed. This plays an important role in contributing to its speed.

> **Less Lines of Code:** Although Spark is written in both Scala and Java, the implementation is in Scala, so the number of lines are relatively lesser in Spark when compared to Hadoop.

Spark Components:

Spark as a whole consists of various libraries, APIs, databases, etc. The main components of Apache Spark are as follows:

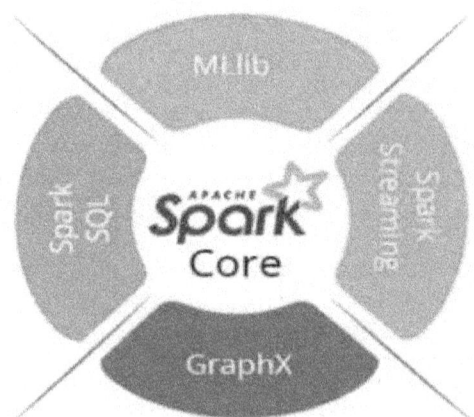

Spark Core: It is the basic building block of Spark, which includes all components for job scheduling, performing various memory operations, fault tolerance, and more. Spark Core is also home to the API that consists of RDD. Moreover, Spark Core provides APIs for building and manipulating data in RDD.

Spark SQL: It works with the unstructured data using its 'go to' tool, Spark SQL. Spark SQL allows querying data via SQL, as well as via Apache Hive's form of SQL called Hive Query Language (HQL). It also supports data from various sources like parse tables, log files, JSON, etc. Spark SQL allows programmers to combine SQL queries with programmable changes or manipulations supported by RDD in Python, Java, Scala, and R.

Spark Streaming: It processes live streams of data. Data generated by various sources is processed at the very instant by Spark Streaming. Examples of this data include log files, messages containing status updates posted by users, etc.

GraphX: It is Apache Spark's library for enhancing graphs and enabling graph-parallel computation. Apache Spark includes a number of graph algorithms which help users in simplifying graph analytics.

MLlib: It comes up with a library containing common Machine Learning (ML) services called MLlib. It provides various types of ML algorithms including regression, clustering, and classification, which can perform various operations on data to get meaningful insights out of it.

Hadoop and Spark Together

There are some scenarios where Hadoop and Spark go hand in hand.

> - Spark can run on Hadoop, stand-alone Mesos, or in the Cloud.
> - Spark's MLlib components provide capabilities that are not easily achieved by Hadoop's MapReduce. By using these components, Machine Learning algorithms can be executed faster inside the memory.
> - Spark does not have its own distributed file system. By combining Spark with Hadoop, you can make use of various Hadoop capabilities. For example, resources are managed via YARN Resource Manager. You can integrate Hadoop with Spark to perform Cluster Administration and Data Management.

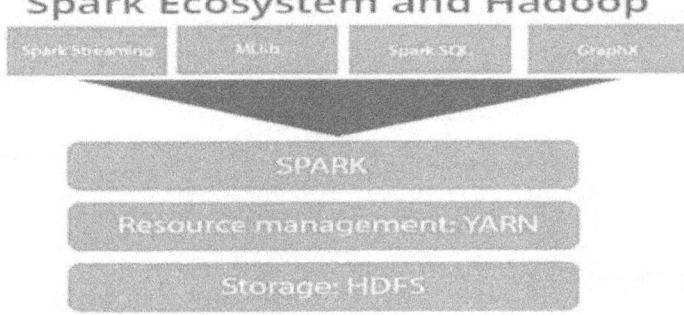

> - Hadoop provides enhanced security, which is a critical component for production workloads. Spark workloads can be deployed on available resources anywhere in a cluster, without manually allocating and tracking individual tasks.

5.3.4 Challenges in Big Data Management for IoT:

The management of IoT data presents a number of key issues that have to be addressed in order for its full potential to be realized:

Scalability: The data management system has to scale as the number of connected devices increases so as to accommodate more data.Interoperability: Different manufacturers make IoT devices using various communication protocols which makes it hard for people to integrate or make them work together; hence they cannot share information easily among themselves.

Data Quality: It is important to ensure high standard quality control measures such as accuracy checks for all collected Information coming from sensors attached on these internet connected gadgets at different locations within an organisation premises.

Security & Privacy – Data Security should also be considered when dealing with large amounts of information being transmitted from one point to another through Public Networks like internet otherwise sensitive customer details might leak out thus leading into financial losses or damaging reputation due to cyber-attacks on the held data. On the other hand, the privacy aspect comes in where by people may wish their personal identities remain anonymous hence they do not want anybody else to know what they are doing online.

Real Time Processing: Most events that occur within a given environment necessitate immediate attention hence requiring quick response Real Time Analytics leveraging Internet Things (IoT) technology so as to bring about suitable controls mechanisms put in place towards stabilizing things during such times of uncertainty.

Solutions for Effective IoT Data Management

To tackle these challenges, several strategies and technologies can be employed:

> - **Edge Computing:** Processing data closer to where it is generated (at the edge) can reduce latency, decrease bandwidth usage, and enhance real-time decision-making capabilities. Edge computing allows for initial data filtering and analytics to be performed locally on devices or edge servers.
> - **Cloud Computing:** Leveraging iot cloud platforms for IoT data storage and processing provides scalability, flexibility, and powerful analytics capabilities. Cloud services offer vast storage solutions and advanced data processing tools that can handle the high volume and velocity of IoT data.
> - **Data Integration Platforms:** Utilizing data integration platforms that support multiple protocols and formats can facilitate the seamless integration of data from diverse IoT devices. These

platforms can aggregate, normalize, and store data in a unified manner, making it easier to manage and analyze.

➢ **Advanced Analytics:** Implementing advanced analytics tools and machine learning algorithms can help in extracting valuable insights from IoT data. Predictive analytics, anomaly detection, and real-time analytics can improve operational efficiency and decision-making.

➢ **Data Governance and Quality Management:** Establishing robust data governance frameworks and quality management practices ensures the integrity, accuracy, and consistency of IoT data. This includes data validation, cleansing, and regular audits to maintain data quality.

➢ **Security Measures:** Implementing comprehensive security measures, such as encryption, secure communication protocols, access management and control mechanisms, is essential to protect IoT data from unauthorized access and breaches. Regular security assessments and updates are also crucial to mitigate potential risks.

Popular IoT Databases Comparison:

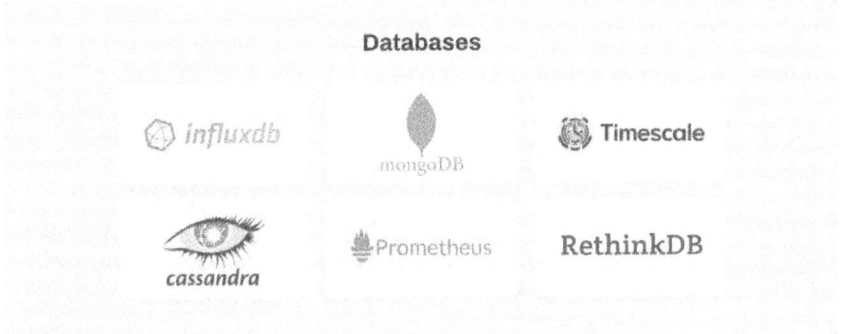

When delving into IoT databases, meticulous assessment of features, performance, and adaptability is paramount. Among the top contenders— InfluxDB, MongoDB, TimescaleDB, Cassandra, Prometheus, and RethinkDB—each offers distinct advantages for efficient IoT data management.

InfluxDB stands out as a potent time-series database, excelling in managing time-stamped IoT data with its optimized storage engine and swift query processing capabilities. Its support for high cardinality and retention policies ensures streamlined storage and handling of historical data, ideal for real-time monitoring and analytics in IoT applications.

MongoDB, a favored document-oriented NoSQL database, provides versatility and scalability for handling diverse IoT data types and structures. Its JSON-like document model caters to complex data schemas, suitable for IoT applications with varying data formats. MongoDB's distributed architecture and horizontal scalability ensure robust performance and availability, making it suitable for large-scale IoT deployments.

TimescaleDB, built atop PostgreSQL, merges the reliability of traditional relational databases with the scalability of time-series databases. Its seamless integration with existing PostgreSQL tools simplifies usage for developers acquainted with SQL. TimescaleDB'shypertable architecture and automatic data partitioning facilitate efficient storage and querying of time-series data, catering to IoT applications necessitating relational database features and time-series capabilities.

Cassandra, a distributed wide-column store NoSQL database, excels in managing high-velocity data streams common in IoT environments. Its decentralized architecture and linear scalability ensure seamless expansion across distributed clusters, guaranteeing fault tolerance and resilience. Cassandra's configurable consistency levels and built-in replication make it suitable for mission-critical IoT applications requiring high availability and data durability.

Prometheus, an open-source monitoring and alerting toolkit, specializes in collecting and querying time-series data. Well-suited for monitoring IoT infrastructure and applications, it offers robust querying capabilities and integrates seamlessly with popular visualization tools.

RethinkDB, a distributed NoSQL database, supports real-time data updates and seamless scaling, making it suitable for IoT applications demanding low-latency data processing and synchronization across distributed systems.

Each of these databases presents unique strengths and use cases, necessitating careful evaluation of specific requirements and priorities when selecting the most suitable database for IoT projects. Understanding these distinctions aids in making informed decisions and optimizing IoT data management strategies for success.

5.4 Digital Twins

5.4.1 Concept of Digital Twins

A Digital Twin of any device/system is a working model of all components (at micro level or macro level or both) integrated and mapped together using physical data, virtual data, and interaction data between them to make a fully functional replica of the device/system and that too on a digital medium.

This digital twin of the physical system is not intended to outplace the physical system but to test its optimality and predict the physical counterparts' performance characteristics.

You can know of the system's operational life course, the implication of design changes, the impact of environmental alters and a lot more variables using this concept. Talking about life course, it invites me to aromatize your awareness of the concept with its origin.

History of Digital Twin

The concept and model of the Digital Twin was officially put forward in 2002 by Dr. Michael Grieves as the conceptual model underlying **Product Lifecycle Management (PLM)**. The concept was being practiced since the 1960s by NASA. They used basic twinning ideas for space programming at that time. They did this by creating physically duplicated systems at ground level to match the systems in space.

Example: When NASA developed a digital twin to assess and simulate conditions on board **Apollo 13**. The efforts were made keeping in mind only a particular mission and because of that, this concept didn't gain recognition until 2002 after **Dr. Grieves** presented it with all the elements including **real space**, **virtual space** and the spreading of data and information flow between **real** and **virtual space**.

The concept of integrating the digital and physical parts as one entity has remained the same since its emergence. Although the terminology has changed over the years till 2010 when it was subsequently called **'Digital Twin'** by **John Vickers** of **NASA in a 2010 Roadmap Report**.

A Digital Twin consists of three distinct parts:

1. The physical part,

2. The Digital Part,

3. The Connection Between the Two.

The **'connection** here refers to the data that flows from physical products to the digital/virtual product and information that is being available from the digital environment to the physical environment.

Types of Digital Twins:

Digital twins can be categorized based on the scope and complexity of the physical entity they represent, forming a tiered hierarchy of functionality. This section outlines the four main types of digital twins:

1. Component Twins

These twins represent the most granular level, focusing on individual components within a system, such as **sensors, actuators,** or **mechanical parts.** They capture intrinsic properties, operational parameters, and behavior characteristics of these components, often relying on sensor data and basic physical models.

For instance, a digital twin of a wind turbine blade might track **temperature, vibration,** and **rotation** speed to predict potential wear and tear.

2. Asset Twins

Moving up the scale, asset twins represent complete physical entities like **vehicles, machines**, or **infrastructure elements.** They integrate data and behavior from individual components (often derived from component twins) into a cohesive model, providing a holistic view of the **asset's performance, health**, and **potential future states**. Asset twins employ more sophisticated models encompassing **physics, thermodynamics**, and other relevant domains, enabling proactive maintenance and performance optimization.

For example, a digital twin of an airplane might **track engine performance, fuel consumption**, and **flight dynamics** to optimize flight paths and predict maintenance needs.

3. System Twins

System twins capture the interactions and dependencies between interconnected assets within a larger system, such as **power grids, transportation networks,** or **manufacturing facilities**. They leverage data and insights from asset twins but incorporate additional layers of complexity to account for emergent behavior arising from inter-asset dynamics. A digital twin of a power grid might simulate how the failure of one generator cascades through the system, impacting other components and potentially causing outages.

4. Process Twins

The most comprehensive digital twins, process twins encompass the entirety of a complex operation, including physical assets, human interactions, environmental factors, and logistical considerations. These twins model the entire **workflow,** enabling **comprehensive optimization,** **scenario simulation**, and **proactive** identification of **potential disruptions**.

A digital twin of a manufacturing process might encompass everything from raw material procurement to finished product delivery, optimizing resource allocation, predicting bottlenecks, and ensuring on-time production.

Advantages of Digital Twins

Digital twins, virtual replicas of physical assets and processes, are rapidly altering the landscape of various industries. These data-driven models, constantly updated with real-time information, offer a multitude of benefits across diverse sectors. Here, we delve into some key advantages of embracing digital twin technology:

1. Enhanced Operational Efficiency:

Predictive Maintenance: Digital twins, empowered by sensor data and artificial intelligence, can forecast equipment failures before they occur. This proactive approach to maintenance minimizes downtime, reduces repair costs, and extends the lifespan of valuable assets. Imagine a digital twin of a wind turbine predicting a potential blade malfunction, allowing technicians to address the issue before it causes costly downtime and energy production loss.

Process Optimization: Real-time data gleaned from digital twins enables continuous monitoring and optimization of processes. Bottlenecks and inefficiencies are readily identified and addressed, leading to enhanced throughput, improved resource utilization, and overall production efficiency. Think of a digital twin of a manufacturing line pinpointing an area causing delays, allowing managers to quickly adjust production schedules and optimize resource allocation.

2. Data-Driven Decision-Making:

Rich Insights: Digital twins provide a comprehensive overview of asset performance, system behavior, and operational data. This wealth of information empowers informed decision-making, enabling businesses to optimize resource allocation, experiment with different scenarios, and predict future outcomes with greater accuracy. Picture a digital twin of a power grid offering insights into energy consumption patterns, allowing utility companies to make informed decisions about resource allocation and grid management.

Reduced Uncertainty: By simulating various scenarios and potential disruptions in the digital twin environment, businesses can mitigate risks, test new strategies, and make informed decisions with greater confidence. Imagine testing a new marketing campaign in a virtual space before launching it in the real world, minimizing potential risks and maximizing its effectiveness.

3. Fostering Innovation and Collaboration:

Accelerated Product Development: Digital twins can be used to virtually test and refine new product designs before physical prototypes are built. This iterative approach reduces development time and costs, fosters innovation, and brings products to market faster. Imagine engineers using a digital twin of a new electric car design to optimize its aerodynamics and battery performance before building a physical prototype.

Enhanced Collaboration: Shared digital twin models can facilitate seamless collaboration between different teams and stakeholders. This improves communication, streamlines workflows, and fosters a more integrated approach to operations. Think of a construction project where architects, engineers, and contractors all have access to a shared digital twin of the building, promoting better coordination and project efficiency.

4. Sustainability and Environmental Impact:

Resource Optimization: Digital twins can help optimize energy consumption, reduce waste generation, and minimize environmental impact by identifying inefficiencies and opportunities for improvement within processes and systems. Imagine a digital twin of a manufacturing plant suggesting ways to optimize water usage and reduce resource waste, contributing to a more sustainable production process.

Sustainable Design and Development: By virtually testing and optimizing product designs for energy efficiency and reduced environmental footprint, digital twins can contribute to the development of more sustainable products and processes. Picture a digital twin of a new building design helping architects optimize its energy efficiency and minimize its carbon footprint before construction begins.

Applications of Digital Twins

1. Manufacturing:

Not only the emergence of Digital Twins helps us manufacture high-grade products. But also, we can salvage money and time both, which would otherwise be wasted on the production. It facilitates these firms to test new designs expeditiously. Talking about Virtualised Testing of a new supply chain, it's a breeze, whereas testing the physical equivalent involves shutting down production, losing profits, which on the other hand can be like opening a Pandora's box. Since digital twins can give a real-time view of what's happening with equipment or other physical assets, they have been very helpful in manufacturing.

2. Automotive:

As automobiles, especially cars, become progressively integrated with IoT and digital technology, the ability to replicate every detail becomes increasingly indispensable. With the help of digital twins, it has become a piece of cake for engineers to predict the performance of the machines. We can construct a digital twin of all sorts of autonomous vehicles and track the vehicle from the day of its creation to the day it goes to the junkyard. Engineers can test new safety features in the digital world, without any need for the new physical vehicle to test changes. For a similar reason, smart car producers are testing their self-driving AI in digital environment too.

3. Healthcare:

A digital twin can help virtualize a hospital system to create a safe environment and test the impact of potential changes on the performance of the system. Furthermore, Digital Twins in the healthcare sector can identify faults with the various equipment (which is often very expensive and needs to operate at optimum levels) involved in various medical fields. Not just that but digital twin has helped doctors to carry out difficult surgeries. Take an example of cardiologists, they used digital twins of the patient's heart to precisely determine the positioning of leads that would work best on this specific patient that too before surgery decreasing the risk of failure.

4. Retail:

The implementation of this concept of a Digital Twin plays a key role in augmenting the retail customer experience by manufacturing a simulation that could accurately represent how a specific model of a product takes place in an individual's life. Not only this but also it lets you test if there is any potential in a new design of the product to cut back expenses without having to make large scale physical changes to your entire product range which can reduce the market price of the product. Having an exact digital copy of your physical asset can lead to trendsetting innovations. Once the innovation works well for digital model, one can start investing in physical assets.

5. Smart Cities:

Cities have numerous moving and interconnected building blocks. With a well suited advanced model, civil engineers, governments and other related companies can test new solutions in the best possible way. This tool can prove highly advantageous for analyzing the different forms of transport and pedestrian movement patterns and for sound planning to ensure that their requirements are met. When prepared with Machine Learning, this model can test possible solutions to problems like traffic management in no time. This model would be beneficial in yet another troublesome situation. Such as, in the case of a fire emergency, firefighters can have access to the 3D model of the building. With the help of Augmented Reality and AI, firefighters could know where people are and how to predict fire's behavior.

5.4.2 Implementing digital twins in iot systems:

What is a digital twin?

Many different kinds of digital twins exist, yet they all share common functionality. The key feature that distinguishes digital twins from other virtual representations, such as simulations, is the continuous, real-time data measurement, which is always anchored in the physical aspect. A simulation of a motor, for instance, might have all the same base data as the digital twin, in the beginning. Over time, however, it is likely inconsistences would emerge as the simulation is operating purely in the hypothetical, virtual realm.

How does a digital twin work?

The exact functioning of a digital twin varies depending on the type, but the principles remain consistent. IoT sensors, smart products, and other computer devices capture the information requested and then feed it into a digital interface. Depending on the application, this data can be analyzed with AI to quickly deduce insights and prioritize the most important information at that moment.

Again, the key feature is consistency. For any digital twin to function properly, the data stream must remain constant. Organizations without proper IoT infrastructure will find trying to create effective digital twins difficult, if not impossible.

Understanding component twins

Component digital twins, as their name suggest, reflect individual pieces of a product. Again think back to a motor, which has numerous gears, screws, and other system parts all working together. Not every piece needs a component twin, however, and teams usually prioritize targeting just those pieces that see tremendous stress, temperature variation, or vigorous usage.

Component twins are used to measure and better understand these particular pieces so that they may be improved in subsequent iterations of product design and refinement. That said, there is nothing to stop an organization from making a component twin for every single piece of the product they are building, provided they have the resources available to do so.

Understanding asset twins

An asset twin is simply another name for a product digital twin. As such, this twin type focuses on reflecting the whole product, and not just individual components. Product digital twins often specialize on analyzing the interactions that occur between all these components, so that the end user can better understand just exactly how the asset is functioning over time.

Understanding systems twins

If many components work together in a product, so too do many products work together in a system. System digital twins (sometimes called unit twins) represent these interactions. One manufacturing line, for instance, typically has numerous hardware types all working together to create one product. A systems twin would measure and record these interactions, helping end users better understand where and how to invest in optimizations that will improve efficiency.

Understanding process twins

Pulling back one level higher, a process twin mirrors the data created within all these systems interacting together. Process twins tend to be some of the most complex digital twins in existence and require impressive digital infrastructure to achieve peak efficiency. A robust process digital twin might reflect the work of an entire manufacturing site, both in terms of various hardware and even employee behavior.

The relationship between digital twins and IoT

Digital transformation has many aspects, and IoT can be seen as a foundational digital transformation initiative. Deploying sensors and creating smart connected products allows organizations access to information that is otherwise impossible to gather. This data can be used in many ways, one of which being to lay the foundation for many types of digital twins. It's very much a cart-and-horse scenario, where the digital twin (the cart) is only made useful through the horse (IoT) as the two together bring tremendous value to the end user.

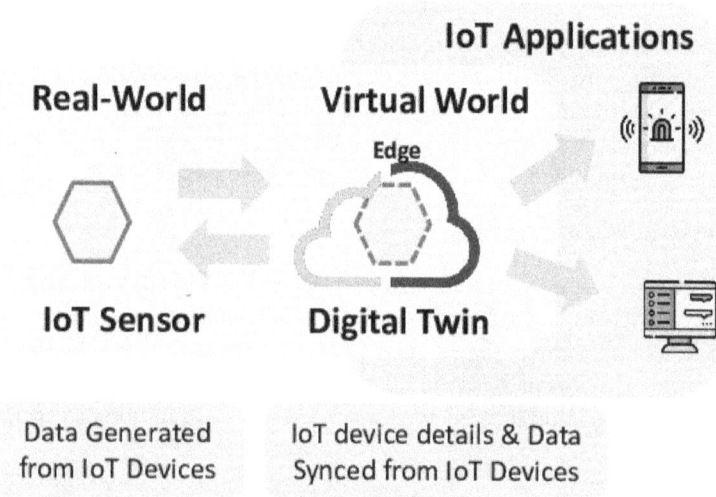

What are the benefits of digital twins in IoT?

Digital twin can be seen as giving structure to IoT. IoT by itself is useful, but the sheer amount of data can be overwhelming. Digital twins break down the information into understandable categories — people, products, places, processes — that are more immediately clear and understandable. Grouping the data is a solid first step to unlocking actionable insights, but often more help is still needed — hence why many digital twin programs use AI in the form of advanced analytics to better provide the user with prioritized information and readouts. That said, categorization is not the only benefit brought by digital twins and IoT. Like many aspects of digital transformation, these investments provide multiple competitive advantages.

Reducing downtime

Predictive maintenance is a crucial advantage for manufacturers, as it allows organizations to more quickly identify and correct problems, sometimes before any downtime occurs. Digital twins are important for any company actively pursuing predictive maintenance, as they provide comprehensive data analysis into exactly how the selected component, asset, unit, or process is performing. Seeing the problems before they occur means reducing downtime, keeping factories operational longer and improving profitability.

Lowering maintenance costs

Predictive maintenance benefits extend further. Not only is downtime reduced, but spotting a problem earlier often means less drastic action needs to be taken. A bolt can be reinforced rather than being replaced, or an entire machine can be salvaged when it would have before had catastrophic failure.

Predictive and preventative maintenance are all about proactively stopping problems before they truly develop, rather than simply reacting to the situation. In any industry, it's better to be thinking ahead. In manufacturing, this translates to reduced downtime and generally lower maintenance costs.

Improving quality

Digital twins don't stop helping at the maintenance level. They provide an incredible look into whatever they've been asked to replicate. As such, the user now has more information and knowledge than ever, and can use this to optimize overall quality. In process twins, this means greatly improving production time through eliminating wasteful behaviors or redirecting energy usage. In product twins, it could mean using after sale data to better track how a product performs, correct any troubled occurrences, then redesign accordingly for superior iterations.

Helping to predict and perform

Whether it's a positive or negative prediction, digital twins provide a window into the future—one that is almost always more accurate than a simulation, given the continuous data feedback. Clearer visions of the future allow organizations to better adjust, positioning themselves for the improvements and success they hope to see. Likewise, general performance standards should also raise, though this also requires action on the part of the user. Digital twins will merely show the data they are supposed to show. The decision making on what to do with this information is still firmly within the hands of its end users, as even digital twins with AI analytical capabilities will not make any drastic decisions without human intervention.

Reducing the time to market

In order to accelerate, it helps to fully know and understand the baseline. If current production rates, for instance, are in fact only using 85% productivity when before it was assumed every machine was at 100% capacity, suddenly there is immediate room to grow. Machines that can be operated more efficiently, while also providing operators with insight into if and when downtime might occur, will produce faster — reducing the time to market and time to value for the manufacturer.

3 ways IIoT is enhancing digital twins

Industrial internet of things (IIoT) is simply a term to express focus on IoT in professional, industrial spaces. The two terms are often used interchangeably, and really it is user preference how they would prefer to describe their IoT operations. That said, regardless of how you express IIoT, there is no denying it brings numerous enhancements to digital twins:

> **Digital twin of products: IoT offers visibility into the full product lifecycle**

Smart connected products have replaced assumptions with facts; real-world IIoT data closes the feedback loop with product usage data, which then informs future iterations — and even business model changes, including product-as-service. Product telemetry also gives engineers and product designers behavioral characteristics of deployed products or fleets of products. Providing a frame of reference to compare the 'as-is' versus 'as-used' product usage is an extremely powerful IIoT-enabled insight that can inform the development of future product iterations. Its applicability can range from replacing or modifying certain features to drilled-down insights into the specific performance of part(s). Expanding visibility into the product lens through cross-functional collaboration can also drive downstream efficiencies. This includes change management in manufacturing and service processes, which lowers scrap, rework, and lead times.

Real-world example: Whirlpool is achieving data-driven design by connecting deployed appliances through IIoT and analyzing operating performance metrics (torque, drum speed, motor temperature, etc.) across fleets of products to improve future iterations.

> **Digital twin of processes: IoT unlocks deeper operational intelligence**

Many operational processes are plagued by two factors: disparate and black-boxed information sources. IIoT unlocks these unknown insights and threads them with different sources both in real-time and historical systems of record. Twins of these connected assets and workers and how they interact are critical to a constructing a process lens — essentially a system-wide view of an industrial environment. IIoT through a process lens can drive critical manufacturing KPIs. For example, improving the uptime of a single asset on a factory floor through IIoT-driven predictive insights can drastically improve throughput while a twin of a production line can reduce bottlenecks through enhanced operational visibility. This connected operational intelligence from diverse assets creates the real-time 360-degree visibility manufacturers need to be flexible and agile — a necessity in today's changing markets and shifting customer demands.

Digital twin elements:

A digital twin is fundamentally composed of three key elements: a physical entity, a digital representation (virtual twin) of that entity, and a data connection linking the two. This connection facilitates real-time data transfer, enabling the digital twin to be updated and reflect the physical entity's current state.

Here's a more detailed breakdown:

1. Physical Entity: This is the real-world object or system being represented. It can be anything from a single component like a motor in a wind turbine to a complex system like an entire manufacturing plant.

2. Digital Representation (Virtual Twin): This is a software-based model that mimics the physical entity. It's a virtual replica of the physical object, often created using CAD, PLM, or other modeling software. This digital twin can be updated with real-time data from the physical entity, making it a dynamic and evolving representation.

3. Data Connection: This element establishes the link between the physical entity and its digital twin. It involves the collection, transmission, and processing of data using technologies like IoT sensors, network infrastructure, and data management middleware. This data connection enables the digital twin to be updated with real-time information, making it a dynamic and accurate representation of the physical entity.

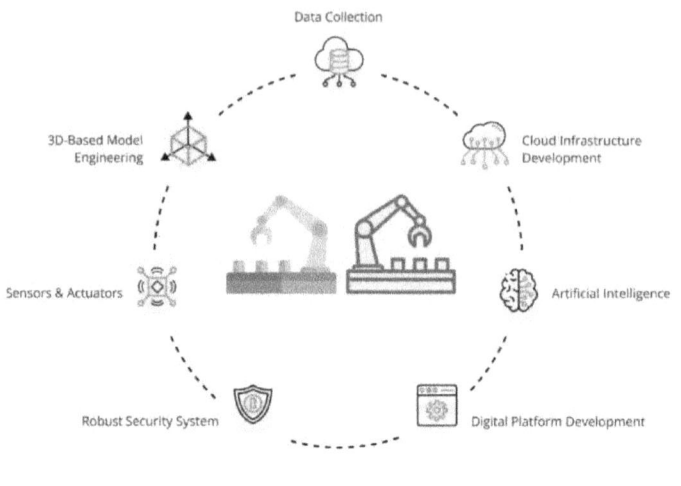

5.4.3 Applications of Digital Twins

Digital twins have become one of the most transformative technologies in the Internet of Things (IoT) ecosystem. A digital twin is a virtual replica of a physical object, system, or process. It leverages IoT data, real-time sensor inputs, and machine learning algorithms to create a dynamic, real-time model of its real-world counterpart. The relationship between digital twins and IoT is symbiotic—while IoT devices collect data from the physical world, digital twins use that data to simulate and predict outcomes in virtual environments. This combination allows organizations to optimize operations, improve performance, and enhance decision-making processes. Here are some key applications of digital twins in IoT:

1. Predictive Maintenance

One of the most powerful applications of digital twins in IoT is predictive maintenance. By monitoring IoT-connected machinery or equipment, digital twins can detect patterns in the data that suggest wear and tear, abnormalities, or impending failure. This early detection allows organizations to perform maintenance only when necessary, reducing downtime, preventing costly repairs, and extending the lifespan of equipment.

Example: In a factory, sensors on a production line provide real-time data to a digital twin of a machine. The digital twin can predict when a part is likely to fail and automatically schedule a maintenance check before the failure occurs.

2. Smart Cities

Digital twins are playing a critical role in the development and management of smart cities. By creating digital replicas of entire urban environments, municipalities can simulate traffic flow, energy consumption, pollution levels, and more. IoT devices embedded in the city's infrastructure send data to these digital twins, helping city planners optimize resources and make data-driven decisions to improve the quality of life for residents.

Example: A city could use a digital twin to simulate traffic patterns. IoT sensors embedded in traffic lights and vehicles send data to the digital twin, which analyzes congestion points and adjusts the traffic signal timings in real-time to alleviate traffic jams.

3. Healthcare and Personalized Medicine

In the healthcare sector, digital twins are enabling more personalized and efficient care. By creating virtual models of patients' bodies or organs, healthcare providers can track real-time health data from IoT-connected medical devices, simulate different treatment scenarios, and predict how a patient's condition might evolve over time. This helps doctors provide more accurate diagnoses and treatments tailored to the individual's unique needs.

Example: A hospital may create a digital twin of a patient's heart using data from IoT-connected sensors such as heart rate monitors. The digital twin can simulate how the heart will respond to different medications or lifestyle changes, helping doctors customize treatment plans.

4. Energy and Utilities

Digital twins are also revolutionizing the energy sector by optimizing the performance and management of energy grids, renewable energy sources, and power plants. IoT sensors in power grids and energy meters collect data, which is fed into digital twins to analyze energy usage, predict equipment failures, and improve energy distribution. This not only reduces energy waste but also ensures more reliable service.

Example: A power company uses digital twins to simulate the operation of wind turbines. IoT sensors collect data on wind speed, turbine rotation, and energy output. The digital twin analyzes this data to optimize turbine performance and predict when maintenance is needed.

5. Supply Chain and Logistics

The integration of digital twins in IoT-driven supply chains allows for enhanced visibility and real-time tracking of goods from production to delivery. By simulating the entire supply chain process, businesses can identify inefficiencies, predict delays, and optimize inventory management. IoT sensors track the location, condition, and status of goods, and digital twins use this information to provide actionable insights.

Example: In a warehouse, IoT sensors monitor the temperature, humidity, and location of sensitive products like pharmaceuticals. A digital twin of the warehouse helps track the conditions in which products are stored, ensuring that they meet required standards for quality and safety.

6. Automotive and Transportation

In the automotive industry, digital twins are used to simulate and improve the design, production, and operation of vehicles. With IoT sensors embedded in vehicles, data can be sent to a digital twin to monitor vehicle performance, predict maintenance needs, and optimize routes for fuel efficiency. This is especially important in the development of autonomous vehicles, where digital twins are used to test and simulate different driving scenarios.

Example: A fleet of delivery trucks is equipped with IoT sensors that monitor engine performance, tire pressure, and fuel consumption. Digital twins of the trucks use this data to predict maintenance needs, optimize delivery routes, and improve overall fleet efficiency.

7. Agriculture

Digital twins are increasingly being used in precision farming, where they enable farmers to monitor and optimize the conditions under which crops grow. IoT-connected sensors gather data on soil moisture, temperature, and weather conditions, and digital twins simulate the growth of crops based on this data. This allows farmers to make informed decisions about irrigation, fertilization, and harvesting, leading to higher crop yields and more sustainable farming practices.

Example: A farmer uses a digital twin of a vineyard to simulate the growth of grapes based on soil conditions, weather patterns, and irrigation schedules. The digital twin helps optimize water usage and predict the best time for harvesting.

8. Building and Facility Management

Digital twins are also transforming the way buildings and facilities are managed. By integrating IoT sensors into building systems such as HVAC, lighting, and security, digital twins provide real-time monitoring of building conditions. This allows facility managers to optimize energy consumption, improve occupant comfort, and reduce operational costs.

Example: A digital twin of a commercial building uses data from IoT sensors to monitor temperature, humidity, and occupancy. The digital twin helps adjust HVAC settings in real-time to ensure energy efficiency and optimal comfort for occupants.

5.4.4 Future Trends in Digital Twin Technology

Digital twin technology has come a long way, and its future holds transformative potential across various industries. As it continues to evolve, several key trends are expected to shape the landscape of this innovative technology. Here are the future trends that are likely to define the next phase of digital twin development:

1. AI and Machine Learning Integration

The future of digital twin technology will heavily rely on Artificial Intelligence (AI) and Machine Learning (ML) to create smarter, more autonomous systems. With AI and ML, digital twins can process vast amounts of data to detect patterns, optimize performance, and predict future behaviors without requiring direct human input. These advancements will allow digital twins to learn from real-time data and evolve their simulations for more accurate predictions and decision-making.

Impact: Real-time optimization, smarter automation, predictive maintenance, and more efficient processes.

2. Edge Computing for Real-Time Processing

Edge computing will play a crucial role in the next generation of digital twins. With the growth of IoT devices and the need for immediate data processing, edge computing allows data to be processed closer to its source rather than being sent to a central cloud server. This reduces latency and ensures that digital twins can operate in real-time, making them more responsive to changes in dynamic environments.

Impact: Real-time decision-making, faster insights, and reduced reliance on centralized cloud infrastructure.

3. Digital Twin Ecosystems and Interoperability

As industries embrace digital twins, there will be a shift toward creating interconnected ecosystems of digital twins. Different digital twins will be able to communicate with each other, sharing information and collaborating to improve overall systems. For instance, digital twins from supply chains, manufacturing, and logistics could work together to optimize operations across multiple sectors, leading to smarter and more efficient workflows.

Impact: Enhanced collaboration between systems, better synchronization, and optimized cross-industry operations.

4. Expansion into Sustainability and Smart Cities

Digital twins will increasingly be used for creating sustainable and resilient smart cities. By modeling urban environments, energy systems, transportation, and infrastructure, digital twins can help cities optimize energy use, reduce emissions, and improve the quality of life for residents. Additionally, digital twins can model climate change scenarios and help cities plan for future environmental challenges.

Impact: Sustainable cities, efficient resource management, reduced environmental footprint, and proactive urban planning.

5. Personalized Medicine and Healthcare

In healthcare, digital twins will evolve from models of machines and systems to models of individual patients. With the integration of IoT devices, wearable sensors, and genomic data, personalized digital twins will provide a real-time, dynamic representation of a patient's health. These models will allow for personalized treatment plans, early detection of diseases, and continuous health monitoring, revolutionizing preventative and precision medicine.

Impact: Proactive healthcare, reduced healthcare costs, and more personalized treatments that improve patient outcomes.

6. Enhanced Simulation and Design Processes

The role of digital twins in product design and development will continue to grow. Future digital twins will not only simulate real-time operational performance but also integrate with design processes from the very beginning. For example, in aerospace or automotive industries, digital twins could model prototypes and simulate various scenarios, enabling better design decisions, faster testing, and reduced time to market.

Impact: Accelerated product development, reduced costs in design and testing, and enhanced innovation.

7. Blockchain for Data Security and Transparency

As digital twins handle increasingly sensitive data, blockchain technology will be integrated to secure data transactions and ensure transparency. Blockchain's decentralized ledger will provide a trusted way to verify the authenticity and integrity of the data used by digital twins, especially in critical industries like healthcare, finance, and supply chains.

Impact: Enhanced security, transparency, and trust in data used by digital twins, particularly for sensitive applications.

8. Autonomous Systems and Digital Twin Feedback Loops

Digital twins will increasingly be linked with autonomous systems, creating continuous feedback loops where the digital twin receives data from its physical counterpart, adapts its model, and makes real-time decisions or optimizations. This will be especially relevant in industries like autonomous vehicles, robotics, and manufacturing, where continuous, real-time data is crucial for performance and safety.

Impact: Self-optimizing systems, reduced human intervention, and faster adaptability to changing environments.

9. Wider Adoption and Democratization of Digital Twins

While digital twins have been primarily adopted by large enterprises, the technology is expected to become more accessible to smaller businesses and industries in the coming years. Cloud platforms, cost-effective sensors, and open-source software will help democratize the use of digital twins, allowing smaller players to leverage the power of this technology without the need for massive investments in infrastructure.

Impact: Increased innovation across industries, with small and medium-sized businesses adopting digital twin technology for greater efficiency and competitiveness.

10. Long-Term, Continuous Data Integration

Digital twins will evolve from simply representing a snapshot of a system to continuously updating and refining their models over time. By integrating long-term data streams, digital twins will offer a holistic view of an asset's lifecycle, helping organizations track performance, make improvements, and predict future behavior with greater accuracy over time.

Impact: Improved asset management, long-term strategic planning, and continuous improvement of systems and processes.

5.5 Federated Learning in IoT

5.5.1 Privacy-Preserving AI Models

Federated learning is an innovative approach to training machine learning models that enhances data privacy by allowing the models to be trained across decentralized devices or servers without the need to share raw data. This technique is especially valuable in sensitive fields such as healthcare and finance where maintaining the confidentiality of personal and financial information is crucial.

What is Federated Learning?

The Federated learning is a distributed machine learning paradigm that enables multiple participants to the collaboratively train a model while keeping their data localized. Instead of centralizing data each participant trains the model on their local data and only shares the model updates with the central server. The server then aggregates these updates to improve the global model.

Key Features of Federated Learning

Data Privacy: The Raw data never leaves the participant's device protecting sensitive information.

Reduced Latency: Training occurs on local devices which can reduce the time required to the send large datasets to the central server.

Decentralization: The approach allows for the collaboration across different institutions without the compromising data integrity.

Advantages of Privacy-Preserving Models:

Compliance with Regulations: FL enables organizations to comply with strict data privacy regulations by keeping user data on local devices.

Reduced Data Breach Risks: Since data isn't stored centrally, the risk of a large-scale data breach is minimized.

Improved User Trust: Users are more likely to engage with services when they know their personal data remains private.

How Federated Learning Works?

Federated learning operates in a few key stages, each designed to protect privacy while ensuring effective model training.

Initialization of the Global Model: The process begins with a central server sending an initial global model to multiple devices. This model serves as the starting point for training.

Local Training on Devices: Each device uses its local data to train the model. For instance, in the context of mobile devices, each smartphone uses its personal data (e.g., browsing history, text input data) to improve the model locally.

Sending Model Updates: Once local training is complete, each device sends the model updates, not the data, back to the central server. These updates typically include parameters such as weights and biases but no raw data.

Aggregating Updates: The central server aggregates the updates received from all devices to refine the global model. Techniques like secure aggregation are often used to ensure the updates themselves do not reveal any sensitive information.

Global Model Update: After aggregation, the global model is updated and sent back to the devices. This process repeats, leading to continuous model improvement while keeping user data secure.

Applications in Federated Learning

Healthcare: In healthcare, federated learning can be applied to train models on sensitive patient data without sharing the actual data. For instance, hospitals can locally train models on medical records to detect diseases like cancer or COVID-19. The updates from each hospital are combined to improve diagnostic accuracy while preserving patient privacy.

Finance: In financial institutions, federated learning can be used to detect fraudulent transactions. Banks can locally train models on customer transaction data to identify anomalies while ensuring the data remains secure within each institution.

Telecommunications: Telecom companies can use FL to improve services like predictive text, personalized recommendations, and network optimization. The training occurs on users' mobile devices, ensuring that personal usage data stays on the device.

Autonomous Vehicles: Federated learning can also support autonomous vehicle systems by allowing cars to train models locally on driving data (like road conditions or driving behavior). The updates are then aggregated to improve the global model, making self-driving systems smarter without sharing sensitive driving information.

Challenges and Considerations

Communication Costs: Since updates must be frequently sent from devices to the server, federated learning can result in high communication overhead. Optimizing communication protocols is crucial for scaling FL across millions of devices.

Device Heterogeneity: Devices participating in federated learning may vary significantly in terms of computational power, memory, and connectivity. Ensuring that the learning process remains efficient across diverse devices is a major challenge.

Data Quality and Bias: The local data on different devices may vary in quality or be biased towards specific groups. Aggregating biased updates may lead to skewed global models, so techniques for handling data imbalance are necessary.

Security Concerns: While federated learning is designed to protect data privacy, there are still potential attack vectors. For example, adversaries may attempt to introduce malicious updates or extract information from the model updates...

5.5.2 Distributed System and IoT Devices

The integration of Distributed Systems and the Internet of Things (IoT) revolutionizes technology management by enabling scalability and real-time responsiveness. This article explores their challenges, architectural considerations, and emerging solutions, helping stakeholders leverage IoT's potential while ensuring resilience and optimal performance in complex environments.

What are Distributed Systems?

Distributed systems are collections of independent computers that work together to perform tasks, often appearing as a single system to users. These systems share resources, coordinate with each other, and communicate over networks. In distributed systems, components may be geographically dispersed but function cohesively. Key Characteristics of distributed systems include:

> Scalability: Distributed systems can handle increasing workloads by adding more nodes.

> Fault Tolerance: If one part of the system fails, the rest can continue functioning.

> Decentralization: The system's control is spread across multiple nodes rather than a central point.

How Distributed Systems Enable IoT?

IoT systems generate massive amounts of data from a wide range of devices, which requires efficient management and processing. Distributed systems play a crucial role in enabling IoT by providing the necessary infrastructure for data collection, analysis, and real-time decision-making across geographically dispersed locations. Key Ways Distributed Systems Power IoT:

Data Distribution: With distributed systems, data collected from various IoT devices can be processed closer to where it's generated (edge computing), reducing latency and bandwidth use.

Scalable Infrastructure: Distributed systems allow IoT networks to grow easily by adding more devices or nodes without overwhelming the system's capacity.

Decentralized Control: Distributed systems avoid bottlenecks by decentralizing control, which is essential in handling the vast scale and dynamic nature of IoT systems.

Resilience: If a part of the network fails, distributed systems ensure that IoT services continue by redistributing the load to functioning parts of the network.

Benefits of Combining Distributed Systems and IoT

Below are the benefits of combining distributed systems and IoT:

1. Improved Scalability:

Combining distributed systems with IoT allows for scalable growth. As more IoT devices are added, distributed systems enable seamless integration by distributing computational load across nodes.

2. Real-Time Processing:

Edge computing, a form of distributed computing, allows data to be processed closer to the source, providing real-time insights. This is especially useful in industries like healthcare and manufacturing, where real-time decision-making is critical.

3. Fault Tolerance:

Distributed systems offer redundancy and fault tolerance. If one node or device fails, the system reroutes data and operations to other functioning parts, ensuring that the IoT network remains operational.

4. Lower Latency:

Edge and distributed computing reduce latency by processing data locally rather than sending it to a centralized cloud. This is crucial for time-sensitive IoT applications like autonomous vehicles or remote surgery.

5. Cost Efficiency:

With distributed systems, IoT applications can process data closer to the edge, minimizing the need for expensive, high-bandwidth connections to centralized cloud services, resulting in cost savings.

Real-World Examples of Distributed Systems and IoT

Below are the real-world examples of distributed systems and iot:

1. Smart Cities:

Smart cities use IoT devices and distributed systems to manage traffic, optimize energy consumption, and enhance public safety. For instance, smart traffic lights rely on distributed systems to adjust signal timings based on real-time traffic data.

2. Healthcare Monitoring:

Wearable devices like smartwatches monitor patients' health and send data to healthcare providers. Distributed systems enable real-time monitoring and alert doctors if abnormalities are detected, ensuring timely intervention.

3. Industrial IoT (IIoT):

Manufacturing plants use IoT devices to monitor equipment, track inventory, and manage supply chains. Distributed systems ensure that real-time data from sensors is processed at various levels to optimize operations and detect issues before they escalate.

4. Autonomous Vehicles:

Autonomous vehicles use IoT and distributed systems to communicate with nearby infrastructure and other vehicles. This ensures real-time navigation, collision avoidance, and traffic management without relying solely on cloud data centers.

Architecture of IoT in Distributed Systems

An IoT-enabled distributed system typically follows a multi-layer architecture, which includes:

Device Layer: This layer consists of the IoT devices (sensors, actuators) that collect data from their environment. These devices are spread across different locations and form the base of the distributed IoT network.

Edge Layer: Edge computing devices process data locally, reducing the need to send all data to a central server. This layer helps in reducing latency and optimizing network bandwidth.

Fog Layer: Fog computing sits between the edge and the cloud, acting as an intermediary for additional processing, storage, and control.

Cloud Layer: The cloud serves as a centralized repository and processing engine for data that requires more intensive computational resources or longer-term storage.

Communication Layer: This layer includes the networking infrastructure that enables communication between devices, edge nodes, fog servers, and the cloud.

Challenges in IoT-Driven Distributed Systems

Below are the challenges in IOT-Driven Distributed Systems:

Interoperability: IoT devices come from various manufacturers, each using different communication protocols, which can make it difficult to integrate them into a unified system.

Latency: In some applications, even minor delays can result in significant issues, such as in autonomous vehicles or healthcare systems. Ensuring low-latency communication is a major challenge in distributed IoT systems.

Network Bandwidth: Managing data traffic across a large number of devices can overwhelm networks, especially when high-bandwidth applications such as video streaming are involved.

Data Privacy: Distributed IoT systems handle vast amounts of sensitive data. Ensuring privacy and compliance with regulations like GDPR while enabling distributed data sharing remains a tough balancing act.

Data Management in Distributed IoT Systems

Below is how data management works in distributed IOT Systems:

Data Collection: IoT devices collect a massive amount of data, often in real-time. Distributed systems help in organizing and routing this data to where it needs to go for processing or storage.

Data Storage: Decentralized data storage can be used to keep data close to the point of generation, minimizing network traffic and storage costs.

Data Processing: Distributed systems support distributed processing, where data is processed at multiple points across the network, including at the edge or fog layer, rather than relying on centralized servers.

Data Replication and Consistency: Ensuring data consistency across distributed nodes is a challenge. Techniques like eventual consistency are often used to strike a balance between performance and data accuracy.

Security Considerations for Distributed IoT Systems

Below are the security considerations for distributed iot systems:

Data Encryption: Encrypting data both in transit and at rest is essential for securing sensitive IoT data in distributed systems.

Access Control: Implement strong authentication and authorization mechanisms to ensure that only authorized devices and users can access the system.

Threat Detection: Implement continuous monitoring and anomaly detection mechanisms to identify and address potential threats in real-time.

Device Security: Securing IoT devices themselves is a critical challenge. Many IoT devices have limited processing power, which makes implementing traditional security measures like firewalls difficult.

5.6 Natural Language Processing (NLP) in IoT

5.6.1 Natural Language Processing's Role in Advancing IoT Applications

Introduction

Natural Language Processing (NLP) has emerged as a revolutionary field in the intersection of computer science, artificial intelligence, and linguistics. It focuses on enabling computers to understand, interpret, and generate human language in a way that is both meaningful and contextually relevant. NLP has paved the way for significant advancements in various industries, including healthcare, finance, and customer service. In this comprehensive guide, we will delve deep into the world of NLP, exploring its history, inner workings, applications, challenges, and future prospects.

History

The roots of NLP can be traced back to the 1950s, when researchers began exploring the possibilities of machine translation. The advent of computers and the increasing availability of textual data sparked interest in developing algorithms that could process and analyze human language. The early years of NLP were marked by rule-based approaches, where linguists manually crafted intricate sets of rules to translate and analyze text. However, these approaches proved to be limited in their ability to handle the complexity and ambiguity of natural language.

The field witnessed a significant breakthrough in the 1980s with the introduction of statistical methods in NLP. This approach involved training models on large amounts of annotated data to learn patterns and make predictions. The rise of machine learning algorithms, such as Hidden Markov Models and Neural Networks, further propelled the progress in NLP. With the advent of deep learning and the availability of massive datasets, NLP has witnessed unprecedented growth, enabling machines to comprehend and generate human language with astonishing accuracy.

How Does Natural Language Processing work?

Natural Language Processing involves a series of intricate steps to process, analyze, and understand human language. The first step is known as tokenization, where the text is broken down into individual words or tokens. These tokens serve as the building blocks for subsequent processing steps. The next step involves part-of-speech tagging, where each word is assigned a grammatical category, such as noun, verb, or adjective. This information helps in understanding the syntactic structure of the text.

Once the text is tokenized and tagged, the next step is to analyze the relationships between words. This is done through syntactic parsing, which involves creating a parse tree that represents the grammatical structure of the sentence. Sentiment analysis is another important aspect of NLP, where the underlying sentiment or emotion expressed in the text is determined. This can be crucial for applications such as social media monitoring or customer feedback analysis.

Applications

Natural Language Processing has found a wide range of applications across various domains. In the healthcare industry, NLP is used to extract important information from medical records, enabling faster and more accurate diagnosis. Sentiment analysis is employed in customer service to gauge customer satisfaction and identify areas for improvement. NLP algorithms are also used in automated translation services, making it easier for people to communicate across different languages and by chatbots to provide personalized assistance and support in various industries, including e-commerce and banking. In the legal domain, NLP is used for e-discovery, where large volumes of legal documents are analyzed to extract relevant information for legal professionals.

Natural Language Processing in the Internet of Things (IoT)

IoT has ushered in a new era of interconnected devices that communicate and share data with each other. NLP plays a vital role in extending this data exchange beyond device-to-device communications to deliver valuable insights to the users of these devices. Voice assistants like Amazon Alexa and Google Assistant utilize NLP algorithms to understand and respond to user commands. By leveraging NLP, IoT devices can interpret and act upon natural language instructions, making them more intuitive and user-friendly.

Voice assistants will also provide a convenient means for drivers to interact with dashcams integrated into fleet telematics solutions with neural network capabilities. Refer to our blog, "Navigating the Neural Network Wave: Unveiling New IoT Capabilities with Neural Networks and Devices" for additional details. As drivers make use of this feature, the dashcam utilizes speech recognition technology to convert spoken language into text. Subsequently, NLP algorithms are activated, carefully analyzing the transcribed text to understand and interpret the driver's instructions or queries. This seamless fusion of voice commands and NLP elevates the driving experience, allowing for intuitive and hands-free control of dashcam functionalities.

In industrial IoT, NLP plays a crucial role in predictive maintenance. By analyzing maintenance logs, manuals, and textual data from sensors, NLP algorithms can identify patterns indicative of potential equipment failures, enabling key personnel to take more proactive maintenance measures to minimize downtime and enhance operational efficiency.

NLP also enhances the functionality of AI-enabled dashcams used in vehicle telematics solutions by accessing and analyzing dashcam footage. As an example, by analyzing the audio information in the dashcam recordings, NLP can identify and extract information related to specific incidents, such as accidents or road events. This facilitates automated incident reporting and documentation.

Challenges in Natural Language Processing

Despite the remarkable progress in NLP, several challenges persist. One major challenge is the ambiguity and complexity of natural language. Words can have multiple meanings, and context is crucial in understanding their intentions. Another challenge is the lack of labeled training data for specialized domains. NLP models often require large amounts of annotated data to achieve high accuracy, which may not be readily available for niche domains. Additionally, ethical considerations regarding privacy and bias in NLP algorithms need to be addressed to ensure fair and responsible use of the technology.

The Future of Natural Language Processing

The future of Natural Language Processing holds immense potential. As research in the field continues to advance, we can expect even greater accuracy and sophistication in language understanding and generation. NLP algorithms will become more adaptable to different domains and languages, enabling machines to understand and communicate with humans in a more natural and human-like manner. As a result, NLP will play a pivotal role in transforming industries such as healthcare, education, and customer service, making our interactions with machines more seamless and intuitive.

5.6.2 Natural Language Processing apply to IoT

The Internet of Things (IoTs) has a deep connection with artificial intelligence. IoT systems generate large amounts of data, and data is the core of artificial intelligence and machine learning. At the same time, with the rapid expansion of connected devices and sensors, the role of smart technology in this field is also growing. Nowadays, the application of computer intelligence in IoT products varies as per the requirements. This article focuses on a specific area of artificial intelligence, Natural Language Processing (NLP). One of the core concepts of natural language processing is the ability to understand human speech. Without NLP, it is impossible to implement voice control on different systems. In IoT, it is difficult to overestimate the value of speech recognition. The hands-free voice interface can bring many benefits to the IoT environment. In some cases, this is just a usability issue; the more complex the system, the harder it is to implement a user-friendly mobile or web interface to control it. In turn, the voice interface is intuitive in nature and does not require a serious learning curve.

In the consumer market, the popularity of voice control is also increasing. About 50% of American households use voice to access online content. Therefore, increasing the number of smart consumer electronic products activated by voice has become a natural step in technological evolution. In addition, NLP not only enables us to integrate speech processing into devices and sensors. Due to the machine translation function, it enables the localization function. With the level of market globalization that we are experiencing today, localization even goes beyond translation and unleashes the benefits of transcreation (creative translation). If the product is focused on cross-border distribution, machine translation is invaluable for any IoT product that enables voice recognition.

Speech recognition is closely related to another NLP concept: question answering system, which is self-explanatory. Question and answer tasks allow us to determine answers to questions given in natural language. Nowadays, more and more devices that support voice recognition use question and answer to provide feedback for user input. The most common examples are popular home assistants such as Amazon Alexa, Google Home etc. These devices are activated and controlled by voice and can answer various questions. Therefore, voice assistants can help people quickly obtain relevant information on the go, thereby improving user work efficiency.

Sentiment Analysis

Customer service can also use sentiment analysis. It can even eliminate invalid investigations. Instead, smart concierges can ask customers questions about their experience and automatically determine their satisfaction. In general, these functions can not only create a competitive advantage for enterprises, but also provide customers with personalized products and services. In addition, due to sentiment analysis and trend monitoring, various connected devices can finally find answers and provide products and services that consumers need or want. The Internet of Things not only connect things, but also connects technology. Imagine a world where devices work with humans, understand their queries, feel their needs, and provide relevant responses.

Understanding APIs

Cognitive APIs are perhaps the most important component of natural language processing, text and video and picture processing to assist consumers in understanding the capability of the voice commands with Watson IoT. The Watson APIs for IoT assist with speeding up the improvement of intellectual IoT arrangements and administrations on Watson IoT.

Natural language processing (NLP): enabling clients to collaborate with frameworks and gadgets by utilizing straightforward human language.

Video and picture processing: enabling clients to screen unstructured information from video feeds and picture depictions to recognize scenes and patters in video information.

Text processing: enabling the mining of unstructured text-based information, including records from client calls at a call place, support methods and investigating, professional upkeep logs, blog remarks, and tweets.

By interfacing the client, the text processing API empowers mining of unstructured literary information coming from sources like records from client call focuses, upkeep specialist logs, blog remarks, and tweets. There are numerous things that should be possible today utilizing the innovation accessible in mix with regular language handling which are something other than making an interpretation of voice into text. Some APIs additionally offer the capacity to get text, semantic, which means, notwithstanding the subtleties related with minor departure from how individuals are asking things.

NLP- A Bridge between Consumers and Frameworks

NLP can assist with working with communications among clients and frameworks. Currently, the common practice to communicate with a framework is through a UI, either a UI in a versatile application, a program or a control place, where a singular press fastens and clicks a bunch of switches. What makes things diverse with Natural Language Processing (NLP) is the means by which an individual can conjure this activity.

NLP adds the option of an elegant 'exchange' to be utilized with similar gadgets, providing orders verbally or questioning them for status and issues. This can be envisioned with a support expert attempting to investigate an issue. The Internet of Things (IoT) is the thing that makes this conceivable availability, robotized information assortment, connection with different information source, like climate, and more installed handling power

Curiously, the bits of knowledge created by existing APIs can be utilized again to retrain the framework, empowering the client to additionally work on the exactness and practicality of the data produced going ahead. Moreover, the APIs of the stage can be joined to acquire data another organization, like sound, into the text information base for Text Analytics. Frameworks are accessible for changing over discourse into text and text into discourse utilizing the Natural Language Processing (NLP) API, which empowers the clients to associate with the framework utilizing straightforward, human language.

NLP based IoT Systems

Applying NLP in IoT frameworks (in various applications) can aid in tackling various issues. For instance, while driving, you notice a light on the vehicle dashboard, rather than pausing and reading the manual, the driver can inquire as to whether they need to stop promptly to get the light checked. Another example is the support specialist who is utilizing his hands and instruments to deal with a resource, and yet needs to interact with the gadget or an upkeep framework.

NLP capacities can assist with working on various cycles. Additionally, by utilizing this profound degree of information handling, and implementing it progressively on data assembled from engineers, field specialists and clients, IoT can assist organizations with making imaginative items and administrations.

www.ingramcontent.com/pod-product-compliance
Lightning Source LLC
Chambersburg PA
CBHW031307150426
43191CB00005B/118